The Descendants of
William England

of Swedesboro, New Jersey

compiled by

Michele England Heckman

Table of Contents

Preface

I never knew much about my father's family. My mother and father were divorced when I was nine years old. I have fond memories of my father and his parents. After the divorce, we never heard from the England family, and my mother felt quite bitter toward them. Now, as an adult, I realize the effects of his alcoholism on our family dynamics. Because of these circumstances, my childhood perception of the England family was quite negative. It is a perception that has changed during the exploration of the documents and through meeting still living members of my grandfather's family.

About twelve years ago, I began exploring this family, and as my family can tell you, the exploration has turned into an obsession. Ancestry.com and FamilySearch.org were just beginning. The US Census documents were gradually made available online. At that time, they were not indexed, and I, painstakingly, went through each page, one by one. I was writing to states for vital records and waiting patiently for them to arrive. I travelled to Seventh Day Adventist libraries to order and review microfilmed documents.

Over the years, the internet has grown. The technology has become more precise and faster. Searching online has become a very efficient way of searching, as the microfilmed documents are available with the click of a mouse.

Even with these advances, there is no substitute to searching dusty books, cardfiles, old newspapers and microfilms in the local historical society. Personal touches and stories have been added to this history because of the contributions previous members of the England family have added to the collections of libraries. And records remain fickle things. They are subject to human error, transcription errors, misinterpretation, and aging.

One of these contributions was a family tree, handwritten by the Reverend Aquila B. England, and found at the Gloucester County Historical Society in Woodbury, New Jersey. These pages are one of my most treasured documents. Cramped and difficult to read, the facts outlined worked to break down some of the brick walls encountered along the way. The document is unsourced, and yet almost all of the facts have been proven to be accurate. Rev. England has made some conclusions about the origins of this family, which he doesn't explain, and I can't prove. I really would have liked to sit down with him over a cup of coffee and talk about what he knew. This is a feeling I have experienced many times along the way.

Another document that was extremely useful, and for which I have a fondness, is the records of the Trinity Episcopal Church in Swedesboro. It is very old and out of print, and now, it is available online at hathitrust.org where it can be viewed in its original handwritten form. This is one of the documents that gave life to the names and dates on the pages.

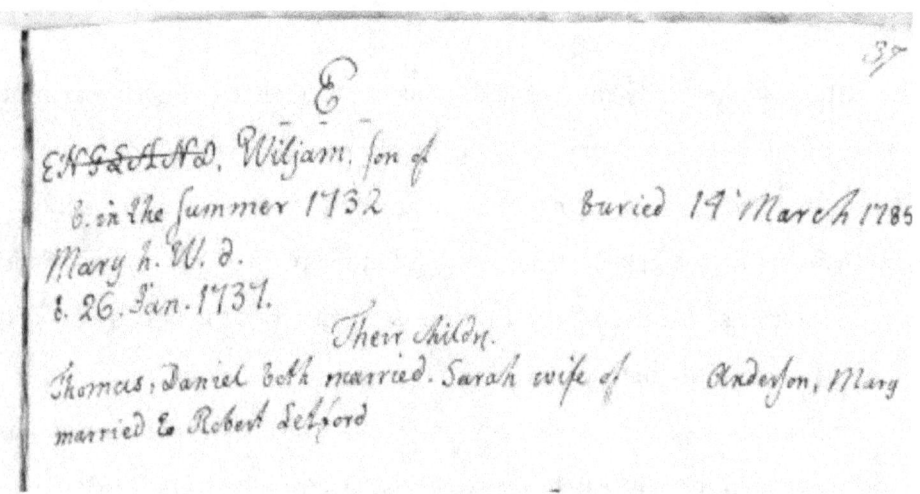

Example of a record from the Trinity Church, Swedesboro, New Jersey

No family history is complete without an exploration of the US Census Records. This census is taken every ten years, and is released to the public when a specific census is 72 years old. The last census that is available was taken in 1940; the 1950 census will be released in 2022. Each census from 1850 lists the name of each person living within the household. Prior to 1850, the census named the head of the household, the number of males, females and slaves, and the number of individuals within specific age ranges. Beginning in 1850, each census asked specific questions about the individuals, their occupations, their maternal and paternal birthplaces, whether they could read and write. The 1900 census asks for the month and year of birth. Another census asks how many children were born to adult women and how many were alive. Two of the censuses asked adult men about their veteran status. You will note some of these descriptions as you read through the records of the descendants.

Example of 1900 US Census

Almost the entire 1890 census was destroyed in a fire. Some states performed a statewide census, which served as a useful substitute for the lost federal census. Some city directories also helped to establish residence for the lost decade, but don't provide the names of minor children. The records of World War I veterans were also lost to a fire. There are very few substitues for those records.

The Family History Format

This document employs the use of the Modified Register System developed by the National Genealogical Society Quarterly (NGSQ). In this system, the family members are presented by generation. Each person is assigned a number, whether or not they have progeny, and regardless of the generation to which they belong. If the individual has progeny, that number is preceded by a "+". That symbol indicates the person and progeny are continued into the next generation. The names, in parentheses, following the descendant's name is a sort of pedigree. Each of those names has a superscript number, indicating the generation to which the ancestors belonged. My pedigree is (George[6], Herbert[5], Oscar[4], Daniel[3], Daniel[2], William[1]): I'm in the seventh generation; George, my father, was the sixth generation; Herbert, my grandfather, was the fifth generation and so on.

Generation 1 looks like this

1. Name of progenitor, dates of birth, death, marriage. Name of spouse.

   +2.   i.   Name of child, dates of birth, death, marriage. Name of spouse.
Names of children will be in generation two. Any interesting facts about this child will be presented in generation 2.

3. ii. Name of second child, dates of birth, death, marriage. Name of spouse. No children to carry into next generation. Any interesting facts about this child will be presented here.

+4 iii. Name of the third child, dates of birth, death, marriage. Name of spouse. Names of grandchildren will be presented in generation two. Any interesting facts about this child will be presented in generation 2.

Generation two continues:

2. Name of child, dates of birth, death, marriage. Name of spouse. Any interesting facts about this person will be presented here.

5. i. Name of grandchild, dates of birth, death, marriage. Name of spouse. Any interesting facts about this grandchild will be presented here.

+6. ii. Name of second grandchild, dates of birth, death, marriage. Name of spouse. Names of great grandchildren will be presented in generation 3.

7. iii. Name of third grandchild, dates of birth, death, marriage. Name of spouse. Any interesting facts about this grandchild will be presented here.

4. Name of the third child, dates of birth, death, marriage. Name of spouse. Any interesting facts about the third child are presented here.

8. i. The name of the grandchild and so on . . . .

9. ii.

10. iii.

Within certain family units, many of the middle names are surnames of one of the parents. To make the reading of these names easier, all surnames are capitalized.

The tiny roman numerals at the end of sentences are endnotes. At the end of the book is a list of corresponding sources from which the information came. To avoid the reader's distraction, I've listed only one source. Usually, more than one source for a fact exists. If you wish, please contact me at ammamichele@gmail.com for your specific information or citation needs.

To protect the confidentiality of persons who are living, I am only including deceased persons in this publication. If any siblings from a family unit are living, none of the siblings will be named. You may notice that, particulary in generations 6 and 7, the records become less complete. This is because information that is contained in the 1950 and later census records is not yet available. Many governmental agencies have established policies that determine the archival age of their records and when they can be released. Information for individuals who have lived in the last 70 years or so is not available, except to next of kin. These policies have been designed to protect people from identity theft. In other words, personal information becomes more difficult to find as the generation gets closer to present day.

And finally, I have made every effort to present this family's history accurately and completely. I have not included any information that I can not, with certainty, link to an individual or family. Comments are offered to explain gaps in information and to support conclusions that I have made. Please forgive me for any errors, misrepresentations, or missing facts that you, the reader, may identify. Please feel free to contact me with your comments, facts, and conclusions.

1

The First Generation

THE ORIGIN OF THIS BRANCH of the England family is not clear. Our progenitor, William England, lived and died in Swedesboro, New Jersey, but the name of his parents and the location of his birth is unknown. A descendant of William, and early England family researcher, the Reverend Aquila Barber England, believed that this line originated in English counties along the Welsh border. He cited the names of several England men and their wives, that were married in a "meeting" in Bristol in 1677. (Although it might seem that the term "meeting" implies a Quaker affiliation, all non-conformist religions of the time called their gatherings "meetings" to avoid the consequences. One of those consequences could be an indentured service in the new colonies in North America and the Caribbean.) The Reverend England did not explain his reasons for linking these English citizens with our American lineage, nor did he cite his sources.

There were many Englands living in what is now the greater Philadelphia area, in Delaware, Maryland, the Isle of Wright (Virginia) and the Barbados Islands. Many of them were Quaker. There was a Daniel England, living in Burlington county, New Jersey, in the mid to late 1600's, a Quaker and a mariner. There was a William England, a contemporary of our William, in Pennsylvania, also a Quaker and a mariner. Interestingly, his wife had the same name as the wife of our William. Our Swedesboro ancestors were members of the Swedish Lutheran Church and continued their membership when the affiliation changed to Episcopalian.

The town of Raccoon was settled in the mid-1600's by Swedish and Finnish settlers as part of the colony of New Sweden. It was an area rich with a variety of trees, sources of lumber, and rich with fertile soil for farming. It was located along the banks of Raccoon Creek, which was deep and fast enough to float lumber to the Delaware River, and then on to Philadelphia for milling and shipping. The creek also provided the main route of transportation for their farm products. In 1765, following the surrender of the Swedes to the British, the town was renamed Swedesboro. Many of the earliest colonists farmed large plantations of tobacco, wheat, and corn. Fur and lumber were important commodities as well. The area is largely supported by farming today.

The earliest settlers worshipped at the Swedish Lutheran Church on Tinicum Island in the Delaware River or the church at Wicaco (present day Philadelphia). One can only imagine what a challenge it must have been to cross the river by boat or canoe in inclement weather. In the late 1600's, the ailing Reverend Andrew Rudman requested that he return to Sweden and that a new minister by sent to replace him. A minister by the name of Lars Tollstadius heard about this opportunity, and needed to escape a scandal in Sweden. He was rejected by his superiors, but he falsified his credentials and came anyway at his own expense. For four controversial years, he served the parishioners at Swedesboro. He immediately recognized the need for a church on the New Jersey side of the Delaware, and built a log cabin structure in 1703. However, he was inconsistent in his duties and in his record keeping. He became involved in a scandal here, involving the daughter of a parishioner. His body was found floating on the shores of the Delaware River while he was awaiting his trial; whether by accident or intention, we will never know. For the next decade or so, the people of Swedesboro shared a succession of ministers with Philadelphia and Fort Christina (present day Wilmington, Delaware).

The Reverend Nicholas Collin arrived from Sweden in 1770. He found the log cabin church in a severe state of disrepair. He designed the plans for the church in its present location on Kings Highway. He organized the labor and finances for its construction, contributing money and physical labor to the project as well. The church thrived under his leadership. Two services were held, one in Swedish, and one in English. Nicholas Collin was transferred to Philadelphia in 1786, where he stayed until his death. By 1787, the Swedish language was almost extinct, and the Swedish service was discontinued. In October 1789, the church began its affiliation with the Episcopal Church, and became known as the Trinity Episcopal Church of Swedesboro, nicknamed "Old Swedes". The journals and records of the Rev. Collin were the primary source of information for our earliest ancestors. The records of the succeeding ministers were also very helpful, but not kept with the same detail and diligence.

This period of time also includes the politics and events of the Revolutionary War. New Jersey saw more battles than any other colony, primarily because of its location on the Delaware River between Philadelphia and New York. Families, churches, and towns were often divided between Loyalists and Patriots. In Swedesboro, Hessian soldiers occupied and vandalized buildings and terrorized families. Nicholas Collin was arrested and confined by the British. Tensions ran high, and yet the town continued to grow and thrive, adapting to the needs of its residents.

The Trinity Episcopal Church of Swedesboro, New Jersey. Photo taken by Michele England Heckman, July 2016.

And so we begin the lineage of this England family:

1. **WILLIAM ENGLAND** was born in the summer of 1732 and died in March 1785, at the age of 53. He married Mary WATSON (daughter of William Watson and Sarah). Mary was born on the 6th of January 1737 and died in 1793, at the age of 56. They are both buried in the churchyard of the Trinity Episcopal Church in Swedesboro.

The diary of Reverend Nicholas Collin notes the death and burial of William. He reflects that William was a faithful church member, although he would frequently be absent because of his duties as the captain of a yacht that sailed between Raccoon (the original name of Swedesboro) and Philadelphia (across the Delaware River). Rev. Collin also notes the hardship of the loss of two of his sons, who "had gone over to the English side and died in distant places." William was indicted for "going into the lines of the enemy" and fined £150. William's son, William, was indicted for high treason, but for unknown reasons, his case was discontinued. [i]

William and Mary had eight children:

+2   i.   Thomas ENGLAND was born on the 17th of April 1753[ii]; his father was 21 and his mother was 16. He died in March 1792 at the age of 38. On the 1st of January 1782, he married Hester ADAMS (daughter of Joseph ADAMS and Elizabeth B. LINCH). She was born on the 18th of October 1759. Her date of death is unknown. She was identified as a "half-Quaker" by Nicholas Collin in his journal.

3.   ii.   William ENGLAND: a handwritten family tree held at the Gloucester Historical Society states that William was born in 1757 and died in 1822. His spouse's name was Mary. No records were located to confirm these facts. He is not named in his father's will. Perhaps he was one of the two sons who "went to the English side."

+4   iii.   Daniel ENGLAND was born on the 27th of January 1760 and died on the 17th of October 1824 in Swedesboro, New Jersey. He married Rebeckah CRAIGHEAD (daughter of Robert CRAIGHEAD and Mary COX) on the 27th of December 1780 at the Trinity Church. She died on the 28th of October 1802. He next married Priscilla HULINGS (daughter of Thomas HULINGS and Priscilla WELCH on the 20th of October 1804. She was the widow of Thomas DERRICKSON. She was born on the 14th of January and died in June 1829. Priscilla's paternal ancestry is historically noteworthy.

5.   iv.   Elias ENGLAND was born in 1762. Again, the only record of his life is in the handwritten tree described above. I am assuming he died as a child as there is no mention of him in other England family histories and he is not named in his father's will. He may also be one of William's two sons who "went to the English side".

6.   v.   Sarah ENGLAND was born in 1764, according to the handwritten family tree. No other records for her life were found. She is not named in her father's will.

7.   vi.   James ENGLAND was born in 1769, according to the handwritten family tree. No other

records for his life were found. He is not named in his father's will. Although a bit young, he may have been lost to the "English side".

+8. vii. Mary ENGLAND was born about 1771. She married Robert LETFORD on the 13th of January 1785 at the age of 14. Her father, William, died two months later. Nicholas Collin describes LETFORD as "a Presbyterian from Ireland".

2

The Second Generation

3. <u>**Thomas ENGLAND**</u> (William[1]) was born on the 17th of April 1753; his father was 21 and his mother was 16. He died in March 1792 at the age of 38. On the 1st of January 1782, he married Hester ADAMS (daughter of Joseph ADAMS and Elizabeth B. LINCH). [iii] She was born on the 18th of October 1759.[iv] Her date of death is unknown. She was identified as a "half-Quaker" by Nicholas Collin in his journal.

Thomas and Hester had four children:

9.   i.   Mary ENGLAND was born on the 27th of March 1783 in Gloucester County, New Jersey.[v] No further records of her life have been found.

+10   ii.   William ENGLAND was born in July 1785. His death is documented in the handwritten family tree as the 29th of October 1826.[vi] On the 6th of November 1806, he married Hannah TITUS.[vii] She was born about 1791 and died the 10th of February 1827.[viii]

11.   iii.   Thomas ENGLAND is recorded as a child in this family on our handwritten tree, but no further records of his life were found.

12.   iv.   David ENGLAND is recorded as a child in this family on our handwritten tree, but no further records of his life were found.

4. <u>**Daniel England**</u> (William[1]) was born on the 27th of January 1760 and died on the 17th of October 1824 in Swedesboro, New Jersey, at the age of 64.[ix] He married Rebeckah CRAIGHEAD (daughter of Robert CRAIGHEAD and Mary COX) at the Trinity Lutheran Church in Swedesboro on the 27th of December 1780.[x] She was born on the 3rd of September 1763 and died on the 28th of October 1802 at the age of 39 in childbirth.[xi] Rebeckah's gravestone is engraved: "Rebeckah, wife of Daniel England; aged 39 years 7 months 8 days; also beside her 4 daughters, Rebeckah, Hannah, Beulah and Kitty who all died in their infancy."[xii]

Daniel married for a second time to Priscilla HULINGS (daughter of Samuel HULINGS and Priscilla WELCH) IN 1804. Priscilla was born on the 14th of January 1776 and died in June of 1829 at the age of 53. Priscilla was the widow of Thomas DERRICKSON; she had four children from this marriage. Priscilla's paternal ancestry is historically noteworthy..

It is not clear how Daniel made his living. His tombstone carries the term "Esq." which implies that he was an attorney. He owned several hundred acres of land in Gloucester County, and it is assumed that he was a farmer as well. There are many official documents that carry his signature, so it is clear that he had some importance in Swedesboro. One of the documents signed was a petition to the King of England to build a road that is still called "Kings Highway" today. Daniel built a large brick home on Kings Highway, directly across the street from the Trinity Episcopal Church, which was torn down in the mid-1800's; a new one was built in its place using some of the brick from the original structure.[xiii] Daniel contributed both financially and with physical labor in the construction of the Trinity Episcopal Church at its current site. His lengthy will provides well for his children and Priscilla in the distribution of cash and property.

Daniel and Rebeckah had ten children:

+13   i.   Sarah C. ENGLAND was born on the 4th of April 1781.[xiv] Her date of death is unknown. She married Samuel Barber of Mantua, New Jersey, on the 26th of February 1801.[xv] Samuel was born on the 1st of September 1776 and died on the 17th of July 1849.[xvi]

+14   ii.   William W. ENGLAND was born on the 6th of April 1783 and died on the 30th of October 1826 in Swedesboro. He married Mary FORD on the 7th of February 1805. She was born about 1781 and died on the 9th of September 1806, seven months after she was married. He married a second time to Meribah BARBER (daughter of Aquila BARBER and Meribah CURRY) on the 17th of March 1808. She was born in 1783 and died in July 1847.[xvii]

+15   iii.   Mary ENGLAND was born on the 27th of November 1785 and died on the 18th of December 1857 in Swedesboro. She married Richard CAMPBELL on the 25th of August 1803. He was born about 1781. He is buried in the churchyard of the Trinity Lutheran Church in Swedesboro; the gravestone is so weathered the date is hard to read, but a guess is 1866.[xviii]

16.   iv.   Elias ENGLAND was born on the 15th of July 1788 and died on the 6th of November 1806, at the age 18.[xix]

17.   v.   Rebeckah ENGLAND was born on the 4th of June 1790 and died on the 22nd of October 1792.[xx]

18.   vi.   Hannah ENGLAND was born on the 17th of August 1792 and died on the 24th of August 1792.[xxi]

19.   vii.   Betsy ENGLAND was born on the 25th of January 1794 and died as an infant.[xxii]

20.   viii.   Beulah ENGLAND was born on the 19th of June 1796 and died on the 28 Jan 1797.[xxiii]

21.   ix.   Kitty ENGLAND was born on the 25th of April 1799 and died on the 1 May 1801.[xxiv]

22.   x.   Rebeckah (2) ENGLAND was born on the 22nd of October 1802. She died on the 6th of March 1803.[xxv]

Between 1790 and her death in 1802, Rebeckah had six children, and buried five of them. The sixth child, born at Rebeckah's death, died six months after her mother.

Daniel ENGLAND and Priscilla HULINGS had five children:

23. i. Priscilla C. ENGLAND was born on the 3rd of September 1805. She died of hypertrophy of the heart on the 15th of February 1868, at the age of 63. She never married.[xxvi]

+24 ii. Daniel ENGLAND was born on the 17th of June 1807. He died on the 11th of December 1887 at the Blackwoodstown Almshouse.[xxvii] He married Sarah T. CLARK (daughter of Joseph V. CLARK and Elizabeth TIERS). She was born about 1812 and died on the 19th of October 1850, at the age of 38 of pertussis in Philadelphia.[xxviii] His second marriage was to Margaret Frances Hess (daughter of Bertis Hess). She was born in 1827 in Pennsylvania and died in December 1885[xxix] in Philadelphia.

+25 iii. James ENGLAND was born on the 31st of July 1809 in Swedesboro. He died on the 22nd of March 1866 in Clarksboro, New Jersey.[xxx] He married Anna Elizabeth DYER on the 2nd of April 1835.[xxxi] She was born in 1818 and died in Philadelphia from valvular heart disease on the 29th of March 1888, at the age of 74.[xxxii]

26. iv. Thomas ENGLAND was born on the 8th of June 1812.[xxxiii] A note on our handwritten tree states that he moved to Little Rock, Arkansas, and this is confirmed with the record of the appointment of his brother, James, as his power of attorney on the 27th of October 1838.[xxxiv] No other records of his life were identified.

27. v. Harriet S. ENGLAND was born in 1820.[xxxv] She married Jacob AMBRUSTER on the 27th of March 1839 by the Rev. John Woast at the home of her father, Daniel.[xxxvi] No further records were found.

8. **MARY ENGLAND** (William[1]), was born about 1771. She is also called "Polly" on several records. She married Robert LETFORD on the 13th of January 1785 at the age of 14.[xxxvii] Her father, William, died two months later. Nicholas Collin describes LETFORD as "a Presbyterian from Ireland".

Robert served in the Captain Francis Nichols Company of the 9th Pennsylvania Regiment as a drummer during the Revolutionary War. He enlisted on the 2nd of March 1777 and was wounded in the arm at the battle of Monmouth or Princeton in May 1778 and spent the next two months in the hospital. He was returned to service. His discharge date is unknown. Drummers were usually too young or too old to fight, so we can assume that Robert was 16 or younger during this time period.[xxxviii] For his service, he was awarded a pension and 200 acres of land.

Robert and Mary had 3 children:

28.   i.   James LETFORD was born on the 12th of August 1788 in Swedesboro.[xxxix] No other records for his life were found.

29.   ii.   William LETFORD was born on the 10th of October 1790.[xl] He is found in the 1860 census living in Philadelphia as a bootmaker.[xli] He died on the 9th of September 1861 in Philadelphia of chronic bronchitis.[xlii] All records indicate he was single; no records of marriage could be found.

30.   iii.   Robert LETFORD died on the 19th of July 1794 in Swedesboro, presumably as an infant.[xliii]

3

The Third Generation

Here is the third generation:

10. William ENGLAND (Thomas[2], William[1]) was born in July 1785. He died on the 29th of October 1826. On the 6th of November 1806, he married Hannah TITUS. She was born about 1791 and died the 10th of February 1827. In his will, William identifies himself as a carpenter.[xliv]

William and Hannah had ten children:

31. i. Thomas ENGLAND was born on the 15th of August 1807 and died on the 3rd of August 1808.[xlv]

32. ii. William ENGLAND was born on the 11th of February 1809.[xlvi] According to our handwritten family tree, he died in 1880.[xlvii] No other records of his life were identified.

33. iii. Hester ENGLAND was born on the 9th of January 1811[xlviii] and died in 1822.[xlix]

+34. iv. Lemuel D. ENGLAND was born on the 29th of October 1812 in New Jersey.[l] He died on the 30th of March 1879 in Philadelphia[li]. He married Mary NEZMOS on the 1st of October 1835. She was born about 1817 in Pennsylvania and died on the 24th of November 1882.[lii]

35. v. Joseph ENGLAND was born on the 13th of August 1814 and died on the 30th of November 1871.[liii] He never married. Joseph was a shoemaker.

+36. vi. Joanna ENGLAND was born on the 22nd of May 1818 and died on the 3rd of November 1894.[liv] She married Jacob ROBERTS about 1835. He was born the 8th of March 1810[lv] and died on the 7th of March 1879 in Camden, New Jersey.[lvi]

+37. vii. Deborah ENGLAND was born in New Jersey on the 22nd of May 1818[lvii] and died in Philadelphia on the 5th of January 1907.[lviii] She married Francis TAWS on the 13th January 1841.[lix] He was born about 1812 and died on the 27th of January 1891.[lx]

+38. viii. Samuel ENGLAND was born on the 12th of April 1820. He married Elizabeth Ann HAINES on the 26th of May 1842. She was born in September 1826 and died on the 19th of December 1912.[lxi]

39. ix. Bodo ENGLAND was born on the 2nd of March 1822 in New Jersey, and died on the 29th of January 1891 of pneumonia.[lxii] He never married. Census records identify his occupation as "artist" and photographer.

+40. x. Robert ENGLAND was born on the 21st of February 1825 and died on the 29th of March 1896 in Philadelphia. He married Louise Rebecca RANCK (daughter of Nathaniel RANCK, MD and Susan KEYSER) on the 18th of July 1855 in Philadelphia[lxiii]. She was born on the 12th of October 1834 and died of bronchitis on the 30th of March 1920.[lxiv]

13. Sarah C. ENGLAND (Daniel^2, William^1) was born on the 4th of April 1781[lxv]. Her date of death is unknown. She married Samuel Barber of Mantua, New Jersey, on the 26th of February 1801.[lxvi] Samuel was born on the 1st of September 1776 and died on the 17th of July 1849.[lxvii]

Sarah and Samuel had three children:

41. i. Daniel BARBER was born on the 2nd of December 1801 in Swedesboro.[lxviii] He died on the 15th of February 1875.[lxix] He never married.

42. ii. William BARBER was born about 1804 and died on the 14th of April 1885 in Greenwich Township, Gloucester County, New Jersey.[lxx] William was a farmer. He never married.

43. iii. Hannah BARBER was baptized in 1807 and died on the 10th of February 1887. She never married.[lxxi]

14. **WILLIAM WATSON ENGLAND** (Daniel^2, William^1) was born on the 6th of April 1783[lxxii] and died on the 1st of January 1856 in Sculltown, New Jersey.[lxxiii] He married Mary FORD on the 7th of February 1805. She was born about 1781 and died on the 9th of September 1806. He married a second time to Meribah BARBER (daughter of Aquila BARBER and Meribah CURRY) on the 17th of March 1808. She was born in 1783 and died in July 1847. He was a member of the Trinity Church vestry, but for a period of time, he and Meribah were "repelled" for an unknown reason. Eventually, his membership was restored when the charges were found to be false.[lxxiv]

William and Mary Ford had one child:

44.   i.   Daniel ENGLAND was born on the 30th of September 1805 in Swedesboro. ^{lxxv} He was eleven months old when his mother died in 1806. He was baptized in 1809. No records of his life after this date are identified. ^{lxxvi}

William and Meribah Barber had eight children:

45.   i.   Elias ENGLAND was born on the 26th of November 1808 in Swedesboro. He died on the 20th of May 1876 in Camden, New Jersey. He married Martha S. BLACKWELL. She was born about 1813 and died on the 18th of December 1904 in Gloucester County, New Jersey. Elias was a house builder. They had no children.

+46.   ii.   Rebecca ENGLAND was born on the 27th of June 1810 in Swedesboro.^{lxxvii} She died on the 25th of November 1886 in Oldmans, New Jersey.^{lxxviii} She married David LYNCH on the 8th of December 1831 at the Trinity Church.^{lxxix} He was born in 1808 and died on the 29th of August 1884 in Oldmans, New Jersey.

+47.   iii.   Aquila Barber ENGLAND was born about 1813 in Swedesboro.^{lxxx} He died on the 27th of August 1896 in Brooklyn, New York.^{lxxxi} He married Elizabeth TOWNLEY. She was born about 1814 in New Jersey ^{lxxxii} and died on the 9th of December 1874.^{lxxxiii}

48.   iv.   Mary ENGLAND was born on the 15th of November 1814.^{lxxxiv} She married Benjamin AVISE on the 18th of April of 1833 in Woolwich, New Jersey. No records of death for Benjamin or Mary were found. There are two children, William and Agnes Ann, in a list of others that were baptized at the Swedesboro Trinity Church. The columns of dates of birth and dates of baptism are empty for these children. No other records for their lives could be found.

+49.   v.   William Watson ENGLAND was born on the 2nd of November 1816^{lxxxv} and died on the 13th of January 1899 in Swedesboro.^{lxxxvi} He married Mary Amanda GREEN on the 21st of December 1850 at a Quaker meeting in Haddonfield.^{lxxxvii} She was born on the 21st of November 1822 in Salem, New Jersey and she died on the 25th of March 1897 in Camden, New Jersey.^{lxxxviii}

+50.   vi.   Sarah Ann ENGLAND was born on the 24th of October 1818.^{lxxxix} She died of throat consumption on the 30th of January 1860.^{xc} She married John AMBRUSTER on the 25th of May 1839 in Gloucester County, New Jersey.^{xci} He was born in 1816 and died on the 10th of January 1885.^{xcii} He married a second time to Virginia "Jennie" ROWLAND in December 1861.^{xciii}

51.   vii.   Elizabeth ENGLAND was born on the 27th of July 1826.[xciv] She died on the 18th of May 1884.[xcv] This information comes from our handwritten tree: no records could be found to validate these dates.

52.   viii.   Meriba ENGLAND died as an infant.[xcvi]

15.   **MARY ENGLAND** (Daniel[2], William[1]) was born on the 27th of November 1785[xcvii] and died on the 18th of December 1857 in Swedesboro, New Jersey.[xcviii] She married Richard CAMPBELL on the 25th of August 1803.[xcix] He was born about 1781. He is buried in the New Trinity Cemetery, but his stone is so worn it is difficult to read.[c]

Mary and Richard had two daughters:

53.   i.   Eliza Trulon CAMPBELL was born about 1810 and died on the 3rd of October 1858 in Swedesboro, New Jersey.[ci] She never married. She preceded her father in death; she included provisions for his care in her will.[cii]

54.   ii.   Rebecca England CAMPBELL was born on the 3rd of May 1811.[ciii] It is probable that she died as a child or infant: she is not named in the 1850 census, and she is not included in her sister's will.

24.   **DANIEL ENGLAND** (Daniel[2], William[1]) was born on the 17th of June 1807. He died on the 11th of December 1887 at the Blackwoodstown Almshouse. He married Sarah T. CLARK (daughter of Joseph V. CLARK and Elizabeth TIERS). She was born about 1812 and died of pertussis on the 19th of October 1850, at the age of 38 in Philadelphia. Around the time of her death, Daniel moved to Camden County, New Jersey. His second marriage was to Margaret Frances Hess (daughter of Bertis Hess). She was born in 1827 in Pennsylvania and died on the 29th of October 1850 in Philadelphia. Margaret's last name is Brethwaite on our handwritten family tree. It is Hess on the death certificate of her son Daniel and on her death record with Camden County. The 1880 census names Bertis A. Wagner as Daniel's step-son, which suggests Margaret was a Wagner at one time. No records were found for Margaret prior to and including her marriage to Daniel. Bertis WAGNER was born in 1852 and died on the 19th of January 1889 in Camden.[civ] He was a railroad car inspector. His death record states he was married, but no records of his marriage were found.

In the 1850 census, Daniel's occupation was listed as "clerk." In the 1860 and 1880 census, he was a day laborer. In the 1870 census, he was without employment. Margaret worked for a washing service in the 1870 census.

Daniel inherited the home on Kings Highway and several other parcels of land, to include the rents, in Swedesboro from his father. It is puzzling to note that he died in the almshouse in Blackwood, New Jersey.[cv]

Daniel and Sarah had six children:

55.   i.   Anna E. ENGLAND was born on the 12th of April 1832.[cvi] She was present in the 1850 census before the death of her mother. No other records of her life were found.

56.   ii.   Joseph C. ENGLAND was born on the 13th of November 1833.[cvii] He was present in the 1850 census before his mother's death. No other records of his life were found.

57.   iii.   Lewis C. ENGLAND was born on the 14th of October 1835[cviii] in Swedesboro, and died on the 11th of April 1858, at the age of 23, of pertussis, in Philadelphia.[cix]

+58.   iv.   Catherine B. ENGLAND was born on the 5th of August 1839 in Swedesboro, and died on the 8th of April 1923 in Chester County, Pennsylvania.[cx] She was 11 years old at the time of her mother's death, and was subsequently adopted by her mother's family and given the surname CLARK.[cxi] She married William Henry IRWIN on the 12th of May 1864 in Philadelphia.[cxii] He was born about 1831 and died on the 14th of September 1874 of typhoid fever at the age of 43.[cxiii] She married a second time to William Arthur CHEYNEY IN 1881.[cxiv] He was born on the 9th of March 1846 in Philadelphia and died the 9th of April 1892 in New York.[cxv]

59.   v.   Lydia C. ENGLAND was born on the 25th of August 1841. She was 8 years old at the time of her mother's death and she, and her sister Emily, went to live with the Tonkin family.[cxvi] She married Harry L. BONSALL on the 6th of December 1865 at the Church of the Epiphany in Philadelphia. No records for Harry could be clearly identified. She died of typhoid fever on the 8th of October 1866, just 11 months after her marriage.[cxvii]

+60.   vi.   Emily T. ENGLAND was born on the 16th of October 1845 in Swedesboro.[cxviii] She was 5 years old at the time of her mother's death and she, and her sister Lydia, went to live with the Tonkin family.[cxix] She died on the 21st of April 1929 in Philadelphia at the age of 83.[cxx] She married Joseph B. CLEMENT IV (son of Joseph B. CLEMENT III and Elizabeth WARWICK[cxxi]) on the 24th of June 1869 in Philadelphia.[cxxii] He was born on the 6th of June 1842 in New Jersey. He died on the 21st of January 1902.[cxxiii]

Daniel and Margaret had four children:

61.   i.   Priscilla ENGLAND was born on the 25th of May 1860[cxxiv] No other records could be found after the 1860 census.

+62.   ii.   Daniel ENGLAND was born on the 2nd of November 1862 in Newton Township, Camden County, New Jersey.[cxxv] He died on the 21st of August 1935 in Philadelphia.[cxxvi] He is identified as Daniel, Jr. in some records, but in fact, he is Daniel III. He married Elena Rachel WILSON (daughter of Joseph WILSON and Rachel STRANG) on the 23rd of March 1877 in Camden, New Jersey.[cxxvii] She was born on the 29th of November

1864 in Clayton Township, Gloucester County, New Jersey[cxxviii] and died on the 11th of February 1937 in Gloucester, New Jersey.[cxxix]

63.   iii.   Huling ENGLAND was born on the 6th of December 1864 in Haddonfield, New Jersey.[cxxx] No other records of his life were found.

+64.   iv.   Oscar Brown ENGLAND was born on the 8th of February 1868 in Camden, New Jersey[cxxxi]. He died on the 26th of April 1937 in Belvidere, Illinois[cxxxii]. He married Frieda RUEDI (daughter of Andrew RUEDI) on the 27th of June 1892[cxxxiii]. She was born on the 11th of January 1870 in Schaffhausen, Switzerland.[cxxxiv] She arrived in this country in 1888.[cxxxv] She died on the 11th of March 1948 in Rockford, Illinois.[cxxxvi]

25.   **JAMES ENGLAND** (Daniel[2], William[1]) was born on the 30th of July 1809 in Swedesboro, New Jersey.[cxxxvii] He died on the 22nd of March 1866 in Clarksboro, New Jersey.[cxxxviii] He married Anna Elizabeth DYER on the 2nd of April 1835.[cxxxix] She was born in 1818 [cxl] and died in Philadelphia on the 29th of March 1888, [cxli] at the age of 74 from valvular heart disease.[cxlii]

James and Anna Elizabeth had three children:

+65.   i.   Mary D. ENGLAND was born about 1837 in Gloucester County, New Jersey.[cxliii] She died of consumption in Philadelphia on the 17th of January 1885, at the age of 48.[cxliv] She married Joseph P. CRAMER.[cxlv] He was born about 1818 and died in Philadelphia on the 1st of May 1880. [cxlvi]

+66.   ii.   Henry C. ENGLAND was born on the 17th of November 1843 in New Jersey. He died on the 10th of October 1910 in Reading, Pennsylvania.[cxlvii] He married Sarah J. GILL (daughter of Matthew GILL and Mary JESSUP) on the 12th of August 1874.[cxlviii] She was born on the 5th of September 1847 in New Jersey and died on the 24th of February 1948.[cxlix]

67.   iii.   Ellen Campbell ENGLAND was born about 1849 in New Jersey. She died on the 24th of May 1903 in Reading, Pennsylvania. She never married. Her will describes her as an invalid for the last ten years of her life, and states that her financial support came from her brother, Henry. She tried to leave $100 to a niece, Annie Westney, who had come upon hard times. That portion of her will was contested by the owner of the building where she resided. The courts found in Ellie's favor through the efforts of Henry.

4

The Fourth Generation

Here is our fourth generation:

34. **LEMUEL D. ENGLAND** (William[3], Thomas[2], William[1]) was born on the 29th of October 1812 in New Jersey. He died on the 30th of March 1879 in Philadelphia.[cl] He married Mary NEZMOS on the 1st of October 1835. She was born about 1817 in Pennsylvania and died on the 24th of November 1882.[cli] He was employed in the dental industry: in the 1860 census, he is identified as a dentist[clii], and in 1870 as "works in dental depot."[cliii] One city directory called him a "toothmkr".[cliv]

Lemuel and Mary had seven children:

68.   i.   Deborah ENGLAND was born about 1837 in Pennsylvania. She died on the 8th of March 1844 in Philadelphia, of tracheitis at the age of 6.[clv]

69.   ii.   Rebecca N. ENGLAND was born about 1838 in Pennsylvania.[clvi] She married William STRICKLAND on the 8th of October 1895.[clvii] She died on the 25th of July 1896 of valvular disease of the heart.[clviii] No further information about William could be identified. Rebecca's death certificate cites her as married; however, her will does not name him. She left several family heirlooms to her siblings. Rebecca worked as a milliner. Because she was in her 50's at the time of her marriage, it is assumed she had no children.

70.   iii.   Jeannette C. ENGLAND was born about 1842 in Pennsylvania.[clix] She died on the 8th of October 1909 in Newark, New Jersey of gastric ulcers.[clx]. She married Major Abram B. GARNER in 1872.[clxi] They had no children.

Here is his published obituary:clxii

A. B. GARNER,
MURPHY VARNISH CO., NEWARK, N. J.,
1838-1909.

Abram Beitler Garner, second vice-president and treasurer of the Murphy Varnish Company, died at his home in Newark, N. J., January 28, 1909. Mr. Garner was born in Philadelphia in 1838. At the age of twenty he enlisted and served with distinction during the civil war, being promoted to the rank of major. After leaving the army Mr. Garner filled a number of positions with prominent Western railroads, the last being purchasing agent of the Denver & Rio Grande, which position he resigned to take charge of the Chicago office of the Murphy Varnish Company. After a short service there Mr. Garner was given the management of the company's New York office, and when that office was closed twenty years ago he was made resident manager of the Newark sales department, a position which he occupied for many years. On the death of Joseph Merrill, Jr., in 1905, Mr. Garner was made the second vice-president of the company.

He was one of the organizers of the National Paint, Oil and Varnish Association, and was elected its first vice-president at the convention held in Philadelphia in 1896, and in the following year he was chosen president, in which capacity he presided at the convention held in New York City in 1898. He was the sixth president of the Paint, Oil and Varnish Club, of New York, and the only man who held that office for two consecutive terms. He was a man of unimpeachable character, and a wonderful charm of manner which endeared him to everyone who had the pleasure of coming in contact with him. He was a member of the Peddie Memorial First Baptist Church, and had been superintendent of its Sunday school for many years. At a regular meeting of the Paint, Oil and Varnish Club of New York a special committee was appointed to draft suitable resolutions in his memory, which resolutions were engrossed and sent to his widow, by whom he is survived.

---

71.   iv.   William Henry ENGLAND was born in March and died in May 1847 of liver disease.

72.   v.   Mary ENGLAND was born on the 18th of December 1847 in Philadelphia.[clxiii] She died on the 9th of December 1907 in Philadelphia.[clxiv] Mary bequeathed financial support for her brother, James.[clxv] She married Joseph BAUGH (son of Jacob and Rachel BAUGH). He was born in 1842 in Chester County, Pennsylvania, and died on the 15th of December 1904.[clxvi] He enlisted in Company G, Pennsylvania, 30th Infantry Regiment on the 6th of June 1861 and mustered out on the 13th June 1864 at Philadelphia.[clxvii] He worked in the hide and tallow industry. They had no children.

73.   vi.   Lemuel D. ENGLAND, Jr was born about 1849 in Pennsylvania[clxviii] and died at 3 years of age.[clxix]

74.   vii.   James M. ENGLAND was born on the 3rd of May 1854 and died on the 2nd of November 1920.[clxx] In the 1900 census, he was living in Philadelphia with his sister, Mary Baugh. It is noted that he had been married for one year, but his wife was not

listed as living with him.[clxxi] In the 1920 census, he was living in a boarding house and was a widower.[clxxii] No records of his marriage can be found. It is doubtful that there were any children.

+75. vi. William Harrison ENGLAND was born on the 4th of March 1857.[clxxiii] He died on the 17th of October 1920 in Winterhaven, Florida.[clxxiv] He married Harriet Kendall TURNER (daughter of C. L. TURNER). She was born on the 1st of February 1875 in Milwaukee, Wisconsin and died on the 18th of July 1941 in Winterhaven, Florida.[clxxv]

36. JOANNA ENGLAND (William[3], Thomas[2], William[1]) was born on the 22nd of May 1818 and died on the 3rd of November 1894. She married Jacob ROBERTS about 1835. He was born on the 8th of March 1810 and died on the 7th of March 1879 in Camden, New Jersey. Jacob was a builder.[clxxvi]

Joanna and Jacob had seven children:

+76. i. Elizabeth ROBERTS was born on the 31st of January 1836 and died on the 22nd of February 1872 in Gloucester County, New Jersey.[clxxvii] She married Oliver CRAWFORD on the 18th of January 1855 in Somerset County, New Jersey.[clxxviii] He was born on the 16th of April 1830 in Pennsylvania and died of tuberculosis on the 26th of May 1880 in Gloucester County, New Jersey.[clxxix]

+77. ii. Isabella E. ROBERTS was born in 1838 and died in Gloucester County on the 10th of May 1879.[clxxx] She married Samuel MYERS (son of Jacob and Letitia MYERS) on the 1st of December 1859 in Swedesboro, New Jersey.[clxxxi] He was born about 1837 in New Jersey.[clxxxii] His date of death is unknown.

+78. iii. Joseph ROBERTS was born in February 1840 and died in 1915 in New Jersey.[clxxxiii] He married Priscilla HILLMAN (daughter of Richard and Ellen HILLMAN) on the 14th of March 1867 in Salem, New Jersey. She was born in 1842[clxxxiv] and died on the 16th of February 1889.[clxxxv]

79. iv. Johanna ROBERTS was born in 1843.[clxxxvi] She did not appear with her family in the 1860 census; at that time, she would have been 17 years of age. No records of her marriage or death were found.

+80. v. Hannah ROBERTS was born about 1846.[clxxxvii] She died sometime after 1900; she was not found in the 1910 census with her husband.[clxxxviii] She married Samuel B. HARBISON (son of Samuel and Sarah Ann HARBISON) on the 26th of November in 1865 in Salem, New Jersey.[clxxxix] He was born about 1809 in New Jersey.[cxc] He died after 1920 (the last census year in which he was found).

+81. vi. Frances "Frank" J. ROBERTS was born on the 13th of September 1846 in New Jersey. He died of tuberculosis on the 23rd of March 1912 in Philadelphia.[cxci] He married

Florence A. SMITH in 1871.[cxcii] She was born about 1852 in Pennsylvania.[cxciii] She died after 1910, the last census year in which she was found.

82.   vii.   Emma ROBERTS was born on the 6th of June 1854 in New Jersey.[cxciv] She died after 1917, the last Camden city directory in which she was found. She married Harry K. HEFLINE in 1870. He was born about 1851 in Pennsylvania and died after 1907 (the last Camden city directory in which he was found). The 1870 census lists a Harry Hefline living in Gloucester County, New Jersey, working as a farmer, and born in France. Emma and Harry had four children, all of whom died in childhood.[cxcv]

37.   **DEBORAH ENGLAND** (William[3], Thomas[2], William[1]) was born in New Jersey on the 22nd of May 1818[cxcvi] and died in Philadelphia on the 5th of January 1907.[cxcvii] She married Francis TAWS on the 13th January 1841.[cxcviii] He was born about 1812 and died on the 27th of January 1891.[cxcix] Francis worked as a machinist and then an engineer for the U.S. Mint.

Deborah and Francis had three children:

83.   i.   Hannah E. TAWS was born about 1845 in Pennsylvania. She died the 10th of October 1929 in Philadelphia.[cc] After the death of her parents, no records of her residence could be found.

84.   ii.   Francis "Frank" TAWS was born about 1848 in Pennsylvania[cci] and died in May 1890 in Philadelphia at the age of 40.[ccii] In all census records, the occupation column is blank. It appears that Frank never married.

+85.   iii.   James B. TAWS was born in 1851 and died on the 6th of November 1894.[cciii] He married Mary E. THOMAS (daughter of Robert THOMAS and Eliza Jane SMITH) on the 22nd of September 1881 in Philadelphia.[cciv] She was born on the 22nd of March 1857 and died on the 1st of June 1942 in Philadelphia.[ccv] After the death of her husband, James, Mary remarried in 1901 to Samuel BORER in Philadelphia.[ccvi]

38.   **SAMUEL ENGLAND** (William[3], Thomas[2], William[1]) was born on the 12th of April 1820. He died of gangrene of the lung on the 8th of June 1879 in Philadelphia. He married Elizabeth Ann HAINES (daughter of Thomas and Elizabeth HAINES) on the 26th of May 1842.[ccvii] She was born in September 1826 and died on the 19th of December 1912.[ccviii] Samuel was a cabinetmaker.

86.   i.   William J. ENGLAND was born in 1843 and died of tuberculosis on the 16th of February 1866 in Philadelphia.[ccix] At the time of his death, he was an infantry soldier, enlisted in the Pennsylvania 114th Regiment, Company D. No marriage records for William were found.[ccx]

87.   ii.   Thomas ENGLAND was born about 1843[ccxi] and died of tuberculosis on the 13th of December 1872 in Philadelphia. He worked as a "gold beater". It is unknown if he married or had children.

+88. iii. Gustavus H. ENGLAND was born in 1847 and died of tuberculosis on the 24th of March 1891 in Philadelphia.[ccxii] He married Ella H. GLESSNER (daughter of Oliver P. and Mary GLESSNER). She was born in 1849 and died on the 28th of November 1875 of typhoid pneumonia.[ccxiii]

40. **ROBERT ENGLAND** (William[3], Thomas[2], William[1]) was born on the 21st of February 1825 and died on the 29th of March 1896 in Philadelphia. He married Louise Rebecca RANCK (daughter of Nathaniel RANCK, MD and Susan KEYSER) on the 18th of July 1855 in Philadelphia.[ccxiv] She was born on the 12th of October 1834 and died of bronchitis on the 30th of March 1920.[ccxv] Robert was a well-known druggist in Philadelphia and, for a short time before his death, owned his own manufacturing company. His son, Joseph, and a number of nephews were employed by him. *Photo from the collection of the Gloucester Historical Society Library (New Jersey); used with permission.*

Robert and Louise Rebecca had nine children:

89. i. Lydia Rebecca MATTHEWS was an adopted daughter. Nothing is known about her parents, but it appears that she was raised in this family, first appearing in the 1870 census at the age of 12. She was born on the 6th of February 1855 and died on the 5th of March 1919. She married Frank KELLEY (son of John Kelley and Catherine LONG). He was born on the 15th of January 1853 and died on the 13th of March 1936.[ccxvi] He never remarried. Lydia and Frank had four children: Edward, Edith, Frank Jr., and William.

90. ii. Anna Ranck ENGLAND was born on the 14th of February 1858 and died on the 31st of May 1939 in Philadelphia.[ccxvii] She married Charles Carson JONES (son of William S. and Mary JONES). He was born about 1855 and died on the 4th of January 1894.[ccxviii] Charles worked as a cutter in the clothing manufacturing industry. The 1900 census indicates that Anna had born one child who was not alive. In his will, Charles left his estate to his wife, but indicated that all financial decisions must be agreed upon by his brother, W. S. Jones, Jr. He explains: "My reason, and the only one, for not giving my wife my property outright is that her heart might run away with her reason, and she may be left in want, in her old age."[ccxix] She never remarried.

91. iii. Susan Louise ENGLAND was born on the 29th of July 1856 and died on the 29th of May 1860 in Philadelphia[ccxx].

92. iv. Robert Mason ENGLAND was born on the 21st of March 1861.[ccxxi] He died on the 5th of July 1862 of hydrocephalus.[ccxxii]

+93. v. Dr. Joseph Winters ENGLAND was born on the 26th of September 1863 in Philadelphia.[ccxxiii] He died in November 1933.[ccxxiv] He married Ella Virginia RUSSELL (daughter of Jacob P. RUSSELL and Anne EMERY) on the 6th of May 1891 in Philadelphia.[ccxxv] She was born on the 30th of May 1863 and died on the 20th of January 1942.[ccxxvi]

94. vi. Louis Nathaniel ENGLAND was born on the 7th of April 1866 and died, at the age of 12, on the 29th of October 1878.[ccxxvii]

95. vii. Mary Estelle ENGLAND was born on the 24th of May 1869 and died on the 28th of November 1941.[ccxxviii] She never married. She was employed as a bookkeeper.

96. viii. Bertha Irene ENGLAND was born on the 16th of February 1878 and died on the 24th of December 1949.[ccxxix] She never married. She was employed as a medical secretary.

46. **REBECCA ENGLAND** (William W.[3], Daniel[2], William[1]) was born on the 27th of June 1810 in Swedesboro.[ccxxx] She died on the 25th of November 1886 in Oldmans, New Jersey.[ccxxxi] She married David LYNCH on the 8th of December 1831 at the Trinity Church[ccxxxii]. He was born in 1808 and died on the 29th of August 1884 in Oldmans, New Jersey. David was a steamboat captain.

Rebecca and David had two daughters:

+97. i. Mary England LYNCH was born on the 9th of September 1832. She died on the 5th of May 1910. She married William HURFF (son of Isaac HURFF and Ann Jane JAGGARD). He was born on the 31st of December 1832 and died on the 13th of April 1894.[ccxxxiii] He is buried in the Trinity churchyard in Swedesboro, New Jersey.

+98. ii. Elizabeth LYNCH was born on the 24th of November 1836.[ccxxxiv] She died on the 15th of February 1924 in Elmwood, Illinois. On the 5th of March 1863, she married Isaac HURFF, Jr. (son of Isaac HURFF and Ann Jane JAGGARD) in Woodbury, New Jersey.[ccxxxv] He was born in September 1835[ccxxxvi] and died on the 14th of January 1903 in Elmwood, Illinois.[ccxxxvii]

47. **AQUILA BARBER ENGLAND** (William W.[3], Daniel[2], William[1]) was born on the 7th of October 1812 in Swedesboro.[ccxxxviii] He died on the 27th August 1896 in Brooklyn, New York.[ccxxxix] He married Elizabeth TOWNLEY. She was born about 1814 in New Jersey [ccxl] and died on the 9th of December 1874.[ccxli].

His obituary from the Brooklyn Daily Eagle:

OBITUARY

Aquila Barber England died at his home, 453 Washington avenue, yesterday, at the age of 83. He was a builder of wide reputation, and was closely identified with the growth of the hill section of the city. The house that he built in 1835 in Washington avenue, near Lafayette, when that street was nothing more than a country road, is still standing and since that time Mr. England has put up many buildings in the Ninth, Eleventh and Twentieth wards. He was born in Swedesboro, N. J., in 1812. His father, who was a vestryman in St. Luke's hospital, was a large landholder in that section. At the age of 16 young England went to Philadelphia, where he learned the trade of a mason. Later, coming to New York on a visit, he was persuaded to remain in the metropolis and he soon gained his first contract by his thorough knowledge of the business in which he was engaged. The contractors for a large building, being unable to fix the ceiling properly asked Mr. England for his opinion and were so pleased with his suggestions that they gave him the contract, and the thoroughness and skill with which he did the work soon gained for him a wide reputation. Most of his work was confined to private houses and it is a significant fact that during his whole career he has never had a lawsuit. He was one of the oldest directors of the National City bank, and was never known to miss a directors' meetng. He was also a director of the Phenix Fire Insurance company for many years. In politics he was a stanch Republican.

Aquila and Elizabeth had five children:

99.   i.   Ophelia M. ENGLAND was born about 1836 in New York.[ccxlii] She died on the 15th of March 1915 at the home of her sister, Emma.[ccxliii] She married Edward DOUGLAS on the 6th of October 1865 in Brooklyn. He was born about 1826[ccxliv] and died on the 12th of November 1868.[ccxlv] His occupation is unknown. There were no children. She next married David J. DEAN on the 30th of June 1880.[ccxlvi] He was born in 1836 in Newark, New Jersey to Isaac DEAN. At the time of his death, he was First Assistant to the Corporation Counsel, and was working on preparing a tentative draft of the charter for Greater New York. He was highly respected and his obituary stated that he "argued more cases in the Court of Appeals than any other lawyer living." Upon his death, the Commission of Greater New York passed a resolution, expressing appreciation for his services. He held the position of First Assistant for twenty-five years, and earned a salary of $10,000 per year. He died on the 10th of January 1897 in San Antonio, Texas. He was on his way to winter in Arizona to care for his tuberculosis and diabetes on the advice of his physicians. [ccxlvii] Full column obituaries ran for four days in the New York newspapers. Ophelia and David had no children. David had four children by a previous marriage, three of whom were living at the time of his death.

+100.   ii.   Benjamin F. ENGLAND was born in April 1840 in New York. [ccxlviii] He died on the 10th of June 1922 in Brooklyn. He married Ella OLLIS in 1868.[ccxlix] She was born in May 1845 in Pennsylvania.[ccl] She died on the 16th of September 1922 in Brooklyn.[ccli]

101. iii. Henry C. ENGLAND was born about 1842 in New York.[cclii] He died on the 5th of March 1881. He married Catherine, born about 1848 in Austria.[ccliii] They had one child, Augusta, born about 1872 and died on the 15th of July 1875.[ccliv] Henry served in the Army during the Civil War. He enlisted at the age of 19, and joined the 5th Independent Battery, New York Light Artillery Division. In his will, dated the 5th of March 1881, he states that he is "very ill" and knows he will die soon. He bequeathed his entire estate to his wife, Catherine.[cclv] Catherine appears in the city directories of 1884 and 1886, as the widow of Henry C. England. No other records for Catherine can be found after 1886.

+102. iv. Emma C. ENGLAND was born about 1847 in New York and she died on the 9th of September 1930 in Brooklyn.[cclvi] She married Thomas J. SODEN who was born about 1841 in Ireland. He died on the 3rd of November 1926 in Brooklyn.[cclvii]

103. v. Annie E. ENGLAND was born in 1855 and died on the 14th of December 1935.[cclviii] She married William READ (son of Thomas and Sarah A. READ) on the 17th of May 1877.[cclix] He died on the 4th of June 1937.[cclx] At the time of their marriage, William was a hat maker. At the time of his death he was president of a plumbing supply company. In his will, he bequeaths $20,000 of personal property to the Methodist Church, to be distributed to people in need. These contributions were given in the name of several of his family members, including his wife, his mother, his mother-in-law and others.[cclxi] Annie and William had no children.

49. **WILLIAM WATSON ENGLAND** (William W.[3], Daniel[2], William[1]) was born on the 2nd of November 1816[cclxii] and died on the 13th of January 1899 in Swedesboro.[cclxiii] He married Mary Amanda GREEN on the 21st of December 1850 at a Quaker meeting in Haddonfield.[cclxiv] She was born on the 21st of November 1822 in Salem, New Jersey and she died on the 25th of March 1897 in Camden, New Jersey.[cclxv] William was a farmer.

William and Mary Amanda had six children:

+104. i. Frances "Fanny" A. ENGLAND was born in 1850 in New Jersey.[cclxvi] She died in 1913 and is buried in the Pedricktown Friends Cemetery in Salem County, New Jersey.[cclxvii] She married George Clark HORNER (son of Elijah Bowers HORNER and Mary CLARK) in 1886.[cclxviii] He was born on the 18th of January 1895 in Swedesboro, New Jersey.[cclxix] and died in November 1930 in Salem County, New Jersey.

105 ii. Mary ENGLAND was born in February 1853 in New Jersey.[cclxx] She died on the 20th of October 1909 in Salem County, New Jersey.[cclxxi] She married Benjamin CARNEY on the 8th of February 1878.[cclxxii] He was born in January 1853 in New Jersey.[cclxxiii] He died in 1940 in Salem County, New Jersey. Benjamin was a farmer. The couple had no children.

+106. iii. Ella K. ENGLAND was born in September 1855.[cclxxiv] She died on the 28th of August 1934 in Gloucester County, New Jersey.[cclxxv] She married Samuel Stratton MATTSON

(son of Jonathon W. MATTSON and Rebecca E. SHILLING) on the 4th of March 1875.[cclxxvi] He was born in December 1850 and died on the 8th of May 1922 in Gloucester County, New Jersey.[cclxxvii]

107.   iv.   Sarah "Sallie" R. ENGLAND was born on the 11th of September 1858.[cclxxviii] The last census in which she is found is 1880, age 21 and living with her parents in Salem County, New Jersey.[cclxxix] There is a marriage record for Sarah R. England, and William Harris, in Cold Spring, New Jersey, March 1887; however, this event can not be definitely linked to our Sallie. [cclxxx] No other records of her life were found.

+108.   v.   William "Willie" ENGLAND was born on the 7th of June 1861 and died on the 13th of February 1929 in Salem, New Jersey.[cclxxxi] He married Hannah CHEESMAN (daughter of Benjamin and Martha CHEESMAN) on the 27th of December 1866 in Woodstown, New Jersey.[cclxxxii] She was born on the 5th of September 1866 in Gloucester County, New Jersey, and died on the 15th of April 1924 in Salem County, New Jersey.[cclxxxiii]

+109.   vi.   Charles ENGLAND was born in February 1864[cclxxxiv] and died in 1948 in Salem, New Jersey. [cclxxxv] He married Mary I. DAVIDSON (daughter of John and Melvina DAVIDSON) in 1892.[cclxxxvi] She was born in March 1874[cclxxxvii] and died in Salem County, New Jersey in 1930.[cclxxxviii]

50.   **SARAH ANN ENGLAND** (William W.³, Daniel², William¹) was born on the 24th October 1818. She died of throat consumption on the 30th of January 1860.[cclxxxix] She married John AMBRUSTER on the 25th of May 1839 in Gloucester County, New Jersey.[ccxc] (Note: his surname is Ambruster, not Armbruster.) He was born in 1816 and died on the 10th of January 1885.[ccxci] He married a second time to Virginia "Jennie" ROWLAND in December 1861.[ccxcii] John was a builder. In the 1850 census, he claimed his real estate value to be $15,000.

Sarah and John had four children:

+110.   i.   William Watson England AMBRUSTER was born on the 19th of August 1845 in Philadelphia.[ccxciii] He died of an intestinal obstruction on the 18th of March 1904 in Philadelphia.[ccxciv] He married Emma Elizabeth EARLEY (daughter of James Wood EARLEY and Deborah CLARK) in Philadelphia on the 10th of June 1873.[ccxcv] She died on the 23rd of February 1895. He next married Isabel C. BINGHAM (daughter of John BINGHAM and Mary GRAYBILL) in Philadelphia in 1896. She was born on the 8th of August 1849 and died on the 17th of October 1931 in Philadelphia.[ccxcvi]

111.   ii.   Edwin AMBRUSTER was born in 1850 in Philadelphia.[ccxcvii] He was recorded as 9 months old in the 1850 census, and he does not appear with his family in the 1860 census. It is, therefore, assumed that he died as an infant or child.

+112.   iii.   Mary AMBRUSTER was born in January 1855.[ccxcviii] She married John Marion ALLEN on the 1st of November 1873 in Camden.[ccxcix] He was born in March 1854 in New Jersey.[ccc] There are no records of their deaths; the last record found in which they appear is the 1920 census.

113.   iv.   Howard AMBRUSTER was born about 1857 and died in January 1878 of cardiac disease, at the age of 21, in Camden, New Jersey. [ccci]

58.   **CATHERINE B. ENGLAND** (Daniel^3, Daniel^2, William^1) was born on the 5th of August 1839 in Swedesboro, and died on the 8th of April 1923 in Chester County, Pennsylvania.[cccii] She was 11 years old at the time of her mother's death, and was subsequently adopted by her mother's family and given the surname CLARK.[ccciii] She married William Henry IRWIN (son of John Cuningham IRWIN and Mary Ann CHEYNEY) on the 12th of May 1864 in Philadelphia.[ccciv] (Yes, it is Cuningham with one 'n'.) He was born about 1831 and died on the 14th of September 1874 of typhoid fever at the age of 43.[cccv] His occupation is unknown. She married a second time to William Arthur CHEYNEY (son of Charles Henry CHEYNEY and Cornelia CONNERY) in 1881.[cccvi] He was born on the 9th of March 1846 in Philadelphia and died the 9th of April 1892 in New York.[cccvii] He was engaged in real estate and served as an auditor for the Franklin Institute (a museum in Philadelphia that still exists today).[cccviii] Catherine and William Cheyney had no children.

Catherine and William Irwin had four children:

114.   i.   William Henry IRWIN was born in 1860 and died in Philadelphia at 5 weeks of age.[cccix]

115.   ii.   Florence IRWIN was born on the 14th September 1865.[cccx] She never married. Her exact date of death is unknown, but she is buried in the Cheyney Family Burying Ground.[cccxi] She traveled to Paris, France five times between 1929 and 1934. Her last found record is the 1940 census, in Greenburgh, New York.[cccxii]

116.   iii.   Helen IRWIN was born on the 29th of April 1867, and died on the 25th of November 1889, at the age of 22. [cccxiii]

+117.   iv.   James Clark IRWIN was born on the 23rd of September 1868 in Cheyney, Pennsylvania.[cccxiv] His exact date of death is unknown; the last record found is the 1940 census. He married Frances Smith MONAGHAN (daughter of Robert Emmet MONAGHAN and Rebecca Darlington SMITH) on the 5th of June 1895 in West Chester, Pennsylvania.[cccxv] She was born about 1873 in Pennsylvania and died in 1943 in Newton, Massachusetts.

58. **EMILY T. ENGLAND** (Daniel[3], Daniel[2], William[1]) was born on the 16th of October 1845 in Swedesboro.[cccxvi] She was 5 years old at the time of her mother's death and she, and her sister Lydia, went to live with the Tonkin family.[cccxvii] She died on the 21st of April 1929 in Philadelphia at the age of 83.[cccxviii] She married Joseph B. CLEMENT IV (son of Joseph B. CLEMENT III and Elizabeth WARWICK[cccxix]) on the 24th of June 1869 in Philadelphia.[cccxx] He was born on the 6th of June 1842 in New Jersey. He died on the 21st of January 1902.[cccxxi] Joseph worked as a commissioned salesman. *Photo from the collection of Kathleen Clement; used with permission*

Emily and Joseph had two children:

+118. i. Joseph B. CLEMENT V was born on the 14th of January 1874 in Woodbury, New Jersey.[cccxxii] He died in 1934 in Schenectady, New York.[cccxxiii] He married Jeanette L. WARD (daughter of Myndert WARD and Mary DUNCAN) in 1896. She was born on the 11th of September 1874[cccxxiv] and died in 1942 in Schenectady, New York.[cccxxv]

+119. ii. Frank West CLEMENT was born on the 14th of July 1883 in Woodbury, New Jersey.[cccxxvi] The date of his death is unknown. He married Anna Knight MARSHALL (daughter of Leander A. MARSHALL and Margaret Levis BARNEY). She was born in February 1889.[cccxxvii] Her date of death is unknown.

62. **DANIEL ENGLAND** (Daniel[3], Daniel[2], William[1]) was born on the 2nd of November 1862 in Newton Township, Camden County, New Jersey.[cccxxviii] He died on the 21st of August 1935 in Philadelphia.[cccxxix] He is identified as Daniel, Jr. in some records, but in fact, he is Daniel III. He married Elena Rachel WILSON (daughter of Joseph WILSON and Rachel STRANG) on the 23rd of March 1877 in Camden, New Jersey.[cccxxx] She was born on the 29th of November 1864 in Clayton Township, Gloucester County, New Jersey[cccxxxi] and died on the 11th of February 1937 in Gloucester, New Jersey.[cccxxxii] Census records tell us that Daniel had several different jobs throughout his lifetime that include making shoes, selling groceries, assistant lineman, and timekeeper.

Daniel and Elena had five children:

120. i. Lillian Frances ENGLAND was born on the 1st of December 1887 in Camden, New Jersey. She died in February 1969 in Moorestown, New Jersey.[cccxxxiii] She married Benjamin F. YARD Jr. (son of Benjamin F. YARD Sr. and Clara WARD) in Haddonfield, New Jersey, on the 8th of April 1914.[cccxxxiv] He was born on the 25th of December 1887 in Camden, New Jersey.[cccxxxv] He died in May 1983 in Pitman,

New Jersey.[cccxxxvi] The couple had no children; they were divorced in the 1920's and Lillian never remarried. [cccxxxvii] She worked as a saleslady in a department store.[cccxxxviii]

121. ii. Bertha Etta ENGLAND was born on the 1st of October 1892 in Camden, New Jersey.[cccxxxix] She died in January 1974 in Collingswood, New Jersey.[cccxl] She married Howard WAKEMAN (son of James Thomas WAKEMAN and Laura LEETY) on the 17th of April 1911 in Camden, New Jersey.[cccxli] He was born on the 11th of February 1891 in New Jersey.[cccxlii] He died in March 1972 in Collingswood, New Jersey.[cccxliii] Howard was a printer with the Lippincott Publishing Company. The couple had seven children.

122. iii. Carrie Estella ENGLAND was born on the 2nd of June 1894 in Camden, New Jersey.[cccxliv] She died on the 14th of October 2001 in New Jersey, at 107 years of age.[cccxlv] She married Albert Meader BROWN (son of Ernest B. BROWN and Bertha SCHERER) in 1907.[cccxlvi] He was born on the 8th of November 1892 in Cambridge, Massachusetts.[cccxlvii] He died on the 1st of March 1946 in Arlington, Virginia, where his son was residing.[cccxlviii] Albert was a manager for a tool company. Carrie and Albert had two children.

123. iv. Daniel Wilson ENGLAND was born on the 6th of May 1898 in Camden, New Jersey.[cccxlix] He died of injuries sustained when he was hit by a trolley car[cccl] in Camden on the 13th of September 1900.[cccli]

124. v. James Milton ENGLAND was born on the 17th of September 1899 in Camden and died on the 1st of September 1926 in Louisville, Kentucky. [ccclii] He was a motorcycle policeman, chasing a bootlegger, when he lost control and hit a tree.[cccliii] He married Catherine M. BECKER (daughter of William BECKER and Anna BORNWASSER) in Chicago, Illinois on the 1st of February 1923. She was born on the 8th of December 1899 in Jefferson County, Kentucky.[cccliv] For a short time, she and her sister, Annetta, lived in an orphanage. She attended nursing school at Hahnemann Hospital in Philadelphia. She died on the 9th of November 1945 in West Chester, Pennsylvania. [ccclv] She next married Frank MARQUETTE in 1930 in Philadelphia. [ccclvi] According to the Officer Down website, James and Catherine had two children.[ccclvii] No records for those children were found. They are not mentioned in his newspaper obituary.[ccclviii] *Photograph from the collection of Lee Weller, used with permission.*

JUNE 12, 1923, PHILA
JAMES MILTON ENGLAND

64. **OSCAR BROWN ENGLAND** (Daniel[3], Daniel[2], William[1]) was born on the 8ᵗʰ of February 1868 in

Camden, NJ.[ccclix] He died on the 26ᵗʰ of April 1937 in Belvidere, Illinois[ccclx]. He married Frieda RUEDI (daughter of Andrew RUEDI) on the 27ᵗʰ of June 1892 at the Church of the Holy Transformation in Chicago, Illinois.[ccclxi] She was born on the 11ᵗʰ of January 1870 in Schaffhausen, Switzerland.[ccclxii] She arrived in this country in 1888.[ccclxiii] She died on the 11ᵗʰ of March 1948 in Rockford, Illinois.[ccclxiv]

Photo from the collection of Jean West; used with permission.

It is not clear why Oscar moved from New Jersey to Illinois. In a letter to her daughter, Oscar's daughter, Dorothy, writes:

> *Dad's info is very sketchy. Think he was born in New Jersey. Never heard how many brothers or sisters his name was Oscar Brown England. So it could be his mother's maiden name was Brown. Whatever – his mother died when he was young his father remarried and he left home as soon as he could for he didn't like his step mother. Marge [Oscar's daughter, Margaret] has said Dad said his grandfather was Billy England the pirate. Never heard that name in history or books so make what you want of that. What he worked at as a young man I don't know. He did do adjustments in White Sewing Machines in Belvidere until he could no longer work. Besides his rheumatism he was diagnosed as tubercular and he also spoke of asthma. I've written I thought Dad a harsh man— maybe that is wrong for I don't recall he and mom ever quarreling but he was impatient at times and when I was older his displeasure when neighbors came to visit mom – which he felt was inconsiderate for it kept her from her work.[ccclxv]*

What we know from the records is that Oscar didn't move to Chicago until after the death of his father, and that there was no step-mother.

In the same letter, Dorothy writes that her mother, Frieda Ruedi, immigrated from Switzerland with a sister to avoid a marriage that her parents had planned to an older man that she didn't like. While living in Cherry Valley, Illinois, Frieda "got hooked on spiritualism". After the move to Belvidere, she "took up with the Jehovah's Witnesses". From this letter and others, it is clear that all of Oscar and Frieda's children, as young adults, worked to support their parents as Oscar was badly crippled with arthritis and couldn't work.

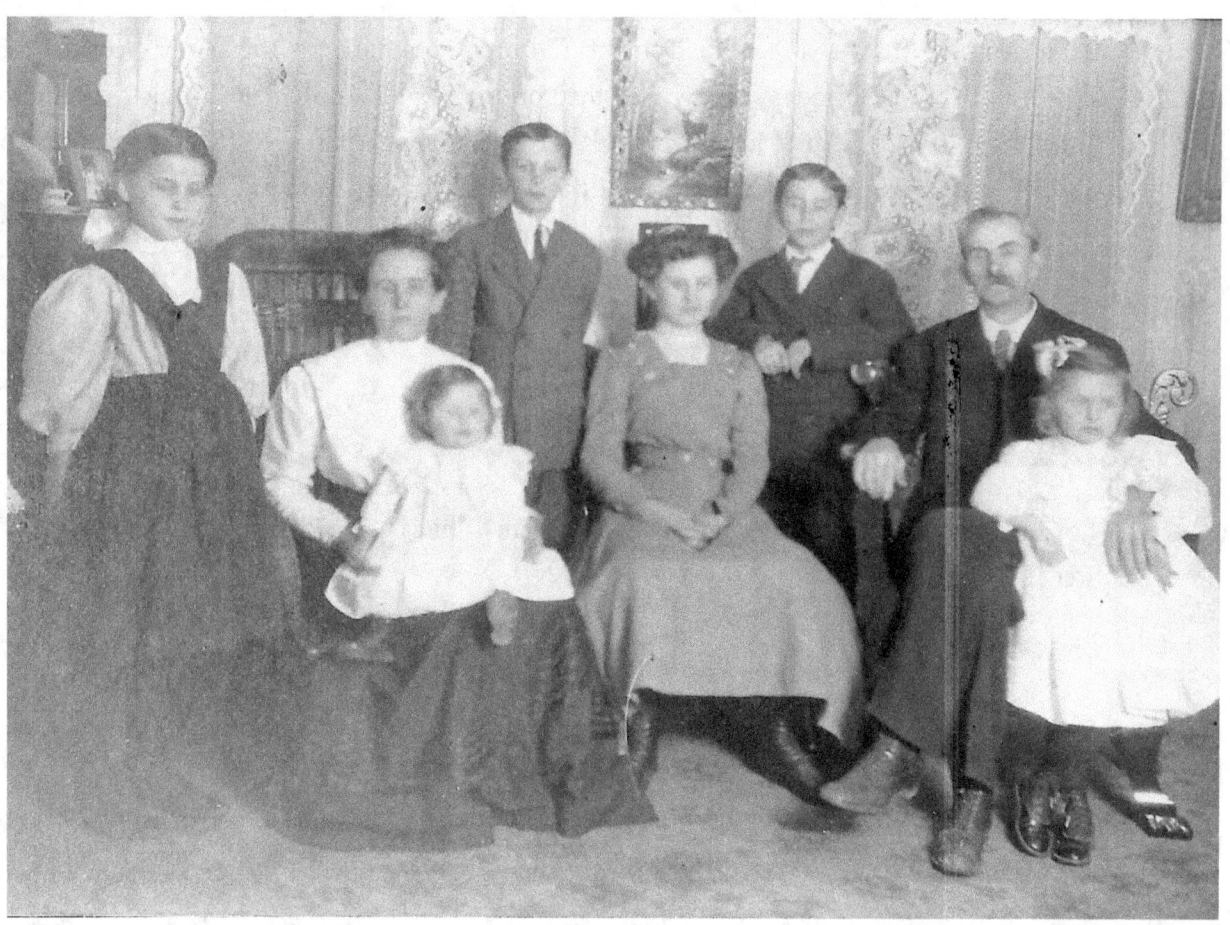

Photo from the collection of Jean West, used with permission

Oscar and Frieda had 6 children:

+125.   i.   Frieda I. ENGLAND was born in April 1894 in Chicago, Illinois.[ccclxvi] She died on the 19th of January 1970 in Belvidere.[ccclxvii] She married William Carlton "Carl" BEAN on the 20th of April 1918 in Belvidere.[ccclxviii] He was born on the 9th of July 1890 in Nebraska.[ccclxix] He died on the 8th of January 1969 in Belvidere.[ccclxx]

126.   ii.   Oscar Daniel ENGLAND was born on the 14th of June 1896 in Chicago, Illinois.[ccclxxi] He died on the 1st of January 1986 in Belvidere, Illinois.[ccclxxii] He married Daisy L. SNYDER (daughter of Martin SNYDER and Cora WEAVER). She was born on the 21st of February 1898 in Blaine, Pennsylvania.[ccclxxiii] She died on the 11th of March 1995 in Belvidere, Illinois.[ccclxxiv] Oscar was the vice-president of the Midwest Bottle Cap Company in Belvidere. After the plant closed, he worked as a printer in Belvidere through the 1950's. There were no children born to Oscar and Daisy.

One of Oscar's nieces recalls Oscar and Daisy:
> *Then came Uncle Oscar who sort of reminded me of my image of our Grandfather [Oscar B. England]. He married Aunt Daisy and they had no children. They lived in Belvidere all their lives. I was "privileged" to spend a week at their home one summer*

but you lived in the basement of the house which was fixed up just like a regular house with a kitchen, livingroom, etc. The upstairs was treated like a museum. We all recall Aunt Daisy have coal black hair all her life. She was a very tiny LADY.[ccclxxv]

+127. iii. Herbert ENGLAND was born on the 22ⁿᵈ of July 1898 in Chicago, Illinois.[ccclxxvi] He died on the 7ᵗʰ of May 1983, at the age of 83, in St. Petersburg, Florida. He was the driver of a battery-powered cart that was hit by a car. He married Rose PIENSCHKE (daughter of Franciszek PIENSCHKE and Rosalia BOLDA) on the 1ˢᵗ of July 1922 in Chicago.[ccclxxvii] She was born on the 20ᵗʰ of February 1901 in Chicago and died on the 3ʳᵈ of October 1974 in St. Petersburg, Florida.[ccclxxviii]

+128. iv. Harriet ENGLAND was born on the 30ᵗʰ of December 1900 in Cherry Valley, Illinois and died in June 1975 in Carlsbad, New Mexico. [ccclxxix] She married Carl BAYLANDER (son of Charles BAYLANDER and Mary LINK) on the 1ˢᵗ of July 1921 in Belvidere.[ccclxxx] He was born on the 1ˢᵗ of May 1900 in Chicago, and died on the 1ˢᵗ of April 1953 in Rockford, Illinois.[ccclxxxi] Harriet then married Dr. Willard C. MORREY on the 21ˢᵗ of January 1961 in Rockford.[ccclxxxii] He was born on the 14ᵗʰ of April 1893 in Ottawa, Ohio.[ccclxxxiii] He died in November 1973 in Carlsbad, New Mexico.[ccclxxxiv]

129. v. Margaret B. ENGLAND was born on the 18ᵗʰ of October 1905 in Cherry Valley, Illinois.[ccclxxxv] She died on the 7ᵗʰ of January 1991 in Oak Park, Illinois.[ccclxxxvi] She never married. She was an office manager and bookkeeper for the Kjos Music Company in downtown Chicago. She is remembered fondly by her nieces, the Venable girls.

Photo from the collection of Jean West, used with permission

130.   vi.   Dorothy I. ENGLAND was born on the 9th of April 1908 in Cherry Valley, Illinois.[ccclxxxvii] She died on the 11th March 1996 in Cherry Valley, Illinois. She married Evan George VENABLES (son of Evan John VENABLES and Mary PERRY) on the 20th of June 1931 in Belvidere, Illinois, at the home of her parents.[ccclxxxviii] He was born on the 30th of April 1905 in Stoufville, Ontario, Canada. He was naturalized as an American citizen on the 15th of December 1942.[ccclxxxix] He died on the 18th June 1993 in Belvidere.[cccxc] Dorothy and George had four children.

From the collection of Lorraine Goodwillie; used with permission

65.   Mary D. ENGLAND (James[3], Daniel[2], William[1]) was born about 1837 in Gloucester County New Jersey.[cccxci] She died of consumption in Philadelphia on the 17th of January 1885, at the age of 48.[cccxcii] She married Joseph P. CRAMER.[cccxciii] He was born about 1818 and died in Philadelphia on the 1st of May 1880.[cccxciv] Joseph worked as a bank clerk.[cccxcv]

Mary and Joseph had two children:

131.   i   George H. CRAMER was born about 1846 in Pennsylvania.[cccxcvi] He died on the 26th of December 1889, at the age of 43, in Philadelphia. He never married and worked as a clerk.[cccxcvii]

+132.   ii.   Anna Elizabeth CRAMER was born on the 29th of January 1871[cccxcviii] and died of tuberculosis on the 30th of October 1899 in Reading, Pennsylvania.[cccxcix] She married William E. WESTNEY in 1892 in Philadelphia.[cd] He was born in March 1870 in New York State.[cdi] His date of death is unknown.

66.   HENRY C. ENGLAND (James[3], Daniel[2], William[1]) was born on the 17th of November 1843 in New Jersey. He died on the 10th of October 1910 in Reading, Pennsylvania.[cdii] He married Sarah J. GILL (daughter of Matthew GILL and Mary JESSUP) on the 12th of August 1874.[cdiii] She was born on the 5th of September 1847 in New Jersey and died on the 24th of February 1948.[cdiv]

Photo from the collection of the Gloucester County Historical Society Library (New Jersey) used with permission

Henry was a very prominent figure wherever he was. There are dozens of newspaper articles written about him and his business activities. The following article was written in 1965[cdv] and best summarizes his life:

Henry C. England was born at Swedesboro, November 17, 1844.
His parents were James and Ann Elizabeth England, descended from

an eminent family of New Jersey, which contributed some of the most distinguished men in its history.

He attended the common schools in Swedesboro until he was fifteen years of age and by that time had acquired a fair education. He was then obliged to assist in helping his parents and secured a position in a general store in that town. One year later, finding he could better himself, he seized the opportunity and came to Paulsboro to work. While engaged in the latter place, the Civil War broke out, so in 1962 he enlisted in the 24th regiment of New Jersey Volunteers.

Though only eighteen years of age he was selected as Third Sergeant of his company and mustered into service for a term of nine months. He fought in the battles at Fredericksburg and Chancellorsville with great bravery and at the end of his term was honorably discharged and mustered out of service.

Sometime after he went to Philadelphia and was employed by the Biddle Hardware Co., as salesman for his native state. He remained with this firm for eight years until July 1872 during which time he became very friendly with the business and on account of his great success in extending the trade and influence of his firm, was recognized as a man of great worth and promise.

He was made manager of the sales department and moved to Reading. Mr. England at once exhibited such marked ability in the management of this department that he was given an interest in its profits and by 1880, he was so valued he was permitted to acquired one-fourth interest in the company.

In 1886 he was elected Treasurer and held that office until a fire, in 1888, destroyed over a million dollars' worth of the plant. In spite of this great loss, the finances of the Henry C. England was born at Swedesboro, November 17. 1844. His parents were James and Ann Elizabeth England, descended from an eminent family of New Jersey, which contributed some of the most distinguished men in its history.

He attended the common schools in Swedesboro until he was fifteen years of age and by that time had acquired a fair education. He was then obliged to assist in helping his parents and secured a position in a general store in that town. One year later, finding he could better himself, he seized the opportunity and came to Paulsboro to work. While engaged in the latter place, the Civil War broke out, so in 1962 he enlisted in the 24th regiment of New Jersey Volunteers.

Though only eighteen years of age he was selected as Third Sergeant of his company and mustered into service for a term of nine months. He fought in the battles at Fredericksburg and Chancellorsville with great bravery and at the end of his term was honorably discharged and mustered out of service.

Sometime after he went to Philadelphia and was employed by the Biddle Hardware Co., as salesman for his native state. He remained with this firm for eight years until July 1872 during which time he became very friendly with the business and on account of his great success in extending the trade and influence of his firm, was recognized as a man of great worth and promise.

He was made manager of the sales department and moved to Reading. Mr. England at once exhibited such marked ability in the management of this department that he was given an interest in its profits and by 1880, he was so valued he was permitted to acquired one-fourth interest in the company.

In 1886 he was elected Treasurer and held that office until a fire, in 1888, destroyed over a million dollars' worth of the plant. In spite of this great loss, the finances of the company were managed by Mr. England in such a manner as to preserve first class credit. The plant was greatly enlarged and now reaches out and dose business all over the world.

When the Reading National Bank was organized in 1893, he was elected a director. Previous to that he was a director for years in the Citizens State Bank. The United Traction Co. selected him as a director in 1896. He was chosen Vice President of the Board of Trade of Reading. In 1896 he assisted in the formation of a company for the extensive production and sale of bicycles. The result of his efforts was the Reading Cycle Mfg. Co., he was President of the Reading Screw Co., Vice Pres. of the Wilder Screw Co. of Philadelphia, President of the Norristown Wire Co., President of the Auburn Nut and Bolt Co., he was director in a chemical and dye plant in Wilmington, a factory that manufactured felt n Phila., also other interests that made door knobs and another that made music rolls in Pennsylvania and New York.

Owing to Mr. England's wide and successful experience he was often consulted and relied upon. While working in the store in Paulsboro, as a young man starting out in the business world, he became acquainted with Sallie Jessup Gill (1847-1948) whom he married on August 12, 1874. They had one child, Mary Gill England (1855-1963), a refined and promising daughter, who married Frank R. Fish, financier and philanthropist of Woodbury. Mrs. Fish was born in the present library and gave it to Paulsboro in memory of her mother. The house was built by John E. Clark in 1811. Both Mr. and Mrs. Fish have given generously to the remodeling and upkeep.

Mr. and Mrs. England resided in Reading about a quarter of a century. In this time, he became thoroughly known and respected by many businessmen. In his social affairs as in other dealings, he was straightforward, frank and honorable. He had a seventeen room home on Perkiomen Avenue, three farms, south of Reading with a half-mile track on each one, to exercise his 123 trotters and pacers.

Mr. England's successful operations deserved much public praise but he preferred to go onward and upward in a quiet manner without ostentatious display. The young lad who worked in the grocery stores in Swedesboro and Paulsboro over one hundred years ago was such a man during his entire life.

Henry and Sallie had two daughters:

133. i. Annie Gill ENGLAND was born on the 26th of September 1875 and died on the 11th of July 1876, at nine months of age.

134. ii. Mary Gill ENGLAND was born on the 15th of September 1885 in Paulsboro, New Jersey.[cdvi] She died on the 18th of May 1963 in Gloucester County, New Jersey.[cdvii] She married Frank Reynolds FISH (son of Harry A. FISH and Laura K. LESLIE) on the 14th of June 1928 in Valley Forge, Pennsylvania.[cdviii] He was born on the 28th of September 1887 and died in December 1977 in Woodbury, New Jersey.[cdix] Frank was a car dealer. He had previously been married to Nancy C. COFFIN who died in 1921. Mary and Frank had no children. Frank was an active member of the Gloucester County Historical Society in Woodbury, New Jersey. He donated a large antique grandfather clock, which is on display in the library.

5

The Fifth Generation

Here is the fifth generation:

75. **WILLIAM HARRISON ENGLAND** was born on the 4th of March 1857.[cdx] He died on the 17th of October 1920 in Winterhaven, Florida.[cdxi] He married Harriet Kendall TURNER (daughter of C. L. TURNER). She was born on the 1st of February 1875 in Milwaukee, Wisconsin and died on the 18th of July 1941 in Winterhaven, Florida.[cdxii] William's occupation in St. Louis, Missouri (where the first two children were born) is not known. The 1910 Census identifies him as secretary for a railway supply in Chicago. It appears that the couple moved to Florida with their son, Garner, just before William's death. William and Harriet had three known children:

135. i. Garner Baugh ENGLAND was born on the 24th of September 1902 in St. Louis, Missouri.[cdxiii] He died on the 19th of October 1978 in Winterhaven, Florida.[cdxiv] He married Marjorie "Maggie" Dale Spann (daughter of George L. Spann and Lessie D. Parker) in 1936.[cdxv] She was born on the 9th of January 1912 in Sasser, Georgia, and died on the 14th of August 1991 in Cobb, Georgia.[cdxvi] She is buried in Winterhaven, Florida. Garner worked as a citrus fruit inspector for the State of Florida. It is unknown if the couple had children.

136. ii. Sarah H. ENGLAND was born on the 1st of May 1904 in St. Louis.[cdxvii] She appears with her family in the 1910 and 1920 census, but no records of marriage or death can be identified.

137. iii. Turner Kendall ENGLAND was born in Chicago on the 5th of August 1906[cdxviii] and

died on the 14th of April 1907 at eight months of age.[cdxix]

76. **ELIZABETH ROBERTS** (Joanna[4], William[3], Thomas[2], William[1]) was born on the 31st of January 1836 and died on the 22nd of February 1872 in Gloucester County, New Jersey.[cdxx] She married Oliver CRAWFORD on the 18th of January 1855 in Somerset County, New Jersey. He was born on the 16th of April 1830 in Pennsylvania and died of tuberculosis on the 26 May 1880 in Gloucester County, New Jersey.[cdxxi] Oliver was a farmer; the 1860 census lists his property value at $21,000.[cdxxii] Oliver died intestate; the court appointed his son-in-law, Thomas W. Smith, as administrator.[cdxxiii]

Elizabeth and Oliver had nine children:

138. i. Hannah B. CRAWFORD was born about 1853 in Gloucester County, New Jersey.[cdxxiv] She is not named in the 1870 census with her parents. She would have been 17 at that time. However, no marriage or death records were found.

139. ii. Twins boy and girl CRAWFORD were born on the 17th of October 1855.[cdxxv] Boy

140. iii. Crawford died on the same day.[cdxxvi] Girl Crawford died on the 2nd of February 1856.[cdxxvii]

141. iv. William CRAWFORD was born about 1857 in Gloucester County, New Jersey.[cdxxviii] He also is not named in the 1870 census with his parents; he would have been 13 in 1870. No death records were found.

+142. v. Annabel CRAWFORD was born about 1859 in Gloucester County, New Jersey.[cdxxix] She married Thomas W. SMITH (son of William F. and Harriet E. SMITH) on the 24th of January 1876 in Camden, New Jersey.[cdxxx] He was born about 1854 in Pennsylvania.[cdxxxi] No death records for either Annabel or Thomas were found.

143. vi. Boy CRAWFORD was born on the 11th of August 1862.[cdxxxii] There is no male child, about 8 years of age, in the 1870 US Census; it is, therefore, assumed that he died as an infant or small child.

144. iv. Sarah CRAWFORD was born about 1863 in Salem County, New Jersey.[cdxxxiii]

145. v. Margarett CRAWFORD was born on the 18th of May 1864 in Gloucester County, New Jersey.[cdxxxiv]

146. vi. Oliver CRAWFORD was born about 1869 in Salem County, New Jersey.[cdxxxv]

Sarah, Margarett, and Oliver would have been 9, 8, and 3 years of age respectively at the time of their mother's death; they would have been 17, 16, and 11 at the time of their father's death. Their father died in 1880, and these children are not found living together in the 1880 census. No clearly identifiable records for these three children could be found after the 1870 census. It is possible that they were "adopted" by neighbors or relatives.

77. **ISABELLA E. ROBERTS** (Joanna[4], William[3], Thomas[2], William[1]) was born in 1838 and died in Gloucester County on the 10th of May 1879.[cdxxxvi] She married Samuel MYERS (son of Jacob and

Letitia MYERS). He was born about 1837 in New Jersey.[cdxxxvii] His date of death is unknown. Samuel was a farmer.

Isabella and Samuel had ten children:

+147. i.   Philena W. MYERS was born on the 15th of August 1860 in Center Square, Gloucester County, New Jersey.[cdxxxviii] She died in 1940 in Center Square.[cdxxxix] She married Stacy C. PANCOAST (son of Charles and Elizabeth PANCOAST) in 1879.[cdxl] He was born in 1854 in Franklin Township, Gloucester County, New Jersey[cdxli] and died in 1929 in Center Square.[cdxlii]

148. ii.   Maria J. MYERS was born about 1862 in Gloucester County, New Jersey.[cdxliii] She would have been 17 at the time of her mother's death. No records of marriage or death were found.

149. iii. Samuel H. MYERS was born in 1864 in Gloucester County, NJ.[cdxliv] He died in 1936 and is buried in Center Square, New Jersey. [cdxlv] He never married and lived with his sister, Minerva, in Pleasantville, New Jersey.[cdxlvi] He was employed as a wagon driver for an express company, a salesman for a fruit company, and a driver for a truck farm.

150. iv.   Jacob MYERS was born on the 16th of December 1866 in Sculltown, New Jersey[cdxlvii] and died on the 11th of September 1868 in Gloucester County, New Jersey.[cdxlviii]

+151. v.   Minerva W. MYERS was born about 1869 in Gloucester County, New Jersey. No death records were found. She married Samuel AMBRUSTER. He was born about 1866 in New Jersey.[cdxlix] He died on the 14th of January 1908 in Pleasantville, New Jersey.[cdl] She then married Edmund HENDRICKSON (son of Edmund W. and Jane HENDRICKSON and twin of William). He was born about 1876 in New Jersey[cdli] and died on the 6th of January 1956 in Burlington, New Jersey.[cdlii]

152. vi.   Florence MYERS was born about 1873 and died in December 1874 in Gloucester County, New Jersey.[cdliii]

153. vii. Harry MYERS, Clara's twin, was born on the 5th of November 1875 and died on the 11th of November 1876 in Gloucester County, New Jersey.[cdliv]

154. viii. Clara MYERS was born on the 5th of November 1875, Harry's twin.[cdlv] No records of marriage or death could be clearly identified. She would have been 4 years old at the time of her mother's death.

155. ix.   Ella MYERS was born on the 5th of September 1877.[cdlvi] No records of her marriage or death were clearly identified. She would have been 2 years old at the time of her mother's death.

156. x.   A child was born to Isabella Roberts and Samuel Myers on the 31st of January 1878 in Gloucester, NJ. No further records for this child were found.

78. **JOSEPH ROBERTS** (Joanna[4], William[3], Thomas[2], William[1]) was born in February 1840 and died in 1915 in New Jersey.[cdlvii] He married Priscilla HILLMAN (daughter of Richard and Ellen HILLMAN) on the 14th of March 1867 in Salem, New Jersey. She was born in 1842[cdlviii] and died on the 16th of February 1889.[cdlix] Joseph was a partner with Edward N. Cohn in Roberts & Cohn, a real estate company.[cdlx]

Joseph and Priscilla had seven children:

157. i. Eleanor "Nellie" D. ROBERTS was born on the 28th of January 1868 in Auburn, New Jersey.[cdlxi] She was living with her father and two sisters in Camden, New Jersey, in the 1910 census, at the age of 42.[cdlxii] She was single. No marriage or death records were found.

158. ii. Johanna ROBERTS was born in December 1869 in Camden, New Jersey.[cdlxiii] She died suddenly at her home on the 25th of January 1931 in Brooklyn, New York.[cdlxiv] She married William John BROWN (son of William BROWN and Eleanor CLAYTON). He was born on the 5th of March 1872 in Vineland, New Jersey.[cdlxv] He is last found in the 1940 census in Camden, New Jersey, living with two of his widowed sisters. William worked as an agent for an electric company. Johanna and William had no children.

159. iii. Elizabeth G. ROBERTS was born in July 1875 in Camden, New Jersey.[cdlxvi] She is last found living in Haddonfield, New Jersey, with her brother, Joseph, in the 1930 census. She was single and working as a librarian in a high school.[cdlxvii] No marriage or death records were found.

+160. iv. Joseph E. ROBERTS was born on the 22nd of December 1878 in Camden, New Jersey.[cdlxviii] He died on the 4th of June 1950 in Camden, New Jersey.[cdlxix] He married Ethel A. ALLEN. She was born on the 30th of August 1855 in New Jersey and died in August 1975 in Short Hills, New Jersey.[cdlxx]

161. v. Herbert ROBERTS was born on the 21st of February 1879 in Camden, New Jersey.[cdlxxi] He died in June of that same year.[cdlxxii]

162. vi. Amy M. ROBERTS was born on the 26th of December 1881 in Camden, New Jersey.[cdlxxiii] No other records of her life were found.

163. vii. Emma A. ROBERTS was born on the 9th of October 1885.[cdlxxiv] She is last found in the 1910 census living with her father and two sisters. No records of marriage or death were found.

80. **HANNAH ROBERTS** (Joanna[4], William[3], Thomas[2], William[1]) was born about 1846.[cdlxxv] She died sometime after 1900; she is not found in the 1910 census with her husband.[cdlxxvi] She married Samuel B. HARBISON (son of Samuel and Sarah Ann HARBISON) on the 26th of November in 1865 in Salem, New Jersey.[cdlxxvii] He was born about 1809 in New Jersey.[cdlxxviii] He died after 1920 (the last census year in which he was found). Samuel worked as a produce dealer.

Hannah and Samuel had five children:

+164. i. William S. HARBISON was born in March 1863. He is found in the 1910 census living with his brother and father in Camden. His last listing in the Camden city directory is 1912. He married Anna M. KLEIN in 1889.[cdlxxix] She was born about 1867 in New Jersey. She is found in the 1900 census living with her husband and son in Camden, New Jersey. Her last listing in the Camden city directory is 1902. There are no records of her death.

+165. ii. Warren G. HARBISON was born in July 1866. No records of his death were identified. The 1900 census lists him as "divorced" but no record of this marriage can be found. In the 1920 census, he is living with his wife, Minnie. In the 1930 census, he is listed as married, but his wife is not named as living in that residence. In the 1940 census, he is identified as a widower. His wife is a bit of a mystery. She is named "Minnie" on census records, but she is "Dolores" on her son's death certificate. No records of her marriage or death can be found. She is last found in the 1920 census in Camden, New Jersey.

166. iii. Minnie HARBISON was born about 1868 in New Jersey.[cdlxxx] No records of her life were found after the 1880 census.

+167. iv. Jacob R. HARBISON was born about 1871 in New Jersey. He married Harriet "Hattie" B. GROSS (daughter of Charles E. GROSS and Sophia FOX) on the 1st of August 1894 in Wilmington, Delaware.[cdlxxxi] She was born in 1870 in Rochester, New York. She died in Philadelphia on the 22nd of October 1899; she committed suicide by inhaling illuminating gas.[cdlxxxii] (Illuminating gas is composed of hydrogen and hydrocarbons and was used for lighting prior to the use of electricity). She is buried in New York with her parents.[cdlxxxiii] He married a second time to Dora MCNEAL on the 22nd of February 1902 in Camden, New Jersey. She was born about 1874 in New Jersey.[cdlxxxiv] No death records for either Jacob or Dora were found.

+168. v. Samuel Bodo HARBISON was born on the 18th of November 1880.[cdlxxxv] He died on the 21st of June 1953 in Audubon, New Jersey.[cdlxxxvi] He married Mary Helen MULLINER (daughter of Joseph MULLINER and Elizabeth PARSONS). She was born on the 24th of September 1884 in Camden, New Jersey.[cdlxxxvii] She died on the 29th of December 1967 in Audubon, New Jersey.

81. **FRANCES "FRANK" J. ROBERTS** (Joanna[4], William[3], Thomas[2], William[1]) was born on the 13th of September 1846 in New Jersey. He died on the 23rd of March 1912 in Philadelphia of tuberculosis.[cdlxxxviii] He married Florence A. SMITH in 1871.[cdlxxxix] She was born about 1852 in

Pennsylvania.[cdxc] She died after 1910, the last census year in which she was found. Frank worked as a salesman.

Frank and Florence had four children:

169.   i.   Milton L. ROBERTS was born about 1871 in New Jersey.[cdxci] It is assumed he died as a child as he is not listed with his parents and siblings in the 1885 New Jersey State Census.[cdxcii]

170.   ii.   Frank V. ROBERTS was born on the 23rd of January 1872 in New Jersey. He died of tuberculosis on the 9th of August 1930 in Janney, Pennsylvania (at the Pennsylvania State Sanitarium).[cdxciii] He never married. He worked laying slate roof tiles.

171.   iii.   Hatty (Hallye) Adele ROBERTS was born in November 1884 in New Jersey and died of tuberculosis on the 29th of April 1926 in Philadelphia.[cdxciv] She married Frank YETTER (son of Frank G. YETTER and Imogene TAFT) in 1917 in Philadelphia.[cdxcv] He was born on the 23rd of April 1888 in River Head, Long Island, New York.[cdxcvi] They had no children.

172.   iv.   Rena F. "Blanche" ROBERTS was born on the 1st of March 1880 in Camden, New Jersey.[cdxcvii] It is assumed that she died as an infant or child because she is not listed in the 1885 New Jersey State Census with her parents and siblings.

85.   **JAMES B. TAWS** (Deborah[4], William[3], Thomas[2], William[1]) was born in 1851 and died on the 6th of November 1894.[cdxcviii] He married Mary E. THOMAS (daughter of Robert THOMAS and Eliza Jane SMITH) on the 22nd of September 1881 in Philadelphia.[cdxcix] She was born on the 22nd of March 1857 and died on the 1st of June 1942 in Philadelphia.[d] After the death of her husband, James, Mary remarried in 1901 to Samuel BORER in Philadelphia.[di] James was a piano tuner.

James and Mary had seven children (per the 1910 census); five are known:

+173.   i.   Florence TAWS was born on the 6th of June 1883 in Philadelphia and died on the 15th of February 1956 in Philadelphia.[dii] She married Alfred James GARBER Sr. (son of Lewis GARBER and Martha MCCANDLES) on the 1st of December 1901 in Philadelphia.[diii] He was born on the 13th of July 1874 in Philadelphia and died on the 2nd of May 1937 in Lansdowne, Pennsylvania.[div]

+174.   ii.   Edith TAWS was born in December 1886 in Pennsylvania.[dv] She died on the 31st of March 1967 in Wethersfield, Connecticut.[dvi] She married George Randall MOORE on the 3rd of July 1907 in Philadelphia.[dvii] He was born on the 5th of November 1883 in Guthriesville, Pennsylvania.[dviii] He died on the 23rd of March 1965 in Wethersfield Connecticut.[dix]

175.   iii.   Willie TAWS was born in January 1888 and died on the 15th of March 1888 in Philadelphia, at the age of 7 weeks.[dx]

176. iv. Mary Lord TAWS was born on the 17th of February 1892 in Philadelphia. She died on the 12th of June 1982 in St. Petersburg, Florida.[dxi] In 1900, she was an "inmate" of the Burd Orphan Asylum in Delaware County, Pennsylvania.[dxii] In 1910, she was living with her sister, Edith, and Edith's family.[dxiii] In 1930 and 1940, she was living in Chicago, and working as a stenographer. Her marital status is "divorced"; however, no records of her marriage could be identified. Her death and burial records are in her maiden name. There are no known children.

Photo from the collection of Robyn Sheets, used with permission.

177. v. Baby Girl TAWS died on the 19th of July 1893, at 6 days of age, in Philadelphia.[dxiv]

88. **GUSTAVUS H. ENGLAND** (Samuel[4], William[3], Thomas[2], William[1]) was born in 1847 and died of tuberculosis on the 24th of March 1891. He married Ella H. GLESSNER (daughter of Oliver P. and Mary GLESSNER). She was born in 1849 and died on the 28th of November 1875 of typhoid pneumonia.[dxv]

Gustavus enlisted in the Union Navy on the 15th of June 1864, and served as paymaster steward aboard the USS Laburnum. On the 14th of January 1865, the USS Laburnum was near the USS Patapsco off the shores of Charleston, when the Patapsco hit a confederate mine and sunk with considerable loss of life. Gustavus participated in the rescue efforts, and presumably caught a cold while doing so. He was confined to sick quarters, and diagnosed with tuberculosis of the throat. He was honorably discharged on the 1st of March 1865.[dxvi] After his discharge, until he became too infirm, Gustavus worked as a compositor for the Methodist Book Society in Philadelphia.

Gustavus and Ella had four daughters:

178. i. Ann Glessner ENGLAND was born on the 5th of December 1866.[dxvii] She died of an inflammation of the bowels at the age of 17 on the 13th of December 1883.[dxviii]

179. ii. Lillie Haines ENGLAND was born on the 12th of December 1867 in Philadelphia.[dxix] She died of rheumatic heart disease on the 18th of November 1949 in Philadelphia.[dxx] She married A. Meredith MYTINGER (son of Frederick A. MYTINGER and Louise H. ZEGGEY) in 1894 in Philadelphia. He was born on the 24th of August 1865 in Philadelphia.[dxxi] He died in August 1949.[dxxii] He worked as an accountant in several industries, a fruit dealer, a steamship line, a bank. The couple had no known children.

+180. iii. Ella V. ENGLAND was born on the 6th of January 1871 and died of carcinoma of the uterus on the 7th of June 1915 in Philadelphia.[dxxiii] She married Charles HOFFMAN in 1889. [dxxiv] He was born in September 1870 in Pennsylvania. Death records, or marriage records after the death of Ella, for Charles could not be clearly identified, complicated by the number of people living in Philadelphia with the same name.

Charles was a police officer, and at one time, was credited with saving the life of a girl who had fallen into the Delaware River.[dxxv]

181.   iv.   Mary O. ENGLAND was born on the 27th of March 1873.[dxxvi] She died of diphtheria on the 15th of January 1879 in Philadelphia.[dxxvii]

93.   **JOSEPH WINTERS ENGLAND, PH. G.** (Robert[4], Willliam[3], Thomas[2], William[1]) was born on the 26th of September 1863 in Philadelphia.[dxxviii] He died in November 1933.[dxxix] He married Ella Virginia RUSSELL (daughter of Jacob P. RUSSELL and Anne EMERY) on the 6th of May 1891 in Philadelphia.[dxxx] She was born on the 30th of May 1863 and died on the 20th of January 1942.[dxxxi] Joseph's entire career was in the drug industry, beginning by working in his father's drug company. He graduated from the Philadelphia College of Pharmacy in 1883. He served as chief druggist for a hospital in Philadelphia. He was active in the Alumni Association, serving as its President in 1891.[dxxxii]

Joseph and Ella had two daughters:

182.   i.   Ethel Virginia ENGLAND was born on the 6th of August 1893 and died of diphtheria on the 28th of June 1894.[dxxxiii]

183.   ii.   Elizabeth R. ENGLAND was born on the 6th of December 1895 and died on the 15th of March 1973.[dxxxiv] She was a lifelong resident of Philadelphia, and was a teacher in the public schools. She never married.

97.   **MARY ENGLAND LYNCH** (Rebecca[4], William W.[3], Daniel[2], William[1]) was born on the 9th of September 1832. She died on the 5th of May 1910. She married William HURFF (son of Isaac HURFF and Ann Jane JAGGARD). He was born on the 31st of December 1832 and died on the 13th of April 1894.[dxxxv] He is buried in the Trinity churchyard in Swedesboro, New Jersey. William was a farmer. The real estate value of is farm was listed as $13,000 in the 1870 census.[dxxxvi]

Mary and William had three known children:

184.   i.   Rebecca HURFF was born on the 4th of December 1853. She died on the 18th of May 1907 and is buried in the Trinity Episcopal Church New Cemetery.[dxxxvii] She never married. In his will, her father claimed she was "not capable of judging for herself" and appointed his sons Aaron and Henry as her guardians.[dxxxviii]

+185.   ii.   Aaron HURFF was born on the 9th of October 1855 in Swedesboro.[dxxxix] He died in Camden County in 1933.[dxl] He married Sarah A. HUNT (daughter of J. B. and Maria HUNT) in November 1876 in Blackwood, New Jersey. She was born on the 19th of March 1858 in New Jersey and died on the 29th of June 1918 in Camden County, New Jersey.[dxli]

+186.   iii.   Henry L. HURFF was born in 1854 in Gloucester County, New Jersey. He died in 1941.[dxlii] He married Elizabeth D. HARVEY on the 3rd of October 1878 in Hurffville, New Jersey. She was born in August 1856[dxliii] and died on the 29th of January 1914.[dxliv] They are both buried in Hurffville, New Jersey.

98. Elizabeth LYNCH (Rebecca[4], William W.[3], Daniel[2], William[1]) was born on the 24th of November 1836.[dxlv] She died on the 15th of February 1924 in Elmwood, Illinois. On the 5th of March 1863, she married Isaac HURFF, Jr. (son of Isaac HURFF and Ann Jane JAGGARD) in Woodbury, NJ.[dxlvi] He was born in September 1835[dxlvii] and died on the 14th of January 1903 in Elmwood, Illinois.[dxlviii]

Isaac moved to Elmwood, Illinois about 1856 to begin work as a nurseryman. When the Civil War broke out, he enlisted in the Union army, the 8th Missouri Volunteer Infantry in 1861. He saw several battles, the last at Corinth, Mississippi. He was discharged in 1864 due to failing health. He enlisted as a private and was promoted to 2nd Lieutenant. After he and Elizabeth married, they made their home in Elmwood.[dxlix]

Elizabeth and Isaac had four children, two died in infancy. The two surviving daughters are:

187.   i.   Georgianna HURFF was born on the 15th of July 1865 in Elmwood, Illinois and died on the 22nd of November 1954 in Sikeston, Missouri.[dl] She married Truman BALL (son of Frank BALL and Ann PHELPS) about 1906.[dli] He was born on the 13th of September 1864 in Trempealeau, Wisconsin and died on the 19th of November 1955 in Sikeston, Missouri.[dlii] He had previously been married and had a daughter, Jessie, who was living with him and Georgianna in 1910, born about 1890 in Wisconsin[dliii]. In his will, he left all of his property to her.[dliv] After their marriage, Georgianna and Truman moved to Marquette, Michigan where they owned and operated the newspaper, *The Evening Chronicle*. They moved to Decatur, Illinois, and then in 1918, move to Sikeston, Missouri, where they had interests in farm lands.[dlv] Georgianna was a graduate of Knox College and the Chicago Musical College.[dlvi] Georgianna and Truman had no children.

188.   ii.   Kate M. HURFF was born on the 22nd of October 1872 in Elmwood, Illinois and died on the 28th of August 1959 in Sikeston, Missouri.[dlvii] She is buried in Elmwood near her parents. She was a graduate of St Mary's School at Notre Dame, Indiana where she specialized in education. She and her sister, Georgianna, bought some undeveloped farmland in New Madrid County, Missouri. Kate lived on this property and supervised its development.[dlviii] She never married.

100. **BENJAMIN FRANKLIN ENGLAND** (Aquila[4], William W.[3], Daniel[2], William[1]) was born in April 1840 in New York.[dlix] He died on the 10th of June 1922 in Brooklyn. He married Ella OLLIS (daughter of Thomas B. and Anna E. OLLIS) on the 20th of February 1868.[dlx] She was born in May 1845 in Pennsylvania.[dlxi] She died on the 16th of September 1922 in Brooklyn.[dlxii]

As a young man, Benjamin worked with his father as a builder. He owned a toy manufacturing business for a short while. For most of his career, he was associated with the Department of Street

Opening in Brooklyn. He was a Civil War Veteran, serving with the 13th Regiment of Brooklyn. He was discharged as a Lieutenant.[dlxiii]

Benjamin and Ella had nine children:

189. i.   Benjamin Franklin ENGLAND was born in Brooklyn on the 19th of March 1869[dlxiv] and died 3 months later on the 3rd of July.[dlxv]

190. ii.   Harry ENGLAND was born in 1870 in Brooklyn.[dlxvi] He was alive and living with his parents and siblings in the 1875 New York State Census, but he does not appear with his family in the 1880 US Census.

191. iii.   Clarence A. ENGLAND was born in April 1870 in Brooklyn. [dlxvii] His date of death is unknown. He married Bessie A. TAYLOR (daughter of Theodore A. and Elizabeth TAYLOR) on the 11th of April 1902 in Brooklyn.[dlxviii] She was born on the 26th of July 1877 and died in February 1968 in White Plains, New York. [dlxix] Clarence and Bessie had two children.

+192. iv.   Ernest Ollis ENGLAND was born in March 1873 in Brooklyn.[dlxx] He died on the 16th of September 1912 in Queens, New York. [dlxxi] He married Ethel Olive JOHNSON on the 3oth of January 1895 in Brooklyn.[dlxxii] She was born in November 1876 in New York.[dlxxiii] In 1919, after the death of her husband, she married Ernest's brother, Herbert. Her date of death is unknown.

193. v.   Bertha ENGLAND was born about 1874 in New York.[dlxxiv] She appears in the 1875 New York State Census, but is not listed with her family in the 1880 US Census.

194. vi.   Herbert F. T. ENGLAND was born on the 27th of August 1876[dlxxv] in Brooklyn, NY. He died on the 17th of May 1948 in Queens, NY.[dlxxvi] He married Ethel O. JOHNSON, the widow of his brother, Ernest, in 1919.[dlxxvii] The couple had no children together, although it appears he cared well for his brother's minor children. He enlisted in the US Army on the 13th of Mary 1899, in Co. A, 6th Infantry. He served in the Spanish American War. He was honorably discharged as a corporal from Co. F of the 22nd NY Volunteers on the 12 March 1902.[dlxxviii] He continued to serve as a field clerk for the US Army until his retirement. This article about a near miss appeared in *the New York Times*, page 1, 23rd July 1890:

DEATH WAS VERY NEAR.

A SNEAK THIEF FIRES POINT-BLANK AT A BOY, BUT MISSES HIM.

Young Herbert England, the fifteen-year-old son of Benjamin F. England of 43 Downing Street, Brooklyn, found a pistol bullet in the hallway of his father's house yesterday that he intends to have mounted and wear as a watch charm. It was fired at him from a pistol in the hands of a sneak thief at point-blank range, and passed through his coat and shirt without doing him any injury.

The family were at the midday meal while the sneak thief was at work ransacking the bureaus up stairs. He had entered through the front door by means of a skeleton key and had stolen noiselessly up stairs when he knew that the family was at dinner. Herbert left the table before the others, and as he was ascending the basement stairs he heard a strange footstep and the next instant caught sight of the thief descending the stairs from the bedroom floor. He is a big strong boy, and without a thought of the danger he made a rush for the intruder with the intention of getting between him and the hall door.

As he did so, he saw the bright gleam of the thief's revolver barrel, and then came the flash of the discharge not three feet away. He was stunned by the suddenness of the shot, and as he cried for help the thief plunged headlong out of the door and down the front steps, disappearing around the corner. The bullet passed through Herbert's coat and shirt without doing any injury. The front bedroom had been thoroughly ransacked, and a pair of gold bracelets worth $15 and $5.75 in cash were to be missing. The thief has not been caught.

195. vii. Boy ENGLAND died in August 1876; the age on the death record is 0.[dlxxix] Perhaps he was a twin to Herbert.

196. viii. Arthur Barber ENGLAND was born on the 30ᵗʰ of January 1880 in Brooklyn.[dlxxx] He died on the 24ᵗʰ of November 1943 in Manhattan.[dlxxxi] He worked as a teller in a bank. He never married.

+197. ix. William Elliott ENGLAND was born on the 17ᵗʰ of September 1885 in Brooklyn.[dlxxxii] He married Hazel SHEAR on the 16ᵗʰ of November 1907 in

Brooklyn.[dlxxxiii] She was born about 1885 in New York.[dlxxxiv] Death records for neither William or Hazel were found.

102. **EMMA C. ENGLAND** (Aquilla[4], William W.[3], Daniel[2], William[1]) was born about 1847 in New York and died on the 9th of September 1930 in Brooklyn.[dlxxxv] She married Thomas Jefferson SODEN who was born about 1841 in Ireland. He died on the 3rd of November 1926 in Brooklyn.[dlxxxvi] Thomas worked as a dry goods and silk fabric salesman for the firm of James McCreery & Co.

Emma and Thomas had four children:

198.   i.   Elizabeth "Lillie" A. SODEN was born on the 16th of February 1871 and died on the 11th of August 1943, a lifelong resident of Brooklyn.[dlxxxvii] She married Charles BURBANK on the 29th of November 1899 in Brooklyn.[dlxxxviii] He was born in December 1869 in New York.[dlxxxix] He was a resident of Colorado Springs at the time of their marriage. He worked as a bookkeeper for a leather goods company. He died on the 21st of November 1951.[dxc] The couple had no known children.

199.   ii.   Meriba "Minnie" England SODEN was born in October 1872 in Brooklyn, New York.[dxci] She married Ernest Augustus DUVAL in 1896.[dxcii] She died on the 29th of March 1945 in Brooklyn. No death records for Ernest were found. Ernest was an accountant. Minnie and Ernest had three children.

200.   iii.   Albert B. SODEN was born 1875 in New York. He enlisted in March 1899 with Company F of the 6th Regiment. In the 1900 US Census, he is listed as a Private with the military in the Philippines. He was honorably discharged in April 1902. He reenlisted in September 1903 with the 16th Regiment. Between October 1903 and October 1904, he was arrested and jailed or fined eight times for charges of being away without leave, selling military clothing and being drunk in quarters. He was dishonorably discharged on October 10, 1904 from Ft. McPherson, Georgia.[dxciii] In June 1908, he reenlisted at Ft. Slocum, New York, under the alias of Albert Hughes. He was court-martialled for this fraudulent enlistment on June 13, 1908, sentenced to one year of hard labor at the military disciplinary barracks at Ft. Leavenworth, Kansas and again, dishonorably discharged.[dxciv] During his testimony at this court martial, he states that he had served the US Navy for 3 years and six months in foreign lands, and was honorably discharged. No record of this service can be found. From this point, he entirely disappears from traditional records using his name and birthdate. He is not named in the obituaries of either parent.[dxcv]

201.   iv.   Edward Douglas SODEN was born on the 8th of July 1878 in Brooklyn, New York.[dxcvi] He died on the 7th of September 1953 in Brooklyn.[dxcvii] He married Isabella PRICE (daughter of George PRICE) about 1906.[dxcviii] She was born about 1881 in New York, and died on the 17th of January 1933 in Brooklyn.[dxcix] The couple had no children. Edward was a manager for the Baseball Magazine Company.

104. **FRANCES "FANNY" A. ENGLAND** (William Watson[4], William W.[3], Daniel[2], William[1]) was born in 1850 in New Jersey.[dc] She died in 1913 and is buried in the Pedricktown Friends Cemetery in Salem County, New Jersey.[dci] She married George Clark HORNER (son of Elijah Bowers HORNER and Mary CLARK) in 1886.[dcii] He was born on the 18th of January 1895 in Swedesboro, New Jersey.[dciii] and died in November 1930 in Salem County, New Jersey. He was a farmer.

Fannie and George had one daughter:

202.   1.   Mary Amanda HORNER was born on the 5th of September 1895 in Oldmans, Salem County, New Jersey.[dciv] She died on the 5th of March 1948 in Salem County.[dcv] She married Joseph C. SCHOCH (son of J. Morton SCHOCH and Ellen RITTERSON) on the 6th of June 1925.[dcvi] He was born on the 18th of January 1894.[dcvii] He died in 1960 in Salem County.[dcviii] For a short time before her marriage, Mary was a high school teacher. Joseph was an assistant chemist at the Dupont Plant. The couple had no children.

106. **ELLA K. ENGLAND** (William Watson[4], William W.[3], Daniel[2], William[1]) was born in September 1855.[dcix] She died on the 28th of August 1934 in Gloucester County, New Jersey.[dcx] She married Samuel Stratton MATTSON (son of Jonathon W. MATTSON and Rebecca E. SHILLING) on the 4th of March 1875.[dcxi] He was born in December 1850 and died on the 8th of May 1922 in Gloucester County, New Jersey.[dcxii]

Stratton was a farmer. The Mattson family was a very large, very prominent family in Woolwich Township, Gloucester County, New Jersey.

Ella and Stratton had eight children:

+203.   i.   John Watson MATTSON was born on the 15th of September 1875, twin to William Watson Mattson, in Swedesboro, New Jersey.[dcxiii] He died on the 20th of May 1945.[dcxiv] He married Ruth BLACK on the 18th of November 1901.[dcxv] She was born on the 9th of January 1880 in Gloucester County, New Jersey.[dcxvi] She died on the 3rd of March 1962.[dcxvii]

+204.   ii.   William Watson MATTSON, twin of John Watson MATTSON, was born on the 15th of September 1875 in Swedesboro.[dcxviii] He died on the 2nd of January 1960.[dcxix] He married Savilla "Annie" TITUS (daughter of Jacob and Annie TITUS) on the 14th of September 1898 in Penns Grove, New Jersey.[dcxx] She was born on the 29th of August 1879 in Pennsylvania.[dcxxi] She died on the 22nd of April 1961. Will was a farmer.

+205.   iii.   Mabel MATTSON was born on the 23rd of July 1877.[dcxxii] She died on the 25th of January 1958.[dcxxiii] She married Chris (or Harry) HOFFMAN on the 6th of September

1897 in Wenonah, New Jersey.[dcxxiv] He was a professional baseball player.[dcxxv] His exact date of death is unknown, but presumed to be about 1900. She next married Harvey TOMLIN on the 1st of September 1907 in Bridgeport at the St. Paul Methodist Church. He was born a Quaker on the 31st of August 1873 in Pedricktown, New Jersey.[dcxxvi] He died on the 22nd of March 1930, and was buried in the Bridgeport Cemetery.[dcxxvii]

206. iv. Edward MATTSON was born on the 9th of May 1879 in Auburn, Salem County, New Jersey.[dcxxviii] He died at the age of 23 on the 23rd of March 1903.[dcxxix] He was employed by his father on the family's farm.

+207. v. Samuel Stratton MATTSON was born in the 1st of May 1883 in Auburn, New Jersey.[dcxxx] He died on the 21st of March 1975 in Williamstown, New Jersey. On the 16th of February 1908, he married Ruth NORTON (daughter of Elmer NORTON and Martha TONKIN) at the Trinity Episcopal Church in Swedesboro.[dcxxxi] She was born on the 13th of July 1885 in Gibbstown, New Jersey.[dcxxxii] She died the 5th of January 1968 in Williamstown, New Jersey.[dcxxxiii] Samuel was a farmer.

208. vi. Charles Parker MATTSON was born on the 26th of April 1889 in Auburn, New Jersey.[dcxxxiv] He died on the 9th of August 1931.[dcxxxv] He married Margaret R. MCKAY (daughter of Andrew MCKAY and Margaret ROBERTS). She was born about 1896 in Pennsylvania.[dcxxxvi] Her date of death is unknown. Charles and Margaret had eight children, two of whom may be living.

209. vii. Arthur Green MATTSON was born on the 24th of March 1890 in Auburn, New Jersey.[dcxxxvii] He died on the 26th of July 1964 and is buried in Woodbury, New Jersey.[dcxxxviii] He married Lillian B. GURLIN (daughter of Charles and Mary GURLIN). She was born on the 11th of May 1900 and died in April 1981.[dcxxxix] The couple had two children, both of whom may be living.

210. viii. Meriba Barber MATTSON was born on the 12th of August 1896.[dcxl] She died in August 1982 in Pittman, New Jersey.[dcxli] She married Harley Monroe PAUL (son of Isaac PAUL and Effie HINES) on the 19th of June 1915 in Camden, New Jersey.[dcxlii] He was born on the 7th of January 1892 in Swedesboro, New Jersey.[dcxliii] He died in January 1951.[dcxliv] Harley was a farmer and tree trimmer. He died following the fall from a tree.[dcxlv] The couple had four children.

108. **WILLIAM "WILLIE" ENGLAND** (William Watson[4], William W.[3], Daniel[2], William[1]) was born on the 7th of June 1861 and died on the 13th of February 1929 in Salem, New Jersey.[dcxlvi] He married Hannah CHEESMAN (daughter of Benjamin and Martha CHEESMAN) on the 27th of December 1866 in Woodstown, New Jersey.[dcxlvii] She was born on the 5th of September 1866 in Gloucester County, New Jersey, and died on the 15th of April 1924 in Salem County, New Jersey.[dcxlviii] Willie was a farmer.

Willie and Hannah had three children:

+211.   i.   Rev. Aquila B. ENGLAND was born on the 7th of September 1887 in Salem County, New Jersey.[dcxlix] He died in December 1974 in Woodbury, New Jersey.[dcl] He was the author of our handwritten family tree so frequently mentioned at the beginning of this work. He married Effie L. THOMAS (daughter of William and Isabella THOMAS). She was born in June 1889 in New York.[dcli] She died in December 1977 in Toms River, New Jersey.[dclii]

+212.   ii.   Benjamin Cheeseman ENGLAND was born on the 1st of August 1890 in Woodstown, Salem County, New Jersey.[dcliii] He died in 1960.[dcliv] He married Louise D. CAWLEY (daughter of William CAWLEY and Martha GREEN). She was born the 13th of September 1899 in Pedricktown, New Jersey.[dclv] She died in Philadelphia on the 14th of June 1962.[dclvi]

213.   iii.   David ENGLAND was born in October 1898.[dclvii] He died on the 28th of August 1991.[dclviii] He married Olga OESTERLE (daughter of Adam and Friedericke OESTERLE). She was born on the 18th of July 1900 in Pilesgrove, Salem County, New Jersey.[dclix] She died on the 28th of January 2001 in Woodstown, New Jersey.[dclx] Olga worked as a bookkeeper and notary for the First National Bank. David worked as a bookkeeper for the South Jersey Farmers Exchange. The couple had no children.

109.   **CHARLES G. ENGLAND** (William Watson⁴, William W.³, Daniel², William¹) was born in February of 1864[dclxi] and died in 1948 in Salem, New Jersey.[dclxii] He married Mary I. "Mamie" DAVIDSON (daughter of John and Melvina DAVIDSON) in 1892.[dclxiii] She was born in March 1874[dclxiv] and died in Salem County, New Jersey in 1930.[dclxv] Charles was a farmer.

Charles and Mary had four children:

214.   i.   Charles Clinton ENGLAND was born on the 30th of September 1899 in Auburn, New Jersey.[dclxvi] He died on the 22nd of June 1989 and is buried in Woodstown, New Jersey.[dclxvii] He married Helen F. DARLINGTON. She was born on the 23rd of June 1901 in New Jersey.[dclxviii] She died on the 23rd of June 1966 and is buried in Woodstown, New Jersey.[dclxix] Charles and Helen had one child, who may be living.

215.   ii.   William Watson ENGLAND was born on the 1st of November 1895 in Auburn, New Jersey.[dclxx] He died in July 1984 in Stirling, New Jersey.[dclxxi] He married Edna BLACKMAN (daughter of Smith S. BLACKMAN and Ethalinda DAVIDSON). She was born on the 21st of June 1893 in Port Norris, New Jersey. She died in May 1988 in Washington, DC.[dclxxii] He worked first as a clerk for the US

government, and then as a clerk for the Columbia Title Insurance Company. The couple had no children.

+216.   iii.   John Davidson ENGLAND was born on the 30th of December 1898 in Olivet, New Jersey.[dclxxiii] He died on the 14th of September 1983 and is buried at Woodstown, New Jersey.[dclxxiv] He married Marion L. WINTER (daughter of William and Carrie WINTER). She was born on the 7th of August 1911 and died on the 21st of June 1992 in Woodbury, New Jersey.[dclxxv]

+217.   iv.   Thomas M. ENGLAND was born in 1907 in Oldmans, New Jersey.[dclxxvi] He died on the 17th of January 1990 in Alexandria, Virginia[dclxxvii] and was buried in Woodstown, New Jersey.[dclxxviii] He married Beatrice E. RAUGAUST (daughter of George O. and Minnie E RAUGAUST) on the 27th of June 1931 in Washington, DC.[dclxxix] She was born on the 3rd of October 1908 in North Dakota and died on the 23rd of August 1986 in Fairfax, Virginia.[dclxxx] She is buried in Woodstown, New Jersey.[dclxxxi] Thomas was a statistical clerk for a railroad. Beatrice was a stenographer.

110.   **WILLIAM WATSON ENGLAND AMBRUSTER** (Sarah[4], William W.[3], Daniel[2], William[1]) was born on the 19th of August 1842 in Philadelphia.[dclxxxii] He died of an intestinal obstruction on the 18th of March 1904 in Philadelphia.[dclxxxiii] He married Emma Elizabeth EARLEY (daughter of James Wood EARLEY and Deborah CLARK) in Philadelphia on the 10th of June 1873.[dclxxxiv] She was born on the 5th of June 1843.[dclxxxv] She died on the 23rd of February 1895. He next married Isabel BINGHAM (daughter of John BINGHAM and Mary GRAYBILL) in Philadelphia in 1896. She was born on the 8th of August 1849 and died on the 17th of October 1931 in Philadelphia.[dclxxxvi]

Watson was the managing editor of *The Evening Telegraph*, a Philadelphia newspaper. He was active in professional organizations and community activities that promoted reading and education. He graduated from the University of Michigan, department of Literary Studies, with a B. S. and a LL. B. in 1864.[dclxxxvii]

There were no children born to Watson and Isabel. Watson and Emma had two children:

218.   i.   Cornelius AMBRUSTER was born on the 8th of December 1875 in Philadelphia, and died on the 14th of June 1958 in Montgomeryville, PA.[dclxxxviii] He married Josephine D. HOEFERT (daughter of Johan Christian Friedrick and Dorothea WALTER) on the 27th of March 1901 in Chicago, Illinois.[dclxxxix] She was born on the 29th of June 1875 in Germany and died on the 21st of September 1939 in Abington, Pennsylvania.[dcxc] She arrived in this country in 1896.[dcxci]

Cornelius worked as an electrical engineer. The couple had no children naturally, but they adopted a son, Richard, between 1905 and 1910. Richard was born on the 4th of March 1905 in England, and died in August 1985. He married Sophia (born in Poland in 1902 and died in Pennsylvania in 1971). Richard and Sophia had two children, a son and a daughter.

+219. ii. Howard Watson AMBRUSTER was born on the 12th of August 1878 in Germantown, Pennsylvania and died on the 10th of January 1961.[dcxcii] He married Florence Ursula FAVREAU (daughter of Fred FAVREAU and Anna D. WILSON) on the 15th of June 1910 in Chicago, Illinois.[dcxciii] She was born on the 30th of April 1890 in Albany, New York [dcxciv] She died on the 30th of November 1970 in Albuquerque, New Mexico.

112. **MARY AMBRUSTER** (Sarah[4], William W.[3], Daniel[2], William[1]) was born in January 1855.[dcxcv] She married John Marion ALLEN on the 1st of November 1873 in Camden. New Jersey.[dcxcvi] He was born March 1854 in New Jersey.[dcxcvii] There are no records of their deaths; the last record found in which they appear is the 1910 census. John worked as a plasterer.

Mary and John had two children:

+220. i. Anna M. ALLEN was born in Feb 1874 in New Jersey.[dcxcviii] She died on the 25th of March 1965 in Merchantville, New Jersey.[dcxcix] Anna was a church organist.[dcc] She first married William Mortimer SKEGGS in 1894 in New Jersey.[dcci] He was born in January 1874; his date of death is unknown. In the 1940 census, Anna is widowed. Mort worked in various positions in the hotel industry. Anna next married William H. WATT. He was born in February 1870 in England.[dccii] He died on the 3rd of November 1950 in New Jersey.[dcciii] His first marriage was to Emma R. BREYER with whom he had two children.

221. iii. Howard Ambruster ALLEN was born on the 15th of April 1895 in Camden, New Jersey.[dcciv] He died on the 17th of November, 1956.[dccv] He married Ethel HOFFLINGER (daughter of William C. and Annie M. HOFFLINGER) on the 30th of December 1917 in Camden.[dccvi] She was born in December 1896 in Camden.[dccvii] She died in 1980.[dccviii] The couple had no children.

Note the 19-year difference between the births of Annie and Howard. Records of siblings born in the years between the two were not found. This difference is unexplained. Mary would have been 50 years of age at the birth of her second child.

117. **JAMES CLARK IRWIN** (Catherine[4], Daniel[3], Daniel[2], William[1]) was born on the 23rd of September 1868 in Cheyney, Pennsylvania.[dccix] His exact date of death is unknown; the last record in which he is found is the 1940 census. He married Frances Smith MONAGHAN (daughter of Robert Emmet MONAGHAN and Rebecca Darlington SMITH) on the 5th of June 1895 in West Chester, Pennsylvania.[dccx] She was born about 1873 in Pennsylvania and died in 1943 in Newton, Massachusetts.

JAMES CLARK IRWIN

James graduated from the University of Pennsylvania in 1890 as a civil engineer. He was associated with the New York Central and Hudson River Railroads.[dccxi] *Photo from this source.*

Catherine and James had five children:

222. i. James Clark IRWIN Jr. was born on the 25th of May 1896 in West Newton, Massachusetts.[dccxii] He died on the 29th of July 1976 in Kansas City, Missouri.[dccxiii] He married Constance ROOT on the 9th of June 1923 in Chicago, Illinois.[dccxiv] She died on the 16th of November 1976.[dccxv] They are buried in Chicago.[dccxvi] James was the vice-president of engineering for the United States Cold Storage Corporation. Constance worked with many community service organizations including the Kansas City Council on Education. The couple had two children, one of whom is living.

Photo from Technique, *yearbook of the Massachusetts Institute of Technology, 1921.*

223. ii. Robert Monaghan IRWIN was born on the 13th of March 1899 in Fonda, New York.^{dccxvii} He died in June 1965 in Newton, Massachusetts. ^{dccxviii} He married Margaret A. BASLEY in 1947 in Massachusetts.^{dccxix} Records for Margaret's birth and death could not be identified. Robert was an assistant manager for the Boston South Terminal train station. It is not known if the couple had children. *Photo from: The Harvard Class Album, yearbook, 1923.*

224. iii. William Henry IRWIN was born on the 28th of April 1901 in New York and died on the 17th of October 1922 in Manhattan, where he was working as an engineer.^{dccxx} He never married.

225. iv. John IRWIN was born on the 22nd of September 1902 in New York and died on the 5th of September 1981 in Newton, Massachusetts.^{dccxxi} He never married. His occupation was a salesman for office supplies.

226. v. Katharine IRWIN was born on the 16th of November 1908 in New York and she died on the 6th of January 1999 in Newton, Massachusetts.^{dccxxii} She never married. She was a French teacher for many years and held administrative positions in a variety of educational systems.

Photo from: The Brimmer and May High School yearbook, 1927, Chestnut, Massachusetts

118. **JOSEPH B. CLEMENT V** (Emily[4], Daniel[3], Daniel [2], Willliam[1]) was born on the 14th of January 1874 in Woodbury, New Jersey.^{dccxxiii} He died in 1934 in Schenectady, New York.^{dccxxiv} He married Jeanette L. WARD (daughter of Myndert WARD and Mary DUNCAN) in 1896. She was born on the 11th of September 1874^{dccxxv} and died in 1942 in Schenectady, New York.^{dccxxvi} Joseph worked as a clerk for General Electric.

Joseph and Jeanette had five known children:

227. i. Joseph B. CLEMENT VI was born on the 23rd of May 1898 in Schenectady, New York.^{dccxxvii} He died in April 1973 in Brentwood, New York.^{dccxxviii} He married Mary B. who was born on the 30th of May 1901 in New York, and died in October 1979. She is buried with her husband in the Long Island National Cemetery. The couple had two known children.

228. ii. Albert W. CLEMENT was born on the 25th of June 1899 in Woodbury, New Jersey.dccxxix He died on the 16th of October 1918 in France while serving in the US Army, 105th Infantry, Co. MG. From the abstract of his service record:

REMARKS: Served overseas from May 17-18 to Oct 16/18. Apld Pvt 1st cl May 7-18 ; Pvt Aug 3/18 ; Pvt 1st cl Oct 4/18. Cited in S.O. 86, 27 Div 1919 :- For great bravery and resourcefulness in carrying messages under heavy fire. This soldier showed great initiative and bravery for obtaining information concerning neighboring units under heavy shell fire until Killed. Thn Sept 29 - Oct 17, 1918.

dccxxx

For his service, he posthumously received the New York State Conspicuous Service Cross.

Albert never married.

229. iii. Robert Lawrence CLEMENT was born on the 16th of August 1901 in Woodbury, New Jersey.dccxxxi He died in December 1979 in Ballston Lake, New York.dccxxxii He married Eleanor Lampard.dccxxxiii She was born on the 30th of April 1894 in New York and died in February 1986 in Schenectady, New York.dccxxxiv The couple had no children. Robert was an inspector for the New York State Department of Horticulture.

+230. iv. James Irwin CLEMENT was born about 1909 in New York.dccxxxv He died in January 1970 in Schenectady, New York.dccxxxvi He married Helene GANOTT (daughter of Baptiste and Natalie GANOTT). She was born on the 6th of September 1914 and died in February 1992 in Schenectady, New York.dccxxxvii

231. v. Richard D. CLEMENT was born on the 10th of January 1915 in Schenectady.dccxxxviii He died on the 17th of June 1993 in Toms River, New Jersey.dccxxxix He married Juanita JOHNSTON, who was born in 1915 and died in 1945. She is buried in Schenectady.dccxl As a young man, he worked on several ships as an oilman and mechanic. He was able to travel all over the world. It is unknown if he and Juanita had children. It is also unknown if he remarried after Juanita's early death.

119. FRANK WEST CLEMENT (Emily[4], Daniel[3], Daniel[2], Willliam[1]) was born on the 14th of July 1883 in Woodbury, New Jersey.dccxli He died on the 8th of November 1957 in Haddonfield, New Jersey.dccxlii He married Anna Knight MARSHALL (daughter of Leander A. MARSHALL and Margaret Levis

BARNEY). She was born in February 1889.[dccxliii] Her date of death is unknown. Most of Frank's working years were as a salesman for an oil company.

Frank and Ann had three children:

232.   i.   Frank West CLEMENT Jr. was born on the 7th of November 1910 in Wenonah, New Jersey.[dccxliv] He died on the 27th of September 1997 in Port Orchard, Washington.[dccxlv] He married Lurene M. BUTLER on the 17th of April 1933 in Philadelphia.[dccxlvi] She was born in 1912 and died in 1982.[dccxlvii] Frank was in the US Navy from March 1939 through January 1948. He was aboard the USS St. Louis in December 1941 when it was dispatched to Pearl Harbor, arriving there on the 12th of December. [dccxlviii] There were no known children born to Frank and Lurene.

233.   ii.   Leander Marshall CLEMENT was born on the 3rd of December 1912 in New Jersey.[dccxlix] He died in November 1981 in Beverly, New Jersey.[dccl] He married Catherine Agatha KAYLOR on the 27th of August 1949 in Washington, D.C. She was born on the 9th of November 1909 and died on the 22nd of April 1997 in Mount Holly, New Jersey.[dccli] In the 1940 census, Leander was in Hawaii as a Pvt. in the US Army. In 1951, he was in the USAF in Orlando. His gravestone is marked with "WW II Korea". The couple had no known children.

234.   iii.   Donald Leeds CLEMENT was born in the 19th of March 1916 in Philadelphia.[dcclii] He died on the 12th of January 2003 in Haddonfield, New Jersey.[dccliii] He served in the US Army between 1942 and 1945. He married Anna Matilda "Tillie" TORR (daughter of William Henry TORR and Edith SHINN) on the 15th of December 1945 at the Grace Church in Haddonfield.[dccliv] She was born about 1921 and died in 2012.[dcclv] She was a member of the Marine Corp Womens Reserve during World War II. She worked at the Haddonfield Library for 24 years, and was very active in community affairs, named Citizen of the Year in 1986. Donald and Tillie had three known children.

124. **FRIEDA I. ENGLAND** (Oscar[4], Daniel[3], Daniel[2], William[1]) was born in April 1894 in Chicago, Illinois.[dcclvi] She died on the 19th of January 1970 in Belvidere.[dcclvii] She married William Carlton "Carl" BEAN on the 20th of April 1918 in Belvidere.[dcclviii] He was born on the 9th of July 1890 in Nebraska.[dcclix] He died on the 8th of January 1969 in Belvidere.[dcclx]

Frieda and Carl were farmers. Frieda was eventually disabled by rheumatoid arthritis. In a telephone conversation with Robert Harnish, a lifelong neighbor and friend of the Beans, he explained that Frieda's feet were so gnarled that she could only wear slippers, and that she needed two canes to walk. He talked about the hard times the Beans had on the farm because of growing conditions, the economy, and that two of their sons were away from the farm in World War II. In a poignant letter to Frieda and Carl, Bob wrote about the death of their son, expressing his condolences. Bob helped out on the Bean farm whenever he could. Bob has since passed away.

Frieda and Carl had three children, one of whom is still alive. One child, Donald England Bean, was killed in the Philippines in World War II. He had been awarded the Purple Heart for injuries received in a previous battle. His obituary:

Belvidere Native

"Donald had been fighting with the 37th division that took Luzon and felt the camaraderie of fighting men as he marched with American forces into Manila, capital of the Philippines.

He was born in Belvidere, May 16, 1921, and moved to a farm in Manchester township with his parents when he was eight years old. He attended the Gray school and was a member of the 4-H club in Manchester township for two years.

Immediately before entering service, Donald was employed in the polishing rooms of the National Sewing Machine company and while in the service corresponded with many friends who he had met at the company and in Belvidere.

After his induction in July, 1942, he trained at Camp Roberts, California, and was later transferred to Angel island off the west coast where his mother visited him before he went overseas. He left for the South Pacific from Camp Stoneman, Cal., in January, 1943.

Donald viewed the war at close range, at the Fiji Islands, at Guadalcanal and the Russell islands, and in the campaign of New Georgia.

Held Purple Heart

In early 1944 he was awarded the Purple Heart for wounds received the preceding August on Munda. It was believed he was wounded while trying to wipe out a Jap machine gun nest with a hand grenade.

On Munda he fought for five weeks in the rain and mud without taking off his boots and on Bougainville, battled with old style guns until he left there in May last year.

Donald had not been home since he entered the service three years ago."[dcclxi]

Bob Harnish described Don as his best friend, a "little guy who was really scrappy".

127. **HERBERT ENGLAND** (Oscar[4], Daniel[3], Daniel[2], William[1]) was born on the 22nd of July 1898 in Chicago, Illinois.[dcclxii] He died on the 7th of May 1983, at the age of 83, in St. Petersburg, Florida. He was the driver of a battery-powered cart that was hit by a car. He married Rose PIENSCHKE  (daughter of Franciszek PIENSCHKE and Rosalia BOLDA) on the 1st of July 1922 in Chicago.[dcclxiii] She was born on the 20th of February 1901 in Chicago and died on the 3rd of October 1974 in St. Petersburg, Florida.[dcclxiv] Herbert began his career working with the Sterling Food Products in Belvidere. This company canned the locally grown food products like beans, peas, and corn. He became superintendent, and in 1934, when the Belvidere plant moved to Sterling, Illinois, he moved with it. Then in 1939, the National Tea Company, who owned Sterling Food Products closed the Sterling plant, Herb continued his employment with National Tea. He retired from National Tea, as head grocery buyer with the New Orleans division, with 43 years of service, on the 30th of April 1966. For his retirement, the company presented him with a brand new, bright red, Ford Mustang.[dcclxv]

Herb and Rose had two children:

235. i. Constance Rose ENGLAND was born on the 2nd of May 1923 in Cook County, Illinois.[dcclxvi] She died on the 30th of December 2004 in Hernando, Florida.[dcclxvii] She married Melvin F. "Bud"  SCHULDT (1921-1983) on the 25th of January, 1943.[dcclxviii] Bud went to war and Connie was one of the thousands of women that went to work in a factory to support herself and the war effort. After Bud returned from the war, the marriage "didn't work out" and ended in divorce. [dcclxix] She then married Edward BERGSTROM. He was born on the 23rd of September 1912 in Michigan and died in

November 1975 in Niles, Illinois.[dcclxx] Connie and Ed had three children all of whom are living. Connie married a third time to Donovan CROFT on the 10th of October 1985 in St. Petersburg, Florida.[dcclxxi]

236. ii. George Allan ENGLAND was my father. He was born on the 9th of March 1930 in Chicago. He died on the 2nd of March 1976 in Tampa, Florida. He married Theresa A. POTEMPA (daughter of Casimir POTEMPA and Mary L. LENCKOS) in Chicago

on the 3rd of February 1952 at St. John Cantius Church. George and Theresa had four children, all of whom are living. George and Theresa were divorced on the 6th of February 1962 in Kalamazoo, Michigan. He married a second time to Janice and they were divorced in 1969. The divorce certificate, with her surname redacted, cited "extreme cruelty" as the reason, and stated that there were no children from this marriage. He married a third time to Winifred Joan Bury on the 29th of October 1970 and divorced in 1972. It is unknown if there were any children from his second marriage. At the time of his death, he was working as a cook on a fishing boat. George was extremely charming and was known as an excellent cook. Unfortunately, he was an alcoholic, and couldn't keep a job. Letters from his father reflect that his parents tried alcohol treatment programs unsuccessfully.

128. <u>Harriet England</u> (Oscar[4], Daniel[3], Daniel[2], William[1]) was born on the 30th of December 1900 in Cherry Valley, Illinois and died in June 1975 in Carlsbad, New Mexico.[dcclxxii] She married Carl BAYLANDER (son of Charles BAYLANDER and Mary LINK) on the 1st of July 1921 in Belvidere.[dcclxxiii] He was born on the 1st of May 1900 in Chicago, and died on the 1st of April 1953 in Rockford, Illinois.[dcclxxiv] Harriet then married Dr. Willard C. MORREY on the 21st of January 1961 in Rockford.[dcclxxv] He was born on the 14th of April 1893 in Ottawa, Ohio.[dcclxxvi] He died in November 1973 in Carlsbad, New Mexico.[dcclxxvii]

Carl was employed by the National Sewing Machine Company in Belvidere and was the spokesperson for their union, the A.F. of L. He was a World War I veteran, attached to the 173rd artillery.

Harriet and Carl had one child:

237. i. Edward BAYLANDER was born on the 11th of August 1921 in Belvidere and died in August 1979 in Rockford, Illinois.[dcclxxviii] He married Marion Louise ESTABROOK (daughter of Levi F. ESTABROOK and Alta I. MABBOTT) on the 30th of September 1942 in Illinois.[dcclxxix] She was born about 1922 in Illinois[dcclxxx] and died on the 10th of September 1960 in Rockford.[dcclxxxi] The couple had no children. Edward worked for

many years as a clerk for the Central Illinois Electric Company and then for the Rockford Transit Company. Marion worked as a stenographer for the Wilson Bottling Company.

132. **ANNA ELIZABETH CRAMER** (Mary[4], James[3], Daniel[2], William[1]) was born on the 29ᵗʰ of January 1871[dcclxxxii] and died of tuberculosis on the 30ᵗʰ of October 1899 in Reading, Pennsylvania.[dcclxxxiii] She married William E. WESTNEY in 1892 in Philadelphia.[dcclxxxiv] He was born in March 1870 in New York State.[dcclxxxv] No records of his death or burial were found.

At the time of Annie's death, William was the owner of the Westney Hat Company, a company that made felted wool hats. The company failed 6 months after Annie's death and William was forced to place the children in an orphanage. He moved back to Yonkers, New York, where his mother was residing and was able to secure employment as a designer for a carpet company, a position that he held for at least 20 years. In 1906, he removed the children from the orphanage and took them to Yonkers. After Annie's death, William married Wilhelmina Popp with whom he had four children.

Annie and William had three children:

238.   i.   Florence Ethel WESTNEY was born on the 3ʳᵈ of July 1884 in Philadelphia.[dcclxxxvi] She died on the 20ᵗʰ of July 1940 in Northampton, Massachusetts.[dcclxxxvii] She married Wallace Addison HOWES (son of Walter K. HOWES and Ida WOLFRAM) in 1917. He was born on the 1ˢᵗ of March 1895 in Ashfield, Massachusetts[dcclxxxviii] He died on the 14ᵗʰ of August 1964 in Northampton, Massachusetts.[dcclxxxix] Wallace was a civil engineer. In 1930, he was employed as a superintendent of a brick manufacturing company. In 1940, he worked for the city of Northampton as the Superintendent of Streets. Florence and Wallace had three children, one of whom is still living.

239.   ii.   Hazel Dyer WESTNEY was born in May 1896 in Philadelphia.[dccxc] She died on the 16ᵗʰ of February 1949 in New York.[dccxci] She married James Salomon LEHREN on the 30ᵗʰ of April 1925 in Yonkers, New York.[dccxcii] He was born on the 16ᵗʰ of July 1888 in Amsterdam, Holland.[dccxciii] He died on the 5ᵗʰ of November 1961 in Greenwich, Connecticut.[dccxciv] He became a US citizen on the 21ˢᵗ of November 1941.[dccxcv] He was President of the Wolverine Supply and Manufacturing Company, which made kitchen utensils and toys. Hazel and James had four children, two of whom are still living.

240.   iii.   Henry "Harry" England WESTNEY was born on the 20ᵗʰ of April 1898 in Reading, Pennsylvania.[dccxcvi] He died on the 8ᵗʰ of October 1947 in Allen Park, Michigan. He was named after his mother's uncle, Henry C. England. Harry served in World War I. He entered the US Navy in April 1915, at the age of seventeen, as an apprentice seaman. He was discharged in April 1919 as a Quartermaster 2ⁿᵈ class. He was a salesman for Monarch Life Insurance Company. He married Grayce KRAMER (daughter of Arend KRAMER and Anna DEKKER) on the 11ᵗʰ of January 1934 in Elkhart, Indiana.[dccxcvii]

She was born on the 3rd of May 1910 in Muskegon, Michigan.[dccxcviii] She died on the 18th of November 1986 in Portage, Michigan. After Harry's death, she married Fred Carl Bode on the 18th of March 1948 in Detroit.[dccxcix] There were no known children born to Harry and Grayce.

Here is the 6th generation:

142.   **ANNABEL CRAWFORD** (Elizabeth[5], Joanna[4], William[3], Thomas[2], William[1]) was born about 1859 in Gloucester County, New Jersey.[dccc] She married Thomas W. SMITH (son of William F. and Harriet E. SMITH) on the 24th of January 1876 in Camden, New Jersey.[dccci] He was born about 1854 in Pennsylvania.[dcccii] No death records for either Annabel or Thomas were found. Thomas was an engineer.

Annabel and Thomas had three children:

241.   i.   Leroy SMITH was born about 1876 in New Jersey.[dccciii] He last appears in the 1895 New Jersey State Census. There are no clearly identifiable records of marriage, residence and death.

242.   ii.   Jesse SMITH was born about 1878 in New Jersey.[dccciv] She died of diphtheria, at the age of 18, on the 11th of July 1896 in Philadelphia.[dcccv]

243.   iii.   Isaac Mulford SMITH was born on the 19th of November 1882 in Camden, New Jersey.[dcccvi] He died on the 13th of January 1963 in Hollywood, Florida, where he and his wife wintered. He married Anna Melissa LEAMING. She was born on the 20th of March 1880 in New Jersey. She died on the 30th of January 1975 in Camden, New Jersey.[dcccvii] I. Mulford was president of the Terminal Building and Loan Association. He retired in 1949 as co-owner of Burr-Smith Company, Camden realtors. The couple had no known children.

147. **PHILENA W. MYERS** (Isabella[5], Joanna[4], William[3], Thomas[2], William[1]) was born on the 15th of August 1860 in Center Square, Gloucester County, New Jersey.[dcccviii] She died in 1940 in Center Square.[dcccix] She married Stacy C. PANCOAST (son of Charles and Elizabeth PANCOAST) in 1879.[dcccx] He was born in 1854 in Franklin Township, Gloucester County, New Jersey[dcccxi] and died in 1929 in Center Square.[dcccxii] Stacy worked as a blacksmith, gunsmith and farmer.

Stacy first married Emma Dunlap in 1874. They had one daughter, Lizzie E. who was born about 1877.

Lena and Stacy had seven children:

+244.　i.　Emma PANCOAST was born on the 19th of July 1880 in Upper Penns Neck, Salem County, New Jersey.[dcccxiii] She died in 1942 and is buried in Center Square, New Jersey.[dcccxiv] She married Fillmore S. DAWSON (son of Franklin and Lucinda DAWSON). He was born in July 1873 in New Jersey.[dcccxv] He died on the 21st of June 1956 and is buried in Center Square, New Jersey.[dcccxvi]

+245.　ii.　Joseph Myers PANCOAST was born on the 26th of February 1882 in Auburn, New Jersey.[dcccxvii] He died on the 21st of October 1957 in Preston, Maryland.[dcccxviii] He married Emilie H. PEPPER in 1905 in Philadelphia.[dcccxix] She was born about 1882 in Pennsylvania.[dcccxx] Her date of death is unknown. Joseph was a machinist for the Baldwin Locomotive Works in Eddystone, Pennsylvania.

+246.　iii.　Herbert Roberts PANCOAST was born on the 1st of March 1885 in Auburn, New Jersey.[dcccxxi] He died on the 19th of May 1960 in Orange, California.[dcccxxii] He married May RISLEY (daughter of Bakley RISLEY and Lizzie SOL) about 1909.[dcccxxiii] She was born on the 19th of May 1886 in New Jersey and died on the 19th of October 1956 in Los Angeles, California.[dcccxxiv]

+247.　iv.　Roger Corliss PANCOAST was born on the 4th of September 1887 in New Jersey.[dcccxxv] He died in September 1962 in Delaware.[dcccxxvi] He married Ruth A. LEIPOLD (daughter of John Harry and Edna L. LEIPOLD) about 1909.[dcccxxvii] She was born in 1899 in Delaware and died on the 23rd of April 1915, at the age of 25. He next married Goldah CONAWAY (daughter of George and Mary CONAWAY) on the 12th of March 1917 in Georgetown, Maryland.[dcccxxviii] She was born on the 31st of January 1900 in Sussex, Delaware.[dcccxxix] She died on the 19th of November 1970 in Smyrna, Delaware. The couple divorced in May 1925.[dcccxxx]

+248.　v.　Foster Richard PANCOAST was born on the 20th of December 1892 in Auburn, New Jersey.[dcccxxxi] He died on the 7th of August 1977 in Jacksonville, Florida.[dcccxxxii] He first married Hazel H. STIMSON (daughter of George G. and Ella STIMSON) in 1917 in Philadelphia. She was born about 1897 in Pennsylvania.[dcccxxxiii] In 1931, Roger sued her for divorce on the grounds of desertion. Her date of death is unknown. He next married Kathryn M. PALMER (daughter of Warren T. PALMER and Grace Mae HELFERSTAY) on the 3rd of March 1942 in Wilmington.

She was born on the 9th of October 1910 in Edgemoor, Delaware.dcccxxxiv She died on the 30th of December 2005 in Wilmington.dcccxxxv

From *The News Journal,* 10 Aug 1922

249.   vi.   Elva K. PANCOAST was born on the 1st of May 1896 in Auburn, New Jersey.dcccxxxvi She died on the 31st of December 1960.dcccxxxvii She married Clarence Dawson NORTON (son of Frank and Blanche NORTON). He was born on the 15th of July 1895 in Gloucester County, New Jersey.dcccxxxviii He died in 1956 and is buried in Center Square, New Jersey.dcccxxxix Clarence was a farmer. The couple had three children.

250.   vii.   Ruth I. PANCOAST was born in 1899 in New Jersey and died in 1959.dcccxl She married James N. DENELSBECK (son of Joseph and Lizzie DENELSBECK) in 1928 in Philadelphia.dcccxli He was born on the 1st of July 1904 in New Jersey.dcccxlii He died on the 28th of June 1977 in Gloucester County, New Jersey.dcccxliii He served in the US Navy from the 14th of October 1922 to the 9th of September 1926.dcccxliv He worked for the DuPont Company in the powder works division. The couple had one known child.

251.   viii.   Stacy C. PANCOAST appears in the 1885 New Jersey State Census, in the 0-4 age group. He does not appear in any subsequent records; it is, therefore, assumed that he died as a child.

151.   **MINERVA W. MYERS** (Isabella[5], Joanna[4], William[3], Thomas[2], William[1]) was born about 1869 in Gloucester County, New Jersey. Her date of death is unknown. She married Samuel AMBRUSTER. He was born about 1866 in New Jersey.dcccxlv He died on the 14th of January 1908 in Pleasantville, New Jersey.dcccxlvi Minerva then married Edmund HENDRICKSON (son of Edmund W. and Jane HENDRICKSON and twin of William) on the 7th of August 1914 in Camden. He was born about 1876 in New Jerseydcccxlvii and died on the 6th of January 1956 in Burlington, New Jersey.dcccxlviii While

living in Camden, Samuel was a driver and teamster. Sometime after 1899, he moved to Pleasantville, New Jersey. Ed Hendrickson was a carpenter. Minnie and Ed had no children.

Minnie and Samuel had five children:

252.   i.   Everett Horner AMBRUSTER was born on the 26th of November 1887 in Auburn, New Jersey.[dcccxlix] He died on the 16th of February 1992 in Somers Point, New Jersey.[dcccl] He married Beatrice CONOVER (daughter of Tunis CONOVER and Elizabeth ELY) on the 8th of January 1913.[dcccli] She was born on the 3rd of January 1891 in Monmouth, New Jersey.[dccclii] She died in 1964 and is buried in Leeds Point, New Jersey.[dcccliii] Everett was a farmer. The couple had no children.

253.   ii.   Elsie E. AMBRUSTER was born on the 17th of December 1887 in Camden, New Jersey.[dcccliv] The last record in which she is found is the 1920 census, living with her parents and siblings. No marriage or death records were found.

254.   iii.   The records for this child are confusing. In the 1910 US Census, the child is Nataniel, a son, born in 1897 in New Jersey. In the 1920 census, the child is Nettie, a daughter, born in 1897 in New Jersey. No records of marriage or death were found for either name.

255.   iv.   Frances (Francisca) M. AMBRUSTER was born about 1904 in New Jersey.[dccclv] The last record in which she was found is the 1920 US Census. No records for marriage or death were found.

256.   v.   Samuel E. AMBRUSTER was born about 1908 in New Jersey.[dccclvi] Records for a Samuel Ambruster exist, but it cannot be confirmed that they are the same individual.

160.   **JOSEPH E. ROBERTS** (Joseph[5], Joanna[4], William[3], Thomas[2], William[1]) was born on the 22nd of December 1878 in Camden, New Jersey.[dccclvii] He died on the 4th of June 1950 in Camden, New Jersey.[dccclviii] He married Ethel A. ALLEN. She was born on the 30th of August 1855 in New Jersey and died in August 1975 in Short Hills, New Jersey.[dccclix] Joseph was a physician, a radiologist, of some distinction in Camden. He was the chief of radiology at St. Joseph's Hospital for five years after his internship. He then became the chief radiologist at Cooper Hospital in Camden, a post he held for 30 years. Dr. Roberts was a member of many professional groups in South Jersey and elsewhere, and was past president of the Camden County Medical Society. He was for many years a trustee of the Broadway Methodist Church in Camden, and later the First Presbyterian Church of Haddonfield.[dccclx]

Photo from http://www.dvrbs.com/people/camdenpeople-drjosepheroberts.htm; used with permission

Joseph and Ethel had three children:

257.   i.   Joseph England ROBERTS III was born about 1911 in New Jersey.[dccclxi] He died on the 24th of August 1930 while swimming in the ocean near Ocean City, New Jersey

while his father helplessly watched.[dccclxii] He was about to enter his senior year at Princeton University.

258. ii. Twin of Joseph England ROBERTS III died about 1917 in an automobile accident which his father witnessed from his office window.[dccclxiii]

259. iii. Richard H. ROBERTS was born about 1923 in New Jersey.[dccclxiv] He died on the 28th of May 1983.[dccclxv] He served in the US Army during World War II from 1943-1946.[dccclxvi] He married Mary MULFORD (daughter of Albert and Mary MULFORD). She was born on the 17th of March 1924 in Philadelphia.[dccclxvii] She died on the 13th of May 2012 in Toms River, New Jersey.[dccclxviii] Richard was a physician with a varied career in private practice, in occupational health for the RCA Company and as a medical advisor to Ciba Pharmaceuticals. There was a brief announcement in the Courier-News in August 1949 that Richard

RICHARD HILLMAN ROBERTS, II

was one of two people who had contracted polio.[dccclxix] The outcome of his disease is unknown. Richard and Mary had six children.

164. **WILLIAM S. HARBISON** (Hannah[5], Joanna[4], Willliam[3], Thomas[2], William[1]) was born in March 1863. He is found in the 1910 census living with his brother and father in Camden. His last listing in the Camden city directory is 1912. He married Anna M. KLEIN in 1889.[dccclxx] She was born about 1867 in New Jersey. She is found in the 1900 census living with her husband and son in Camden, New Jersey. Her last listing in the Camden city directory is 1902. There are no records of her death. William was a coal merchant.

William and Anna had one son:

+260. i. Warren Grant HARBISON was born on the 7th of November 1889 in Camden, New Jersey.[dccclxxi] He died the 5th of October 1940 in Manhattan.[dccclxxii] He married Violet MATHIS on the 7th of May 1910 in Birmingham, Alabama.[dccclxxiii] She was born about 1888 in New Jersey.[dccclxxiv] She died in March 1986.[dccclxxv]

165. **WARREN G. HARBISON** was born in July 1866. No records of his death were identified. The 1900 census lists him as "divorced" but no record of this marriage can be found. In the 1920 census, he is living with his wife, Minnie. In the 1930 census, he is listed as married, but his wife is not named as living in that residence. In the 1940 census, he is identified as a widower. His wife is a bit of a mystery. She is named "Minnie" on census records, but she is "Dolores" on her son's death certificate.

No records of her marriage or death can be found. She is last found in the 1920 census in Camden, New Jersey.

Warren was the father of two children:

261.   i.   Warren Pershing HARBISON was born on the 30th of August 1919 in Camden, New Jersey.[dccclxxvi] He died on the 26th of October 1947 in Jacksonville, North Carolina. He enlisted in the US Marine Corps in 1939 and saw action in the Pacific, where he earned the Purple Heart and several other awards. He remained in the Corps after the war and was killed in an automobile accident while on active duty at Camp Lejeune.[dccclxxvii] He never married.

262.   ii. Ronald G. HARBISON was born about 1921 in New Jersey.[dccclxxviii] He died on the 2nd of March 2013 in Vineland, New Jersey.[dccclxxix] He is survived by his wife and three children. He made his career as a merchant marine, retiring as a Captain with the Mobile Oil Company.

168.   **JACOB R. HARBISON** (Hannah[5], Joanna[4], Willliam[3], Thomas[2], William[1]) was born about 1871 in New Jersey. He married Hattie B. GROSS (daughter of Elias A. GROSS and Sophia FOX) on the 1st of August 1894 in Wilmington, Delaware. Hattie died on the 2nd of October 1899 in Philadelphia. She committed suicide by inhaling illumination gas (the gas used to provide indoor lighting before electricity was available).[dccclxxx] She is buried with her parents in Rochester, New York.[dccclxxxi] She never had children. He married a second time to Dora MCNEAL on the 22nd of February 1902 in Camden, New Jersey. She was born about 1874 in New Jersey.[dccclxxxii] No death records for either Jacob or Dora were found. Jacob was a fruit salesman.

Jacob and Dora had two children:

263.   i.   Robert J. HARBISON was born about 1909 in New Jersey.[dccclxxxiii] He died in June 1980. It is unknown if he married or had children.

264.   ii. John W. HARBISON was born about 1911 in New Jersey.[dccclxxxiv] He died in March 1960 in Camden, New Jersey.[dccclxxxv] It is unknown if he married or had children.

167.   **SAMUEL BODO HARBISON** (Hannah[5], Joanna[4], Willliam[3], Thomas[2], William[1]) was born on the 18th of November 1880.[dccclxxxvi] In 1908, he married Mary Helen MULLINER (daughter of Joseph MULLINER and Elizabeth PARSONS). She was born on the 24th of September 1884 in Camden, New Jersey.[dccclxxxvii] No death records for either Bodo or Mary Helen could be found. Bodo worked for Wanamaker's Department Store.

Bodo and Mary Helen had two children:

265.   i.   Helen Grace HARBISON was born in 1910 in Camden, New Jersey.[dccclxxxviii] She died in January 1968 in Camden.[dccclxxxix] She never married. A graduate of Glassboro State

Teachers College, Grace taught for 48 years the Haviland Avenue Elementary School.^{dcccxc}

266. ii. Neil Bodo HARBISON was born on the 31st of January 1916 in Audubon, New Jersey.^{dcccxci} He died on the 6th of May 2004 in Pennsauken, New Jersey.^{dcccxcii}. He married Dorothy M. LUDWIGSEN (daughter of George LUDWIGSEN and Ida MCWATTERS). She was born on the 15th of November 1928 in Camden, New Jersey and died on the 2nd of October 1988 in Audubon, New Jersey.^{dcccxciii} It is unknown if the couple had children.

173. **FLORENCE TAWS** (James[5], Deborah[4], William[3], Thomas[2], William[1]) was born on the 6th of June 1883 in Philadelphia and died on the 15th of February 1956 in Philadelphia.^{dcccxciv}

She married Alfred James GARBER Sr. (son of Lewis GARBER and Martha MCCANDLES) on the 1st of December 1901 in Philadelphia.^{dcccxcv} He was born on the 13th of July 1874 in Philadelphia and died on the 2nd of May 1937 in Lansdowne, Pennsylvania.^{dcccxcvi} Alfred worked as a machinist for the railroad.

Photo from the collection of Robyn Sheets, usesd with permission

Florence and Arthur had three children:

267. i. Alfred J. GARBER Jr. was born on the 12th of November 1904 in Philadelphia.^{dcccxcvii} He died on the 10th of October 1945 in Delaware.^{dcccxcviii} He married Sarah T. WALTZ (daughter of Cleveland T. WALTZ and Sarah TRAYER) in 1928 in Philadelphia.^{dcccxcix} She was born about 1906 in Maryland.^{cm} Alfred was an electrician for the railroad and Sarah was a teacher. No death records were identified for Sarah; however, she may have remarried. There were no known children born to Alfred and Sarah.

268. ii. Elizabeth GARBER was born on the 13th of June 1906^{cmi} and died of enterocolitis on the 23rd of June 1906.^{cmii}

+269. iii. Mahlon GARBER was born on the 28th of June 1909 in Philadelphia.^{cmiii} He died on the 1st of October 1969 in Philadelphia.^{cmiv} He married Anna WALTZ (daughter of Cleveland T. WALTZ and Sarah TRAYER). She was born the 4th of March 1910 in Philadelphia and died on the 21st of August 1993 in Media, Pennsylvania.^{cmv}

174. **EDITH TAWS** (James[5], Deborah[4], William[3], Thomas[2], William[1]) was born in December 1886 in Pennsylvania.[cmvi] She died on the 31st of March 1967 in Wethersfield, Connecticut.[cmvii] She married George Randall MOORE on the 3rd of July 1907 in Philadelphia.[cmviii] He was born on the 5th of November 1883 in Guthriesville, Pennsylvania.[cmix] He died on the 23rd of March 1965 in Wethersfield Connecticut.[cmx] George owned and operated his own wallpaper hanging business. He was blind in the left eye.[cmxi]

Edith and George had four children:

+270.　i.　Violet Elizabeth MOORE was born on the 3rd of July 1908 in Philadelphia.[cmxii] She died in June 1984 in Grand Junction, Colorado.[cmxiii] She married Arthur M. BAKER on the 18th of September 1926 in Philadelphia. He was born about 1906 in Pennsylvania.[cmxiv] His record of death was not found.

271.　ii.　Dorothy R. MOORE was born on the 9th of February 1911 in Philadelphia.[cmxv] She died on the 24th of May 1999 in Quakertown, Pennsylvania.[cmxvi] She married Edgar A. PATTERSON (son of Frank PATTERSON and Lydia WARREN) in 1930 in Philadelphia.[cmxvii] He was born on the 27th of May 1912 in Philadelphia and died in March 1972.[cmxviii] He is buried in Downington, Pennsylvania.[cmxix] The couple had one child.

272.　iii.　Hazel Amanda MOORE was born on the 27th of April 1915 in Philadelphia.[cmxx] She died in December 1995 in Glenwood, Illinois.[cmxxi] She married Russell H. GIBSON (son of Robert GIBSON) in 1940 in Philadelphia.[cmxxii] He was born on the 29th of September 1909 in Philadelphia[cmxxiii] and died in March 1974 in Cook County, Illinois.[cmxxiv] He was a World War II veteran. Hazel and Russell had one child. Hazel married a second time to a John A. Roberts, who died in 1991 in Chicago.

273.　iv.　Florence May MOORE was born on the 15th of June 1919 in Philadelphia.[cmxxv] She died on the 4th of May 2012 in Bloomfield, Connecticut.[cmxxvi] Florence never married. She was a teacher and librarian.

180. **ELLA V. ENGLAND** (Gustavus[5], Samuel[4], William[3], Thomas[2], William[1]) was born on the 6th of January 1871 and died of carcinoma of the uterus on the 7th of June 1915 in Philadelphia.[cmxxvii] She married Charles HOFFMAN in 1889.[cmxxviii] He was born in September 1870 in Pennsylvania. Death records, or marriage records after the death of Ella, for Charles could not be clearly identified. Charles was a police officer, and at one time, was credited with saving the life of a girl who had fallen into the Delaware River.[cmxxix] Charles married a second time to Mary Ellen LOGAN with whom he had one child.

Ella and Charles had five children:

274.　i.　Gustavus Allen HOFFMAN was born on the 18th of December 1899 in Philadelphia.[cmxxx] He died of pancreatic cancer on the 2nd of February 1951 in Philadelphia.[cmxxxi] He married Clara A. STRUBE (daughter of Frederic and Henrietta STRUBE) in 1927 in

Philadelphia.[cmxxxii] She was born in May 1889 in Pennsylvania.[cmxxxiii] Her date of death is unknown. Gustav enlisted in the US Army on the 22ⁿᵈ of November 1917, was assigned to Co. F of the 304ᵗʰ Ammunition Train until April 1918, was transferred to the 103ʳᵈ Ammunition Train, and was honorably discharged on the 20ᵗʰ of May 1919.[cmxxxiv] Both trains saw battle in France. Chaplains of both trains wrote histories that are available online, the 304ᵗʰ at Google Books[cmxxxv], and the 103ʳᵈ at Hathitrust.org.[cmxxxvi] Gustav managed a soda fountain at a local pharmacy, and considered himself an "ice cream maker". There were no known children.

275. ii. Charles Daniel HOFFMAN was born on the 7ᵗʰ of February 1892 in Philadelphia.[cmxxxvii] He died on the 26ᵗʰ of November 1971 in Broward County, Florida.[cmxxxviii] He married Marion SPENCER in 1910 in Philadelphia.[cmxxxix] She was born in 1891 in Philadelphia.[cmxl] She died in 1940 and is buried in Cherry Hill, New Jersey.[cmxli] He next married the widow Lorraine E. DUTROW Dean (daughter of Harry Elsworth DUTROW and Cora May COLEMAN) on the 20ᵗʰ of February 1950 in Washington, DC.[cmxlii] She was born on the 27ᵗʰ of October 1897 In Martinsburg, West Virginia and died in May 1985 in Ft. Lauderdale, Florida.[cmxliii] Charles and Marion had two children, one of whom is living.

276. iii. Elizabeth HOFFMAN died of congestion of the brain at the age of 14 months on the 2ⁿᵈ of August 1899 in Philadelphia.[cmxliv]

277. iv. Raymond HOFFMAN was born on the 10ᵗʰ of January 1906 in Philadelphia.[cmxlv] He died on the 2ⁿᵈ of December 1993 in Stratford, New Jersey.[cmxlvi] He married Eva Mary OZLOWSKI. She was born on the 1ˢᵗ of July 1911 in Blackwood, New Jersey.[cmxlvii] She died on the 26ᵗʰ of June 1985 in Camden.[cmxlviii] Raymond was a police officer for the city of Camden for 20 years. He played the snare drum, and was a member of several bands. He played Santa Claus at area shopping malls.[cmxlix] Raymond and Eva Mary had two children, one of whom is living.

278. v. Cooper HOFFMAN was born on the 13ᵗʰ of March 1907, and died on the 19ᵗʰ of May 1907.[cml] He had been born prematurely.

185. **AARON HURFF** (Mary⁵, Rebecca⁴, William W.³, Daniel², William¹) was born on the 9ᵗʰ of October 1855 in Swedesboro.[cmli] He died in Camden County in 1933.[cmlii] He married Sarah A. HUNT (daughter of J. B. and Maria HUNT) in November 1876 in Blackwood, New Jersey. She was born on the 19ᵗʰ of March 1858 in New Jersey and died on the 29ᵗʰ of June 1918 in Camden County, NJ.[cmliii] Aaron was a produce merchant.

Aaron and Sarah had three children:

+279. i. Mabel B. HURFF was born on the 20th of March 1879 in Haddonfield, New Jersey.[cmliv] She died in April 1971 in Haddonfield.[cmlv] She married Harry C. AVIS (son of Harry AVIS and Henrietta LIPPINCOTT) about 1902.[cmlvi] He was born on the 11th of September 1878 in Harrisville, New Jersey.[cmlvii] He died on the 10th of February 1935 in Jefferson, Pennsylvania.[cmlviii] Harry was a clerk at a lumber business. He was a veteran of the Spanish American war, serving with Co. G of the Pennsylvania Volunteers.

280. ii Linda M. HURFF was born in December 1883 in New Jersey. She married Charles Albert SCHAFER. He was born on the 14th of July 1887 in Bridgeton, New Jersey.[cmlix] He died on the 16th of January 1966 in Bellmawr, New Jersey.[cmlx] In his obituary, Linda is referred to as his "late" wife, so it is assumed that she died before 1966, but no record of her death can be found. Charles owned and operated a light hauling company. Charles and Linda had eight children, one of whom is living.

+281. iii. Virginia S. HURFF was born on the 11th of September 1886 in Camden, New Jersey.[cmlxi] She died in December 1976 in Haddonfield, New Jersey.[cmlxii] She married Charles E. MAGILL, who was born about 1872 in Pennsylvania.[cmlxiii] His date of death is unknown. Charles was a veterinarian.

186. **HENRY L. HURFF** (Mary[5], Rebecca[4], William W.[3], Daniel[2], William[1]) was born in 1854 in Gloucester County, New Jersey. He died in 1941.[cmlxiv] He married Elizabeth D. HARVEY on the 3rd of October 1878 in Hurffville, New Jersey. She was born in August 1856[cmlxv] and died on the 29th of January 1914.[cmlxvi] They are both buried in Hurffville, New Jersey. Henry was a farmer.

Henry and Elizabeth had five children:

282. i. Amy HURFF was born on the 29th of March 1879 in Glassboro, New Jersey.[cmlxvii] No records of marriage or death were found. The 1910 US Census indicates that Elizabeth had five children, and four were living in 1910. It is assumed that Amy died as an infant or child.

+283. ii. Ada HURFF was born in September 1880.[cmlxviii] She died on the 25th of October 1953 in Seattle, Washington.[cmlxix] She married William Thompson CAMPBELL (son of Thomas J. CAMPBELL and Sophia C. TICE) on the 25th of July 1903 in Monroe, New Jersey[cmlxx]. He was born on the 25th of July 1880 in Williamstown, New Jersey.[cmlxxi] He died on the 25th of October 1950 in Seattle, Washington.[cmlxxii] William was an insurance agent.

+284. iii. Walter Henry HURFF was born on the 28th of June 1883 in Washington Township, Gloucester County, New Jersey.[cmlxxiii] He died on the 9th of February 1948[cmlxxiv] and is buried in Hurffville.[cmlxxv] He married Ida Mae SCOTT. She was born on the 17th of March 1892 and died in October 1971 in Glassboro, New Jersey.[cmlxxvi]

+285. iv. Grover Cleveland HURFF was born on the 14ᵗʰ of January 1884.[cmlxxvii] He died on the 16ᵗʰ of October 1964.[cmlxxviii] He married Edythe Mae DOWN (daughter of John Franklin DOWN and Elizabeth DAUGHERTY). She was born on the 4ᵗʰ of July 1890 and died on the 17ᵗʰ of April 1977.[cmlxxix] Grover was a farmer.

286. v. Ella HURFF was born on the 21ˢᵗ of September 1886[cmlxxx] and died on the 11ᵗʰ of October 1886 in Gloucester County, New Jersey.[cmlxxxi]

192. **ERNEST OLLIS ENGLAND** (Benjamin⁵, Aquilla⁴, William W.³, Daniel², William¹) was born in March 1873 in Brooklyn.[cmlxxxii] He died on the 16ᵗʰ of September 1912 in Queens, New York.[cmlxxxiii] He married Ethel Olive JOHNSON (the adopted daughter of William SHARPE and Lillian A. WRIGHT) on the 30ᵗʰ of January 1895 in Brooklyn.[cmlxxxiv] She was born in November 1876 in New York.[cmlxxxv] On the 4ᵗʰ of October 1919, she married Ernest's brother, Herbert.[cmlxxxvi] She died on the 19ᵗʰ of February 1963.[cmlxxxvii] Ernest was an electrician with the telephone company. Herbert and Ethel had no children together. Two of Ernest's children listed Herbert as their father on their social security applications.

Ernest and Ethel had four children:

287. i. Florence Violet ENGLAND was born in January 1886.[cmlxxxviii] She died at the age of 16 on the 18ᵗʰ of August 1912 in Queens, New York.[cmlxxxix]

288. ii. Harold F. ENGLAND was born on the 20ᵗʰ of March 1897 in Brooklyn.[cmxc] He died on the 3ʳᵈ of July 1967 in Fresno, California.[cmxci] He married Emma Matilda Eskilson (daughter of August ESKILSON and Emma J. MOELLER). Harold was a real estate broker. Harold and Matilda had two children, both of whom are living.

289. iii. Benjamin Franklin "Frank" ENGLAND was born on the 5ᵗʰ of August 1901 in Brooklyn.[cmxcii] He died on the 13ᵗʰ of May 1981.[cmxciii] He married Ida R. FORMAN on the 1ˢᵗ of July 1933 in Kings, New York.[cmxciv] She was born on the 19ᵗʰ of April 1898 in New York.[cmxcv] She died in October 1973. She had been previously married to and divorced from Thomas Lambert HEWITT. He was a lifelong resident of Mackinac County, Michigan. Lambert and Ida had two children. There were no children born to Frank and Ida. Frank and Ida are both buried in Mackinac County, Michigan.[cmxcvi] Frank was a US Navy Seal, serving from April 1921 to January 1925.[cmxcvii] Ida was a secretary for the Wall Street Stock Exchange.

290. iv. Ethel Lillian ENGLAND was born on the 15ᵗʰ of August 1909 in Queens, New York.[cmxcviii] She died on the 21ˢᵗ of April 2001 in Midland, Texas.[cmxcix] She married Lester Bonnington in June 1931 in Brooklyn. He died on the 6ᵗʰ of February 1969.[m] The couple had one child who is living.

197. **WILLIAM ELLIOTT ENGLAND** (Benjamin[5], Aquilla[4], William W.[3], Daniel[2], William[1]) was born on the 17th of September 1885 in Brooklyn.[mi] He married Hazel SHEAR on the 16th of November 1907 in Brooklyn.[mii] She was born about 1885 in New York.[miii] Their dates of death are unknown. He was a compositor for the Country Life Press Corporation, part of the Doubleday printing empire.

William and Hazel had two children, twins:

291. i. William E. ENGLAND Jr. was born on the 14th of September 1908 in Kings, Brooklyn, New York. He is last found in the 1930 US Census, living with his parents and working as a clerk for a brokerage firm. No records of marriage or death were found. He is not mentioned in his twin sister's obituary of 1998.

292. ii. Ella F. ENGLAND was born on the 14th of September 1908 in Kings, Brooklyn, New York.[miv] She died on the 15th of October 1998 in Broward County, Florida.[mv] On the 17th of September 1929, she married Oscar George NUBEL.[mvi] He was born on the 7th of February 1902[mvii] and died on the 16th of November 1983 in Florida.[mviii] Ella and Oscar had one known child.

203. **JOHN WATSON MATTSON** (Ella[5], William Watson[4], William W.[3], Daniel[2], William[1]) was born on the 15th of September 1875, twin to Will Watson Mattson, in Swedesboro, New Jersey.[mix] He died on the 20th of May 1945. He married Ruth BLACK on the 18th of November 1901. She was born on the 9th of January 1880 in Gloucester County, New Jersey.[mx] She died on the 3rd of March 1962. John was a farmer.

John and Ruth had three children:

293., i., The Mattson twins died shortly after birth in 1909.
294. ii.
295. iii. Joseph S. MATTSON was born about 1906 and died in November 1929 in New Jersey.[mxi] He married Helen Audrey HOMAN (daughter of Harry E. and Honora J. HOMAN) in September 1923.[mxii] She was born on the 16th of April 1907 in Swedesboro, New Jersey.[mxiii] She died on the 20th of July 1965 in Gloucester County, New Jersey.[mxiv] After Joseph's death, Helen married J. Cooper MUNYAN. Joseph and Helen had four children, one of whom is living.

204. **WILLIAM WATSON MATTSON**, (Ella[5], William Watson[4], William W.[3], Daniel[2], William[1]) twin of John Watson MATTSON, was born on the 15th of September 1875 in Swedesboro, New Jersey.[mxv] He died on the 2nd of January 1960.[mxvi] He married Savilla "Annie" TITUS (daughter of Jacob and Annie TITUS) on the 14th of September 1898 in Penns Grove, New Jersey.[mxvii] She was born on the 29th of August 1879 in Pennsylvania.[mxviii] She died on the 22nd of April 1961. Will was a farmer.

Will and Annie had two daughters:

+296.   i.   Ethel S. MATTSON was born on the 1st of July 1900 in Bridgeport, Gloucester County, New Jersey.[mxix] She died in April 1982 in Paulsboro, New Jersey.[mxx] She first married George W. OSBORN on the 24th of December 1918. He was born about 1899 in New York[mxxi] and died in May 1920 of an accident while working in the New York shipyard.[mxxii] She next married John Ralph SMALLEY Jr. (son of John Ralph SMALLEY, Sr, and Ruthella MATLACK) in August 1925 in Camden, New Jersey.[mxxiii] He was born about 1903 in Pennsylvania. He worked as a telephone linesman and installer. His date of death is unknown.

297.   ii.   Blanch E. MATTSON was born about 1903 in New Jersey. She died on the 9th of December 1965.[mxxiv] She first married Howard Jackson (son of Charles Earp JACKSON and Annie WARDELL) in October 1925.[mxxv] He was born on the 27th of April 1900 in Long Island, New York. His date of death is unknown. In the 1930 census, he is living with Blanch and their three children in Westville, New Jersey and working as a house painter. In the 1940 census, Blanche is living with her children and is listed as married. There is also a boarder, named James Patrick ANDERSON, who became her second husband. He was born in May 1895 in Philadelphia, the son of James Patrick ANDERSON and Susan CAULEY. He was the widower of Anna CASSIDY with whom he had nine children.[mxxvi] Blanche divorced James in June 1956 in Camden, New Jersey.[mxxvii] She then married Eugene T. GIBBONS on the 29th of September 1956 in New Jersey.[mxxviii] His dates of birth and death are unknown.

205. **MABEL MATTSON** (Ella[5], William Watson[4], William W.[3], Daniel[2], William[1]) was born on the 23rd of July 1877.[mxxix] She died on the 25th of January 1958.[mxxx] She married Chris (or Harry) HOFFMAN on the 6th of September 1897 in Wenonah, New Jersey. He was a professional baseball player. His exact date of death is unknown, but presumed to be about 1900. She next married Harvey TOMLIN on the 1st of September 1907 in Bridgeport at the St. Paul Methodist Church. He was born a Quaker on the 31st of August 1873 in Pedricktown, New Jersey.[mxxxi] He died on the 22nd of March 1926.

Photo from the collection of Elizabeth Horton, used with permission

Mabel and Chris (or Harry) had one child:

+298. i. Myrtle HOFFMAN was born on the 12th of December 1897.[mxxxii] She died in November 1980 in Gloucester County.[mxxxiii] She married Leon WILSON (son of George M. and Sarah WILSON) on the 24th of June 1915 in Gibbstown, New Jersey.[mxxxiv] He was born in September 1894 in New Jersey.[mxxxv] He died on the 17th of May 1916, the result of an accident while working at the DuPont Company.[mxxxvi] She then married Daniel Boody CARSON, Jr., (son of Daniel B. CARSON and Elvina G. TREADWAY) on the 28th of June 1924. He was born on the 20th of March 1896 in Paulsboro, New Jersey.[mxxxvii] He died on the 10th of May 1957 in Philadelphia.[mxxxviii]

Mabel and Harvey had six children, four of whom are living.

207. **SAMUEL STRATTON MATTSON** (Ella[5], William Watson[4], William W.[3], Daniel[2], William[1]) was born in the 1st of May 1883 in Auburn, New Jersey.[mxxxix] He died on the 21st of March 1975 in Williamstown, New Jersey. On the 16th of February 1908, he married Ruth NORTON (daughter of Elmer NORTON and Martha TONKIN) at the Trinity Episcopal Church in Swedesboro.[mxl] She was born on the 13th of July 1885 in Gibbstown, New Jersey.[mxli] She died the 5th of January 1968 in Williamstown, New Jersey.[mxlii] Samuel was a farmer.

The couple had six children:

299. i. Walter Charles MATTSON was born on the 24th of July 1908 in Gloucester County, New Jersey, and was baptized at the Trinity Church in Swedesboro.[mxliii] He died on the 19th of October 1987 in Clarksboro, New Jersey.[mxliv] He married Margaret VIGNOLA (daughter of Tony VIGNOLA and Mary ABDIGO). She was born on the 22nd of October 1913 in Havre Grace, Maryland.[mxlv] She died on the 14th of September 1999 in Clarksboro, New Jersey. They had four children, one of whom is deceased.

300. ii. Robert MATTSON was born on the 11th of March 1911.[mxlvi] He died on the 5th of July 1988 in Miami, Florida.[mxlvii] He married Jeanette KIESEL (daughter of Robert KIESEL and Maude PHILLIPS). She was born on the 22nd of June 1918 in Carney's Point, New Jersey.[mxlviii] She died on the 7th of June 2004 in Hudson, New Hampshire.[mxlix] Robert was a chemical worker in Salem, New Jersey.[ml] The couple had three known children, who may all be living.

301. iii. Margaret Eleanor MATTSON was born about 1913 in New Jersey.[mli] She is last found in the 1940 US Census living with her parents and siblings, with her maiden surname and is listed as married. No records of marriage or death could be clearly identified.

302. iv. Eugene MATTSON was born on the 6th of January 1916 in Swedesboro, New Jersey.[mlii] He died on the 31st of August 1994 in Whittier, California.[mliii] He married Theresa ASTA (daughter of Henry P. ASTA and Sidonie GUICHARD). She was born on the 24th of January 1920 in Oak Park, Illinois.[mliv] She died on the 16th of July

2007 in Whittier, California. Eugene was a chemical worker for Lever Brothers. It is unknown if the couple had children.

303. v. Alice May MATTSON was born about 1919 in New Jersey. She is last found in the 1940 US Census living with her parents and siblings as single.[mlv] No records of marriage or death could be clearly identified.

304. vi. Samuel S. MATTSON, Jr. was born on the 22nd of March 1928 in Center Square, New Jersey.[mlvi] He died on the 5th of December 1996 in Tacoma, Washington.[mlvii] He served two tours of duty in the US Army, between July 1946 and December 1947 and again between March 1957 and October 1975.[mlviii] It is unknown if he married or had children.

211. **REV. AQUILA B. ENGLAND** (William "Willie"[5], William Watson[4], William W.[3], Daniel[2], William[1]) was born on the 7th of September 1887 in Salem County, New Jersey.[mlix] He died in December 1974 in Woodbury, New Jersey.[mlx] He was the author of our handwritten family tree so frequently mentioned at the beginning of this work. He married Effie L. THOMAS (daughter of William and Isabella THOMAS). She was born in June 1889 in New York.[mlxi] She died in December 1977 in Toms River, New Jersey.[mlxii]

Photo from the collection of the Gloucester Historical Library, Woodbury, NJ, used with permission

Aquila and Effie had three children:

305. i. Lillian Ella ENGLAND was born on the 25th of June 1913 in Alfred, New York.[mlxiii] She died on the 12th of May 2003.[mlxiv] She married Josef Walter LIENER (son of Charles LIENER and Theresa VOLKS). He was born on the 10th of September 1909 in Salem, New Jersey.[mlxv] He died on the 20th of January 2002 in Wittman, Maryland.[mlxvi] He served with US Navy during World War II, and is buried in the National Cemetery at Alloway, New Jersey.[mlxvii] Lillian and Josef had no known children.

306. ii. Marie Annabelle ENGLAND was born on the 7th of November 1916 in New York.[mlxviii] She died on the 1st of June 2011.[mlxix] She married George Cortlandt HOWARD (son of George G. HOWARD and Flora B. SNEATH) on the 8th of October 1941 in Williamsburg, Virginia.[mlxx] He was born on the 3rd of August 1911 and died on the 30th of June 1984.[mlxxi] He served with the US Army during World War II. The couple had no known children.

307. iii. Milton Thomas ENGLAND was born on the 29th of March 1929 in New Jersey.[mlxxii] He died on the 1st of August 1961.[mlxxiii] He married Iris Frances BUDD (daughter of

William Francis BUDD and Marie BOND) on the 31st of August 1951 in Pasquotank, North Carolina. [mlxxiv] She was born on the 1st of September 1929 in Norfolk, Virginia. [mlxxv] She died on the 9th of September 1991. [mlxxvi] Milton served in the US Navy between 1947 and 1951. [mlxxvii] The couple had one known child, **BRENDA LEE ENGLAND**, who died at 2 days of age in 1962. [mlxxviii]

212. **BENJAMIN CHEESEMAN ENGLAND** (William "Willie"[5], William Watson[4], William W.[3], Daniel[2], William[1]) was born on the 1st of August 1890 in Woodstown, Salem County, New Jersey. [mlxxix] His exact date of death is unknown but he preceded his wife in death. He married Louise D. CAWLEY (daughter of William CAWLEY and Martha GREEN). She was born the 13th of September 1899 in Pedricktown, New Jersey. [mlxxx] She died in Philadelphia on the 14th of June 1962. [mlxxxi] Benjamin was a farmer.

Benjamin and Louise had three children:

308.   i.   Elizabeth Martha "Peg" ENGLAND was born on the 19th of January 1914 in Pilesgrove, New Jersey. [mlxxxii] She died on the 6th of August 2010 in Swedesboro, New Jersey. [mlxxxiii] She married Horace W. KRAGLER (son of Louis and Emma B. KRAGLER). He was born on the 27th of August 1917 and died in October 1965. [mlxxxiv] The couple had three children, one of whom is living.

+309.   ii.   Ruth K. ENGLAND was born on the 18th of October 1915 in Sharptown, New Jersey. [mlxxxv] She died on the 22nd of July 2005. [mlxxxvi] She married Horace C. DOUGHTEN. He was born on the 25th of January 1910 and died on the 20th of May 1989 in Mullica Hill, New Jersey. [mlxxxvii]

310.   iii.   Vernon W. ENGLAND was born on the 29th of April 1921 and died on the 6th of April 2008 in Pedrickstown, New Jersey. [mlxxxviii] It is unknown if he married or had children.

216. **JOHN DAVIDSON ENGLAND** (Charles[5], William Watson[4], William W.[3], Daniel[2], William[1]) was born on the 30th of December 1898 in Olivet, New Jersey. [mlxxxix] He died on the 14th of September 1983 and is buried at Woodstown, NJ. [mxc] He married Marion L. WINTER (daughter of William and Carrie WINTER). She was born on the 7th of August 1911 and died on the 21st of June 1922 in Woodbury, NJ. [mxci] Davidson was a truck driver. Marion was a licensed practical nurse.

Davidson and Marion had one child:

311.   i.   Davidson Winter ENGLAND was born about 1937 and died in July 1971 in Swedesboro, NJ. [mxcii] It is unknown if he married or had children.

217. **THOMAS M. ENGLAND** (Charles[5], William Watson[4], William W.[3], Daniel[2], William[1]) was born in 1907 in Oldmans, New Jersey. [mxciii] He died on the 17th of January 1990 in Alexandria, Virginia [mxciv]

and was buried in Woodstown, New Jersey.[mxcv] He married Beatrice E. RAUGAUST (daughter of George O. and Minnie E RAUGAUST) on the 27ᵗʰ of June 1931 in Washington, DC.[mxcvi] She was born on the 3ʳᵈ of October 1908 in North Dakota and died on the 23ʳᵈ of August 1986 in Fairfax, Virginia.[mxcvii] She is buried in Woodstown, New Jersey.[mxcviii] Thomas was a statistical clerk for a railroad. Beatrice was a stenographer.

Thomas and Beatrice had one child:

312. i. William W. ENGLAND was born on the 9ᵗʰ of November 1933 in Washington, D.C. He died on the 4ᵗʰ of September 2016 in Peoria, Arizona.[mxcix] He was married and had three children. Bill served in the US Navy from 1953 to 1957. He made a career as a senior analyst for the Interstate Commerce Commission until his retirement in 1987.[mc]

219. **HOWARD WATSON AMBRUSTER** (William W. E.[5], Sarah[4], William W.[3], Daniel[2], William[1]) was born on the 12ᵗʰ of August 1878 in Germantown, Pennsylvania and died on the 10ᵗʰ of January 1960.[mci] He married Florence Ursula FAVREAU (daughter of Fred FAVREAU and Anna D. WILSON) on the 15ᵗʰ of June 1910 in Chicago, Illinois.[mcii] She was born on the 30ᵗʰ of April 1890 in Albany, New York.[mciii] She died on the 30ᵗʰ of November 1970 in Albuquerque, New Mexico.

Howard's obituary from the New York Times, 11 January 1961:

Howard Watson Ambruster, who spent a lifetime fighting for the strict enforcement of pure food and drug laws and against the international chemical trusts, died here last night in his home at 158 Forest Road. His age was 82.

Mr. Ambruster was a chemical engineer, writer and lecturer. He gave up a promising career as a chemical consultant in 1927 to campaign for a ban on the importation of substandard ergot which he declared had caused the death of thousands of mothers in childbirth through its use in various medicines.

He filed suits against a number of prominent Government officials for what he called failure to enforce the drug laws, and charged complicity between them and the big chemical combines of Europe.

Mr. Ambruster appeared before Congressional committees, grand juries and other investigative bodies and spoke to platform and radio audiences, repeatedly demanding investigation of "German cartel influence inside the United States."

He lectured at Columbia and New York Universities and the University of Pennsylvania and his articles and special columns appeared in newspapers in New York and other cities.

Mr. Ambruster attended the University of Pennsylvania, which awarded him an honorary B. S. degree in economics in 1939. Early in his career he was a reporter for The Philadelphia Evening Telegraph, the first paid football coach at Rutgers University, a clearing house clerk at the Philadelphia Stock Exchange, a construction engineer, an editorial writer for The Philadelphia Times and secretary and director of the General Artificial Silk Company.

After 1905 he was an organizer and director of various chemical and textile enterprises.

He was a consulting engineer to the insecticide industries beginning in 1921. Five years later he began a wide survey of the distribution and use of arsenic compounds for control of the boll weevil and other pests to publicize his belief in the danger to the public in arsenical spray residue.

In 1927, Mr. Ambruster entered the pharmaceutical industry. After making attempts to insure a supply of pure ergot to the medical profession, he began his anti-chemical trust career.

*His book, "Treason's Peace", was one of the vehicles through which he claimed to "trace the gigantic criminal conspiracy against this nation, beginning with the operations of the big German dye companies prior to World War I * * *." He also wrote "The Sanctity", a documentary work dealing with German spy activities. Others of his books dealt with the arsenic problem and the question of proper food and drug law enforcement.*

Howard and Florence had two children:

313.   i.   Watson AMBRUSTER II was born on the 8th of March 1911 in Haddonfield, New Jersey.[mciv] He died on the 9th of May 1984 in Albuquerque, New Mexico. He married Helen HUTCHINGS on the 11th of June 1935.[mcv] She was born on the 5th of February 1912.[mcvi] She died the 12th of August 1995 in New Mexico.[mcvii] He retired, a Lieutenant Colonel, from the US Air Force in 1962 and taught at Sandia High School in Albuquerque for twelve years. Watson and Helen had three children, two of whom are living.

314.   ii.   Albert L. AMBRUSTER was born about 1915 and died as a child.

220.   **ANNA M. ALLEN** (Mary[5], Sarah[4], William W.[3], Daniel[2], William[1]) was born in February 1874 in New Jersey.[mcviii] She died on the 25th of March 1965 in Merchantville, New Jersey.[mcix] Anna was a church organist.[mcx] She first married William Mortimer SKEGGS in 1894 in New Jersey.[mcxi] He was born in January 1874; his date of death is unknown. In the 1940 census, Anna is widowed. Mort worked in various positions in the hotel industry. Anna next married William H. WATT. He was born in February 1870 in England.[mcxii] He died on the 3rd of November 1950 in New Jersey.[mcxiii] His first marriage was to Emma R. BREYER with whom he had two children.

Anna and Mort had one daughter:

315. i.   Lavenia SKEGGS was born on the 8th of August 1903 in Pennsylvania.^{mcxiv} She died

on the 1st of May 1975 in Merchantville, New Jersey.^{mcxv} She married Samuel Herbert Taylor (son of Samuel H. TAYLOR, Sr. and Sara WELSH). He was born on the 26th of April 1901 in Pennsauken, New Jersey. He died on the 24th of January 1960 in Philadelphia from complications of surgery for colon cancer.^{mcxvi} Lavenia served in various positions with the Federation of Women's Clubs on the local, state and national levels. She held numerous positions in community organizations, including the Governor's Conference on Education. She also organized and served with theatre and drama groups in the Camden area. S. Herbert was a civil engineer in a firm that beared his name. He was instrumental in the design of highway systems in the New Jersey/Philadelphia area. He held positions in many councils and professional organizations. The couple had two children.

230. James Irwin CLEMENT (Joseph⁵, Emily⁴, Daniel³, Daniel ², Willliam¹)was born about 1909 in New York. ^{mcxvii} He died in January 1970 in Schenectady, NY.^{mcxviii} He married Helene GANOTT (daughter of Baptiste and Natalie GANOTT). She was born on the 6th of September 1914 and died in February 1992 in Schenectady, New York.^{mcxix}

Photo from the collection of Kathleen Clement, used with permission

James and Helene had one child:

316. i.    James Irwin CLEMENT, Jr. was born on the 30th of October 1937.^{mcxx} He died on the 15th of August 2000 in Norwalk, Connecticut. He was married and had children.

Photo from the collection of Kathleen Clement, used with permission

7

The Seventh Generation

Here is the seventh generation:

244. **EMMA PANCOAST** (Philena[6], Isabella[5], Joanna[4], William[3], Thomas2, William[1]) was born on the 19th of July 1880 in Upper Penns Neck, Salem County, New Jersey.[mcxxi] She died in 1942 and is buried in Center Square, New Jersey.[mcxxii] She married Fillmore S. DAWSON (son of Franklin and Lucinda DAWSON). He was born in July 1873 in New Jersey.[mcxxiii] He died on the 21st of June 1956 and is buried in Center Square, New Jersey.[mcxxiv] Fillmore was a farmer.

Fillmore and Emma had five children:

317.   i.   Willis M. DAWSON was born on the 17th of November 1901 in New Jersey.[mcxxv] He died in December 1959 and is buried in Center Square, New Jersey.[mcxxvi] He married Leona KIRBY about 1929.[mcxxvii] She was born in 1906 in New Jersey. She died in 1957 and is buried in Center Square, New Jersey.[mcxxviii] Willis was a farmer. The couple had no known children.

318.   ii.   Herbert P. DAWSON was born on the 31st of August 1907 in New Jersey.[mcxxix] He died in October 1982 in Pennsville, New Jersey. [mcxxx] He married Clementine STANSBURY (daughter of Alfred E. and Hattie STANSBURY about 1930.[mcxxxi] She was born in 1909 in New Jersey. She died on the 25th of April 1969.[mcxxxii] The couple

had one known child. In the 1940 Census, Herbert was working as an explosives operator for the US Government.

319. iii. Beatrice M. DAWSON was born on the 27th of February 1910.[mcxxxiii] She died in June 1955 in Pedricktown, New Jersey.[mcxxxiv] She married Samuel Chattin MCCOLLISTER (son of William E. MCCOLLISTER and Caroline MYERS). He was born on the 13th of December 1904 and died on the 22nd of February 1975 in Pedricktown, New Jersey.[mcxxxv] Samuel was an explosives operator. The couple had one known child, **SHIRLEY ANN MCCOLLISTER**. She was born on the 2nd of November 1937 in Bridgeton, New Jersey.[mcxxxvi] She died on the 24th of January 2001 in Pedricktown, New Jersey.[mcxxxvii]

320. iv. Mildred DAWSON was born about 1914. Her date of death is unknown. She married Norman SIMPKINS. He was born on the 5th of January 1912. He died on the 10th of March 1977 in St. Lucie, Florida and is buried in Woodstown, New Jersey.[mcxxxviii] Norman was an operator at a dye works plant. The couple had two known children.

321. v Elva Viola DAWSON was born about 1915 in New Jersey.[mcxxxix] Her date of death is unknown. She married William H. KROUSE (son of Harry KROUSE and Jennie Marie WOLFFBRANDT) on the 3rd of August 1931 in BelAir, Maryland.[mcxl] He was born on the 23rd of January 1908 in Glassboro, New Jersey. He died on the 26th of January 1993 in Fairview, Oklahoma. His second marriage was to Olivia YOUNG on the 7th of June 1949 in Fairview, Oklahoma. He was a schoolteacher and a photographer with his own studio in Fairview. (This information was taken from an unsourced obituary posted on ancestry.com). Elva and William had two known children.

245. **JOSEPH MYERS PANCOAST** (Philena[6], Isabella[5], Joanna[4], William[3], Thomas[2], William[1]) was born on the 26th of February 1882 in Auburn, New Jersey.[mcxli] He died on the 21st of October 1957 in Preston, Maryland.[mcxlii] He married Emilie H. PEPPER in 1905 in Philadelphia.[mcxliii] She was born about 1882 in Pennsylvania.[mcxliv] Her date of death is unknown. Joseph was a machinist for the Baldwin Locomotive Works in Eddystone, Pennsylvania.

Joseph and Emilie had four children:

322. i. Joseph M. PANCOAST, Jr. was born on the 5th of April 1906 in Philadelphia.[mcxlv] He died of pneumonia on the 9th of October 1972 in Paoli, Pennsylvania.[mcxlvi] He married Virginia F. MENDELL on the 6th of November 1943 in Joplin, Missouri. She was born on the 19th of June 1916 and died on the 6th of June 1998. She is buried in the same cemetery in Adair, Oklahoma as her brother-in-law Raymond. Joseph was an outdoor columnist for the *Evening Bulletin* for 25 years. He began writing the column upon his return from military service in 1947. Prior to the war, he was a sports reporter

for the Philadelphia *Public Ledger*.[mcxlvii] He served in the US Army from March 1942 to December 1946.[mcxlviii] The couple had one known child.

323.   ii.   Wynfield Scott PANCOAST was born on the 18th of July 1908 in Philadelphia.[mcxlix] He died on the 12th of July 1993 in Manchester, New Hampshire.[mcl] He married Barbara Louise STROUT (daughter of Delmar STROUT and Edna HARRIS). She was born on the 13th of November 1916 in Oxford, Maine. At the age of 5, she was orphaned and adopted by her Aunt Florence Harris FARRIS. She died on the 17th of October 2012 in Ipswich, Massachusetts. Wynfield's occupation is not known. He served in the US Army from 1946 to 1946. Barbara worked for many years as an electronics assembler in special top secret government projects at (Lockheed) Sanders' Associates in Nashua and then Merrimack, New Hampshire, until her retirement in 1987.[mcli] The couple had five children.

324.   iii.   Raymond W. PANCOAST was born on the 6th of April 1910 in Pennsylvania. He died in August 1969 in Adair, Oklahoma.[mclii] He married Hilda Jane CALVERT (daughter of George CALVERT and Hattie DAVIS) on the 1st of Aprill 1940 in Tulsa, Oklahoma.[mcliii] She was born on the 20th of June, 1921 in Adair, Oklahoma.[mcliv] She died on the 8th of July 1996 in Adair.[mclv] It is assumed that the couple had children, because the word "Daddy" is inscribed on Raymond's tombstone.

325.   iv.   Charles G. PANCOAST was born on the 20th of July 1913 in Philadelphia. He died on the 3rd of September 1990 in Middletown, Pennsylvania.[mclvi] He was a sheet metal worker at the shipyards. He married Charlotte SHAFFER (daughter of Walter F. SHAFFER and Annie S. BYRUM). The couple had two known children.

246. **HERBERT ROBERTS PANCOAST** (Philena[6], Isabella[5], Joanna[4], William[3], Thomas[2], William[1]) was born on the 1st of March 1885 in Auburn, New Jersey.[mclvii] He died on the 19th of May 1960 in Orange, California.[mclviii] He married May RISLEY (daughter of Bakley RISLEY and Lizzie SOL) about 1909.[mclix] She was born on the 19th of May 1886 in New Jersey and died on the 19th of October 1956 in Los Angeles, California.[mclx] Herbert was a carpenter.

Herbert and May had five children:

326.   i.   Grace Elizabeth PANCOAST was born on the 17th of November 1909 in New Jersey.[mclxi] She died on the 15th of March 1991 in California.[mclxii] She married Richard W. TURBEVILLE (son of Benjamin TURBEVILLE and Lizzie CARTY). He was born on the 3rd of August 1907.[mclxiii] He died on the 1st of July 1992 in California.[mclxiv] Grace and Richard had six children. Richard was a railroad conductor.

327. ii. Phylena Myers PANCOAST was born about 1912 in New Jersey.[mclxv] She died on the 3rd of February 1978 in Orange County, California.[mclxvi] She first married James B. WINTERMUTE in 1928.[mclxvii] He was born about 1908, his date of death is unknown. It is also unknown if James and Phylena had any children. She next married Frederick Walter SEARCH in 1935.[mclxviii] He was born on the 27th of December 1910 in Alabama.[mclxix] He died on the 24th of February 1969 in Los Angeles.[mclxx] Phylena and Fred had one known child. Fred was a superintendent for the Richfield Oil Company.

328. iii. Herbert PANCOAST was born on the 15th of June 1913 in Los Angeles.[mclxxi] He died at the age of 18 on the 25th of July 1931 in Los Angeles.[mclxxii]

329. iv. Harry Myers PANCOAST was born on the 9th of March 1919 in Los Angeles, California.[mclxxiii] He died on the 27th of April 1956 in Los Angeles.[mclxxiv] It is unknown if he married or had children.

330. v. Samuel J. PANCOAST was born on the 9th of November 1926 in Los Angeles, California.[mclxxv] He died on the 27th of June 1982 in South ElMonte, California.[mclxxvi] He married Kay Frances LAROCCA (daughter of James LAROCCA and Josephine GIUNTA) on the 12th of June 1956 in Los Angeles.[mclxxvii] She was born on the 23rd of November 1923 and died in March 1979 in Los Angeles.[mclxxviii] The couple divorced in May 1977.[mclxxix] He served in the US Navy from 1944 to 1946.[mclxxx] It is unknown if the couple had children. It is also unknown if Samuel remarried.

247. **ROGER CORLISS PANCOAST** (Philena[6], Isabella[5], Joanna[4], William[3], Thomas[2], William[1]) was born on the 4th of September 1887 in New Jersey.[mclxxxi] He died in September 1962 in Delaware.[mclxxxii] He married Ruth A. LEIPOLD (daughter of John Harry and Edna L. LEIPOLD) about 1909.[mclxxxiii] She was born in 1899 in Delaware and died on the 23rd of April 1915, at the age of 25, 17 days after the birth of her youngest son. He next married Goldah CONAWAY (daughter of George and Mary CONAWAY) on the 12th of March 1917 in Georgetown, Maryland.[mclxxxiv] She was born on the 31st of January 1900 in Sussex, Delaware.[mclxxxv] The couple divorced in May 1925.[mclxxxvi] Roger was the superintendent of the Delaware Power and Light Company.

Roger and Ruth had four children:

331. i. Howard Roger PANCOAST was born on the 2nd of June 1910 in Delaware.[mclxxxvii] He died on the 9th of May 1997 in High Point, North Carolina.[mclxxxviii] He married Mazie E. OUTTEN (daughter of Walter J. OUTTEN and Josephine MILES) on the 28th of March 1933 in Wilmington, Delaware.[mclxxxix] She was born on the 28th of May 1908 in Wilmington.[mcxc] She died on the 7th of June 1995 in High Point.[mcxci] Howard was general manager, vice-president, and president of Bryant Electric

Company. On March 20, 1960, he was named "High Pointer of the Week" by the *High Point Enterprise.*[mcxcii] Prior to her marriage, Mazie was secretary to Judge Speakman, Quaker Judge of Delaware.[mcxciii] Howard and Mazie had three children.

332. ii. Helen PANCOAST was born on the 18th of September 1911 in New Castle, Delaware.[mcxciv] She died in December 1980 in Rehoboth Beach, Delaware.[mcxcv] She married John P. McLAUGHLIN (son of James McLAUGHLIN and Ellen CROSSAN). He was born on the 27th of September 1907 in Wilmington, Delaware.[mcxcvi] He died on the 17th of December 2001 in Newark, Delaware.[mcxcvii] For many years, he operated a gas station with his father-in-law, Roger C. Pancoast. He was found guilty on two occasions of accepted counterfeit gas ration coupons in 1944.[mcxcviii] From 1952 to 1975 he was a chemical operator for the DuPont Company.

Helen and John had one son: **JOHN P. MCLAUGHLIN, JR.** was born on th 17th of February 1932 in Wilmington.[mcxcix] He died on the 27th of February 2013 in Wilmington.[mcc] He was married and had five children. John, Jr. was a magistrate for the Delaware State Court.[mcci] He served in the Korean War with the US Navy.

333. iii. Harry R. PANCOAST was born on the 21st of May 1913 in New Castle, Delaware.[mccii] He died on the 8th of December 1997 in Wilmington, Delaware.[mcciii] He married Naomi C. TRESSLER (daughter of Grant and Annie TRESSLER) on the 5th of September 1936 in Wilmington.[mcciv] She was born on the 9th of April 1912 in Delaware.[mccv] She died in June 1992 in Delaware.[mccvi] Harry worked for the Budd Company (metal fabrication) for 35 years. The couple had two children.

334. iv. Leroy Warren PANCOAST was born on the 6th of April 1915 in Wilmington.[mccvii] He died on the 3rd of November 1998 in Greenfield, North Carolina.[mccviii] His death certificate states that he was widowed, but his wife's name is not known. It is not known if he had children.

Roger and Goldah had two children:

335. i. Roger Sheridan PANCOAST was born in 1918 in Delaware.[mccix] He enlisted in the US Army on the 23rd of October 1941. On the 19th of June 1942, he married Lillian Ann CURTIN (daughter of Robert E. and Lillian M. CURTIN) in Commanche, Oklahoma.[mccx] On the 7th of August 1944 he was killed in action and is buried at Normandie, France. Lillian next married Walter E. KEE in 1949, with whom she had three children.

Roger and Lillian had one child: **RONALD SHERIDAN PANCOAST** was born on the 7th of April 1944.[mccxi] His father died four months later without ever seeing his son. Ronald died on the 5th of January 2004 and is buried in San Diego, California.[mccxii] He married Jean A. BECK (daughter of Howard and Wilman BECK). Jean was born on the 27th of May 1944 in Terre Haute, Indiana.[mccxiii] She died on the 29th of April 2015 in California.[mccxiv] Ronald was an attorney. Jean and Ronald had one child. Jean had three children from a previous marriage.

336. ii. Kenneth Stacy PANCOAST was born on the 17th of December 1920 in Wilmington.[mccxv] He died on the 30th of October 2007 in Delaware.[mccxvi] He served in the US Army during World War II. He was a laboratory technician with the DuPont Company for 37 years.[mccxvii] He married Jean Rita COLLINS (daughter of Jerome COLLINS and Lillian MONCK). She was born on the 5th of February 1923 in Wilmington.[mccxviii] She died on the 29th of August 1983.[mccxix] She was a registered nurse and served in the US Army during World War II. The couple had four children.

248. **FOSTER RICHARD PANCOAST** (Philena[6], Isabella[5], Joanna[4], William[3], Thomas[2], William[1]) was born on the 20th of December 1892 in Auburn, New Jersey.[mccxx] He died on the 7th of August 1977 in Jacksonville, Florida.[mccxxi] He first married Hazel H. STIMSON (daughter of George G. and Ella STIMSON) in 1917 in Philadelphia. She was born about 1897 in Pennsylvania.[mccxxii] In 1931, Roger sued her for divorce on the grounds of desertion.[mccxxiii] Her date of death is unknown. He next married Kathryn M. PALMER (daughter of Warren T. PALMER and Grace Mae HELFERSTAY) on the 3rd of March 1942 in Wilmington. She was born on the 9th of October 1910 in Edgemoor, Delaware.[mccxxiv] She died on the 30th of December 2005 in Wilmington.[mccxxv] Foster owned an auto supply store in Wilmington. Kathryn was a self-employed hairdresser and interior decorator for Sears Roebuck. There were no children born to Foster and Kathryn.

Foster and Hazel had one daughter:

337. i. Dorothy PANCOAST was born on the 7th of August 1918 in Wilmington, Delaware.[mccxxvi] She died on the 3rd of April 1992 in Wilmington.[mccxxvii] She married Richard W. ROBINSON, Jr. (son of Richard W. ROBINSON, Sr. and Laura E. DERRY) on the 15th of January 1938 in Wilmington.[mccxxviii] He was born on the 5th of September 1915 in Wilmington.[mccxxix] He died on the 20th of December 1998 in Wilmington.[mccxxx] Richard had a twenty-year career with the Wilmington Police Department, retiring as a Detective Lieutenant.[mccxxxi] In May 1970, their home was burglarized; the burglar held a knife to Dorothy's throat. Dorothy screamed and the burglar escaped.[mccxxxii] The couple had four children.

260. **WARREN GRANT HARBISON** (William S.[6], Hannah[5], Joanna[4], Willliam[3], Thomas[2], William[1]) was born on the 7th of November 1889 in Camden, New Jersey.[mccxxxiii] He died the 5th of October 1940 in Manhattan.[mccxxxiv] He married Violet MATHIS on the 7th of May 1910 in Birmingham, Alabama.[mccxxxv] She was born about 1888 in New Jersey.[mccxxxvi] She died in March 1986.[mccxxxvii] Warren was a draftsman with the Tennessee Coal, Iron and Railroad Company, a major steel producer of the 18th century. The company merged with its rival, the United States Steel Company, in 1907.

Warren and Violet had one child:

338. i. Warren Grant HARBISON was born in 1911 in Alabama. He died in 1964 and is buried in Hurleyville, New York.[mccxxxviii] He married Margaret THORNHILL (daughter of Arthur A. and Pearl E. THORNHILL). She was born on the 1st of May 1919 in Liberty, New York and died on the 11th of March 2011 in Manhattan.[mccxxxix] The couple had no known children.

269. **MAHLON GARBER** (Florence[6], James[5], Deborah[4], William[3], Thomas[2], William[1]) was born on the 28th of June 1909 in Philadelphia.[mccxl] He died on the 1st of October 1969 in Philadelphia.[mccxli] He married Anna WALTZ (daughter of Cleveland T. WALTZ and Sarah TRAYER). She was born the 4th of March 1910 in Philadelphia and died on the 21st of August 1993 in Media, Pennsylvania.[mccxlii] Mahlon served with the US Army during World War II.

Mahlon and Anna had two children:

339. i. June Phyllis GARBER was born on the 6th of June 1931 in Philadelphia.[mccxliii] She died on the 15th of September 2007 in Prescott, Arizona.[mccxliv] She married Eddie West FRAZIER on the 27th of December 1954 in Kansas City, MO.[mccxlv] They divorced in February 1956 in Okaloosa, Florida.[mccxlvi] They had one child. She married a second time to Edward Jacob PAULISON on the 4th of May 1961; there were no children.[mccxlvii] He  died in 2004.[mccxlviii] Her third marriage was to Robert Bryan COX on the 14th of May 1962. They had one child.[mccxlix] Cox died in 2001. In June 1981, she married Thomas Eugene MERRYMAN. He died on the 9th of December 2010.[mccl] Thomas served with the US Navy during World War II. June served with the US Air Force during the Korean War. After her discharge, she was employed by the US Postal Service.

Photo from the collection of Robyn Sheets, used with permission.

340. ii. Robert Mahlon GARBER was born on the 8th of January 1934 in Philadelphia.[mccli] He died on the 15th of January 1990 in Philadelphia.[mcclii] He served in the US Army from 1956 to 1960, and he is buried in the National Cemetery in Beverly, New Jersey. He is survived by his wife, two children and four step-children.

270. VIOLET ELIZABETH MOORE (Edith[6], James[5], Deborah[4], William[3], Thomas[2], William[1]) was born on the 3rd of July 1908 in Philadelphia.[mccliii] She died in June 1984 in Grand Junction, Colorado.[mccliv] She married Arthur M. BAKER on the 18th of September 1926 in Philadelphia. He was born about 1906 in Pennsylvania.[mcclv] Arthur's record of death was not found.

Arthur and Violet had one daughter:

341. i.  Barbara Edith BAKER was born on the 4th of August 1928 in Philadelphia.[mcclvi] She died on the 13th of December 2005 in Grand Junction, Colorado.[mcclvii] She married Paul E. MARTIN (son of Edward A. MARTIN and Helen MAHARG) on the 14th of June 1952 in Philadelphia.[mcclviii] He was born on the 16th of November 1930 in Delta, Colorado.[mcclix] He died on the 30th of September 1997 in Grand Junction.[mcclx] James worked in the family's mortuary business. The couple had four children, all of whom are living.

Photo from her obituary posted at http://www.legacy.com/obituaries/gjsentinel/obituary.aspx?n=barbara-edith-martin-baker&pid=16049190

279. MABEL B. HURFF (Aaron[6], Mary[5], Rebecca[4], William W.[3], Daniel[2], William[1]) was born on the 20th of March 1879 in Haddonfield, New Jersey.[mcclxi] She died in April 1971 in Haddonfield.[mcclxii] She married Harry C. AVIS (son of Harry AVIS and Henrietta LIPPINCOTT) about 1902.[mcclxiii] He was born on the 11th of September 1878 in Harrisville, New Jersey.[mcclxiv] He died on the 10th of February 1935 in Jefferson, Pennsylvania.[mcclxv] His death is recorded in Quaker records.[mcclxvi] Harry was a clerk at a lumber business. He was a veteran of the Spanish American war, serving with Co. G of the Pennsylvania Volunteers.

Mabel and Harry had three children:

342. i. Eleanor B. AVIS was born about 1904 in New Jersey.[mcclxvii] Her date of death is unknown. She married Emlen Paul WAYNE (son of Franklin A. WAYNE and Emma P. GRIFFITH). He was born on the 25th of September 1894 in Haddonfield, New Jersey.[mcclxviii] He died on the 13th of August 1989 in St. Petersburg, Florida. The 1940 US Census finds the couple living apart. Paul is living in Puerto Rico and is listed as divorced. Eleanor is living in Gaithersburg, Maryland and is working as a private duty nurse. The children are living together at a separate residence in Gaithersburg. Paul had a career in the US Navy in the Finance Division. In 1953,

he survived a plane crash in which two people were killed at the Idlewild Airport (now called JFK). Because he is buried with "Ruth", it appears that Paul remarried; no records of this marriage can be found. Eleanor may have also remarried, but no records can be identified. Eleanor and Paul had seven children, one of whom is living.

343.   ii.   Virginia Lippincott AVIS was born on the 13th of January 1910 in Camden, New Jersey.[mcclxix] She died on the 27th of March 1983. She never married. Virginia was a nurse.

344.   iii.   Paul Hurff AVIS was born on the 22nd of June 1917.[mcclxx] He died on the 13th of June 2008 in Westminster, California.[mcclxxi] He served in the US Army during World War II. It is unknown if he married or had children.

281.   **VIRGINIA S. HURFF** (Aaron[6], Mary[5], Rebecca[4], William W.[3], Daniel[2], William[1]) was born on the 11th of September 1886 in Camden, New Jersey.[mcclxxii] She died in December 1976 in Haddonfield, New Jersey.[mcclxxiii] She married Charles E. MAGILL, who was born about 1872 in Pennsylvania.[mcclxxiv] His date of death is unknown. Charles was a veterinarian.

Virginia and Charles had four children:

345.   i.   Elizabeth Cooper MAGILL was born on the 19th of September 1914 in Camden, New Jersey.[mcclxxv] She died on the 19th of March 1990 in Haddonfield, New Jersey.[mcclxxvi] Elizabeth never married. Her obituary names one child. Elizabeth was a teacher.

346.   ii.   Sarah Elizabeth MAGILL was born on the 15th of August 1916 in Haddonfield, New Jersey.[mcclxxvii] No records of marriage or death were found. She is not named in her mother's obituary in 1976.

347.   iii.   Charles E. "Mike" MAGILL was born on the 8th of February 1920 in Haddonfied, New Jersey.[mcclxxviii] He died on the 31st of August 2006 in Collingswood, New Jersey.[mcclxxix] He married Jeanie HOLLIS. She died on the 18th of October 2001 in Haddonfield. Mike was a World War II Veteran serving as a night fighter pilot in the Pacific. He was also a well-known race car driver, nicknamed "Iron Mike". He raced in the Indianapolis 500 in 1957, 1958 and 1959.[mcclxxx] Jeanie was a legal secretary and served as the secretary to Cherry Hill (New Jersey) Mayor John Gilmour.[mcclxxxi] The couple had two children, one of whom is living.

348.   iv.   John R. MAGILL was born about 1923 in New Jersey. No records of his marriage or death were found. He also is not mentioned in his mother's obituary of 1976.

283.   **ADA HURFF** (Henry[6], Mary[5], Rebecca[4], William W.[3], Daniel[2], William[1]) was born in September 1880.[mcclxxxii] She died on the 25th of October 1953 in Seattle, Washington.[mcclxxxiii] She married William Thompson CAMPBELL (son of Thomas J. CAMPBELL and Sophia C. TICE) on the 25th

of July 1903 in Monroe, New Jersey.[mcclxxxiv] He was born on the 25th of July 1880 in Williamstown, New Jersey.[mcclxxxv] He died on the 25th of October 1950 in Seattle, Washington.[mcclxxxvi] William was an insurance agent.

Ada and William had three children:

349. i.   Raymond H. CAMPBELL was born on the 29th of February 1904 in Williamstown, New Jersey.[mcclxxxvii] He died of typhoid fever on the 25th of December 1929 in Lakewood, Ohio.[mcclxxxviii] At the time of his death, he was a newspaper reporter. He never married.

350. ii. Thomas Earl CAMPBELL was born about 1908 in New Jersey. He is last found in the 1920 US Census living with his parents in Philadelphia. No records of his marriage or death were found.

351. iii. Alice E. CAMPBELL was born on the 13th of November 1910 in New Jersey.[mcclxxxix] She died on the 18th of October 1954 in Seattle, Washington.[mccxc] She married Perry Edmunds JACOBY (son of Mathias M. JACOBY and Emma M. EWING). He was born on the 4th of March 1909 in Pennsylvania.[mccxci] He died on the 9th of March 1992 in Santa Clara, California. He remarried in 1955. There were no children born to Perry and Alice.

284. **WALTER HENRY HURFF** (Henry[6], Mary[5], Rebecca[4], William W.[3], Daniel[2], William[1]) was born on the 28th of June 1883 in Washington Township, Gloucester County, New Jersey.[mccxcii] He died on the 9th of February 1948[mccxciii] and is buried in Hurffville, New Jersey.[mccxciv] He married Ida Mae SCOTT. She was born on the 17th of March 1892 and died in October 1971 in Glassboro, New Jersey.[mccxcv] Walter was a farmer.

Walter and Ida Mae had two children:

352. ii. Henry Walter HURFF was born on the 28th of October 1917 in Sewell, New Jersey.[mccxcvi] He died on the 31st of August 1999 in Woodstown, New Jersey.[mccxcvii] He married Edna Freda TROENDLE (daughter of William TROENDLE and Edna BAUSCH). She was born on the 25th of October 1916 in Philadelphia.[mccxcviii] She died in July 1984 in Woodstown, New Jersey.[mccxcix] Henry was a farmer. There were no known children.

353. iii. Florence Ada HURFF was born on the 4th of March 1919 in Bunker Hill, New Jersey.[mccc] She died on the 18th of July 1996 in Pilesgrove, New Jersey.[mccci] She married Michael CHISARIK. He was born on the 10th of December 1912.[msccii] He died on the 17th of November 1975 in Sewell, New Jersey.[mccciii] Michael was a World War II veteran and a marine machinist at the Philadelphia Naval Base.[mccciv] Florence and Michael had one child.

285. **GROVER CLEVELAND HURFF** (Henry[6], Mary[5], Rebecca[4], William W.[3], Daniel[2], William[1]) was born on the 14th of January 1884.[mcccv] He died on the 16th of October 1964.[mcccvi] He married Edythe Mae DOWN (daughter of John Franklin DOWN and Elizabeth DAUGHERTY). She was born on the 4th of July 1890 and died on the 17th of April 1977.[mcccvii] Grover was a farmer.

Grover and Edythe had four children:

354. i. Walter C. HURFF was born on the 21st of December 1913 in Gloucester County, New Jersey.[mcccviii] He died on the 29th of April, 2002 in Sewell, New Jersey.[mcccix] He married Priscilla HOAR. She was born on the 27th of August 1915.[mcccx] She died on the 3rd of December 1986 in Sewell, New Jersey.[mcccxi] Walter was a farmer and tractor salesman. He was active in a number of organizations related to agriculture. There were no known children born to the couple.

355. ii. Miriam HURFF was born on the 2nd of May 1918 in Hurffville, New Jersey.[mcccxii] She died on the 2nd of November 2009 in Hurffville.[mcccxiii] She never married. She was a teacher and elementary school principal.

356. iii. Lewis A HURFF was born on the 15th of August 1919 in Hurffville.[mcccxiv] He died on the 14th of November 2000 in Pitman, New Jersey.[mcccxv] He is survived by his wife and one child.

357. iv. Ruth A. HURFF was born on the 25th of August 1925 in Hurffville.[mcccxvi] She died on the 24th of December 2016 in Vineland, New Jersey.[mcccxvii] She married John M. SCHOCH. He was born on the 11th of August 1929.[mcccxviii] He died in November 1978 in Vineland.[mcccxix] The couple had three children, one of whom is living.

296. **ETHEL S. MATTSON** was born on the 1st of July 1900 in Bridgeport, Gloucester County, New Jersey.[mcccxx] She died in April 1982 in Paulsboro, New Jersey.[mcccxxi] She first married George W. OSBORNE on the 24th of December 1918. He was born about 1899 in New York[mcccxxii] and died in May 1920 in an accident while working in the New York shipyard.[mcccxxiii] She next married John Ralph SMALLEY Jr. (son of John Ralph SMALLEY, Sr, and Ruthella MATLACK) in August 1925 in Camden, New Jersey.[mcccxxiv] He was born about 1903 in Pennsylvania. He worked as a telephone linesman and installer. His date of death is unknown.

Ethel and George had one child:

358. i. Ethel Mae OSBORNE was born on the 9th of October 1919 in Swedesboro, New Jersey.[mcccxxv] She died on the 4th of September 2005 in Haddonfield, New Jersey.[mcccxxvi] She married James H. SHOLDERS (son of Wilmer C. SHOLDERS

and Lois H. WITSEE).   He was born on the 4th of September 1917 in Bridgeport, New Jersey.[mccccxxvii] He died on the 12th of November 1990 in Glassboro, New Jersey.[mccccxxviii] James was a pipefitter for Hercules, Inc. in Gibbstown and was a member of the Greenwich Township Planning Board.[mccccxxix] Ethel and James had three children.

Ethel and Ralph had one child:

359.   i.   John R. SMALLEY was born on the 3rd of April 1928 in Collingswood, New Jersey.[mccccxxx] He died on the 11th of November 1990.[mccccxxxi] He served in the US Army from 1946-1948 and again from 1950-1960.[mccccxxxii] It is unknown if married or had children.

298.   **MYRTLE HOFFMAN** (Mabel[6], Ella[5], William Watson[4], William W.[3], Daniel[2], William[1]) was born on the 12th of December 1897.[mccccxxxiii] She died in November 1980 in Gloucester County.[mccccxxxiv] She married Leon WILSON (son of George M. and Sarah WILSON) on the 24th of June 1915 in Gibbstown, New Jersey.[mccccxxxv] He was born in September 1894 in New Jersey.[mccccxxxvi] He died on the 17th of May 1916, the result of an accident while working at the DuPont Company.[mccccxxxvii] She then married Daniel Boody CARSON, Jr., (son of Daniel B. CARSON and Elvina G. TREADWAY) on the 28th of June 1924. He was born on the 20th of March 1896 in Paulsboro, New Jersey.[mccccxxxviii] He died on the 10th of May 1957 in Philadelphia.[mccccxxxix] Daniel was a foreman of the dynamite factory at the Repauno Chemical Works in Gibbstown, New Jersey.

Myrtle and Leon had one child:

360.   i.   Leon WILSON was born on the 9th of December 1916 in Gibbstown.[mccccxl] He died on the 23rd of January 1995 in Gibbstown.[mccccxli] He served in the US Army in World War II. Leon married Elizabeth Rose ATHEY (daughter of Allen ATHEY and Elizabeth MAGUIRE). She was born on the 17th of January 1918 in Philadelphia. She died on the 26th of December 1995 in Mantua, New Jersey. Leon and Elizabeth had two children.[mccccxlii]

Myrtle and Daniel had one child:

361.   i.   Daniel George CARSON was born on the 1st of July 1927 in Paulsboro, New Jersey.[mccccxliii] He died on the 24th of November 1995 in Gibbstown.[mccccxliv] He married Dora Mary BRILL. She was born on the 4th of November 1937. She died on the 21st of February 2008 in Salem County, New Jersey.[mccccxlv] Daniel and Dora had one child.

309. **RUTH K. ENGLAND** (Benjamin[6], William "Willie"[5], William Watson[4], William W.[3], Daniel[2], William[1]) was born on the 18th of October 1915 in Sharptown, New Jersey.[mcccxlvi] She died on the 22nd of July 2005.[mcccxlvii] She married Horace C. DOUGHTEN. He was born on the 25th of January 1910 and died on the 20th of May 1989 in Mullica Hill, New Jersey.[mcccxlviii]

Ruth and Horace had one known child:

362. i. Marlene Ruth DOUGHTEN was born in 1938 and died in 1985. Her tombstone is inscribed "Navy Recruit CPO".

And so ends the seventh generation. The eighth, ninth and tenth generations continue, but are not named in this edition to protect their confidentiality and privacy.

About the Author

Michele England Heckman and her husband, Rory, have retired to northwestern Michigan near the Sleeping Bear Dunes National Lakeshore. Michele and Rory have two children. In her retirement, she has enjoyed her obsession in exploring her family history. When she is not working on genealogy, you can find her working in the garden, knitting, and playing with her four grandchildren.

Acknowledgments

This journey could not have been completed without the help of many. I'd first like to acknowledge my husband. He's always there for me, and interested in what I'm finding. Along the way, I've met cousins that I didn't know I had, and they have been supportive in sharing photos, letters and memories with me. Thank you to Jean Bean West, Cathy Dionne, Lorraine Goodwillie, William Bean, Lee Weller, Kathleen Clement, and Robyn Sheets. The staff at the Gloucester County Historical Society, the Burlington Historical Society and the Camden Historical Society have been wonderful and helpful, and they've worked hard to find the answers to my questions.

Index to the Descendants of William England

(Note: female descendants are listed by their maiden names only)

England, Lillian Frances (1887-1969): 37

England, Lillian Haines (1867-1949): 53

England, Louis Nathaniel: 32

England, Lydia C.: 25

England, Marie Anabell: 87

England, Margaret B. (1905-1991): 41

England, Mary (1771-): 15, 19

England, Mary (1783-): 17

England, Mary (1785-1857): 18, 24

England, Mary (1814-): 23

England, Mary (1847-1907): 28

England, Mary (1853-1909): 34

England, Mary Estelle (1869-1941): 32

England, Mary D. (1837-1885): 26, 42

England, Mary Gill (1885-1963): 45

England, Mary O. (1873-1879): 54

England, Meriba: 24

England, Milton Thomas: 88

England, Thomas: 17

England, Oscar B. (1868-1937): 26, 39

England, Oscar Daniel (1896-1986): 40

England, Priscilla (1860-): 25

England, Priscilla C. (1805-1868): 19

England, Rebecca (1810-1886): 23, 32

England, Rebecca N. (1838-1896): 27

England, Rebeckah (1) (1790-1792): 18

England, Rebeckah (2) (1802-1803): 19

England, Robert (1825-1896): 22, 31

England, Robert Mason (1861-1862): 31

England, Ruth K.: 88, 104

England, Samuel: 22, 30

England, Sarah (1764-): 14

England, Sarah Ann (1818-1860): 23, 35

England, Sarah C. (1781-): 18, 22

England, Sarah H. (1904-): 47

England, Sarah R. "Sallie" (1858-): 35

England, Susan Louise: 31

England, William Watson (1816-1899): 23, 34

Myers, Minerva W.: 49, 75

Myers, Philena M: 49, 74

Myers, Samuel H.: 49

Osborne, Ethel Mae: 103

Pancoast, Charles G.: 95

Pancoast, Dorothy: 98

Pancoast, Elva K.: 75

Pancoast, Emma: 74, 93

Pancoast, Foster Richard: 74, 98

Pancoast, Grace Elizabeth: 95

Pancoast, Harry Myers (1919-1956): 96

Pancoast, Harry R. (1913-1997): 97

Pancoast, Helen: 97

Pancoast, Herbert (1913-1931): 96

Pancoast, Herbert Roberts (1885-1960): 74, 95

Pancoast, Howard Roger: 96

Pancoast, Joseph Myers (1882-1957): 74, 94

Roberts, Frances J. "Frank" (1846-1912): 29, 51

Pancoast, Kenneth Stacy: 98

Pancoast, Leroy Warren: 97

Pancoast, Phylena Myers: 96

Pancoast, Raymond W.: 95

Pancoast, Roger Corliss (1887-1962): 74, 96

Pancoast, Roger Sheridan (1919-1944): 97

Pancoast, Ronald Sheridan: 98

Pancoast, Ruth I.: 75

Pancoast, Samuel J.: 96

Pancoast, Stacy C.: 75

Pancoast, Wynfield Scott: 95

Roberts, Amy: 50

Roberts, Eleanor D. "Nellie": 50

Roberts, Elizabeth (1836-1872): 29, 48

Roberts, Elizabeth G. (1875-): 50

Roberts, Emma (1854-): 30

Roberts, Emma A. (1885-): 50

Smith, Leroy: 73

Endnotes

[i] Johnson, Amandus. 1936. The Journal and Biography of Nicholas Collin, 1746-1831. The New Jersey Society of Pennsylvania: Camden New Jersey

[ii] England, Aquila B., Rev. Handwritten England family tree. England family file: Gloucester Historical Society, Woodbury, NJ.

[iii] Historical Society of Pennsylvania. Pennsylvania and New Jersey Church and Town Records, 1708-1895, Reel 779. 2011. Ancestry.com, Provo, UT.

[iv] Historical Society of Pennsylvania. Pennsylvania and New Jersey Church and Town Records, 1708-1895, Reel 779. 2011. Ancestry.com, Provo, UT.

[v] Historical Society of Pennsylvania. Pennsylvania and New Jersey Church and Town Records, 1708-1895, Reel 779. 2011. Ancestry.com, Provo, UT.

[vi] England, Aquila B., Rev. Handwritten England family tree. England family file: Gloucester Historical Society, Woodbury, NJ.

[vii] Dodd, Jordan, Liahona Research. New Jersey Marriages, 1684-1895. 2001. Ancestry.com. Provo, UT.

[viii] England, Aquila B., Rev. Handwritten England family tree. England family file: Gloucester Historical Society, Woodbury, NJ.

[ix] Historical Society of Pennsylvania. Pennsylvania and New Jersey Church and Town Records, 1708-1895, Reel 779. 2011. Ancestry.com, Provo, UT.

[x] Historical Society of Pennsylvania. Pennsylvania and New Jersey Church and Town Records, 1708-1895, Reel 779. 2011. Ancestry.com, Provo, UT.

[xi] Historical Society of Pennsylvania. Pennsylvania and New Jersey Church and Town Records, 1708-1895, Reel 779. 2011. Ancestry.com, Provo, UT.

[xii] Miscellaneous Gloucester County Cemeteries, vol. 4, Gloucester County Historical Library, file no. 10893.

[xiii] Personal conversation with Lois Stanley, Swedesboro historian, at her home in Swedesboro, June 27, 2016

[xiv] Historical Society of Pennsylvania. Pennsylvania and New Jersey Church and Town Records, 1708-1895, Reel 779. 2011. Ancestry.com, Provo, UT.

[xv] Dodd, Jordan, Liahona Research. New Jersey Marriages, 1684-1895. 2001. Ancestry.com. Provo, UT.

[xvi] England, Aquila B., Rev. Handwritten England family tree. England family file: Gloucester Historical Society, Woodbury, NJ.

[xvii] Historical Society of Pennsylvania. Pennsylvania and New Jersey Church and Town Records, 1708-1895, Reel 779. 2011. Ancestry.com, Provo, UT.

[xviii] Historical Society of Pennsylvania. Pennsylvania and New Jersey Church and Town Records, 1708-1895, Reel 779. 2011. Ancestry.com, Provo, UT.

[xix] Historical Society of Pennsylvania. Pennsylvania and New Jersey Church and Town Records, 1708-1895, Reel 779. 2011. Ancestry.com, Provo, UT.

[xx] Historical Society of Pennsylvania. Pennsylvania and New Jersey Church and Town Records, 1708-1895, Reel 779. 2011. Ancestry.com, Provo, UT.

[xxi] Historical Society of Pennsylvania. Pennsylvania and New Jersey Church and Town Records, 1708-1895, Reel 779. 2011. Ancestry.com, Provo, UT.

xxii Historical Society of Pennsylvania. Pennsylvania and New Jersey Church and Town Records, 1708-1895, Reel 779. 2011. Ancestry.com, Provo, UT.

xxiii Historical Society of Pennsylvania. Pennsylvania and New Jersey Church and Town Records, 1708-1895, Reel 779. 2011. Ancestry.com, Provo, UT.

xxiv Historical Society of Pennsylvania. Pennsylvania and New Jersey Church and Town Records, 1708-1895, Reel 779. 2011. Ancestry.com, Provo, UT.

xxv Historical Society of Pennsylvania. Pennsylvania and New Jersey Church and Town Records, 1708-1895, Reel 779. 2011. Ancestry.com, Provo, UT.

xxvi Pennsylvania, Philadelphia Death Certificates, 1803-1915, familysearch.org.

xxvii Historical Society of Pennsylvania. Pennsylvania and New Jersey Church and Town Records, 1708-1895, Reel 779. 2011. Ancestry.com, Provo, UT.

xxviii Pennsylvania, Philadelphia Death Certificates, 1803-1915, file no. 004009858. familysearch.org.

xxix West Jersey Press, Margaret England obit 6 January 1886

xxx *Find A Grave*. Find A Grave. http://www.findagrave.com/cgi-bin/fg.cgi.

xxxi Historical Society of Pennsylvania; Philadelphia, Pennsylvania; Collection Name: *Historic Pennsylvania Church and Town Records*; Reel: *779*

xxxii *Find A Grave*. Find A Grave. http://www.findagrave.com/cgi-bin/fg.cgi.

xxxiii England, Aquila B., Rev. Handwritten England family tree. England family file: Gloucester Historical Society, Woodbury, NJ.

xxxiv Stewart, Frank H.,. *Notes on old Gloucester County, New Jersey : historical records published by the New Jersey Society of Pennsylvania*. New Jersey: unknown, 1917.

xxxv England, Aquila B., Rev. Handwritten England family tree. England family file: Gloucester Historical Society, Woodbury, NJ.

xxxvi Historical Society of Pennsylvania. Pennsylvania and New Jersey Church and Town Records, 1708-1895, Reel 779. 2011. Ancestry.com, Provo, UT.

xxxvii New Jersey State Archives. *New Jersey, Published Archives Series, First Series*. Trenton, New Jersey: John L Murphy Publishing Company.

xxxviii Fife, Drum and Bugle during the Revolutionary War. http://www.fifeanddrum.army.mil/kids_fife_drum.html

xxxix Historical Society of Pennsylvania; Philadelphia, Pennsylvania; Collection Name: *Historic Pennsylvania Church and Town Records*; Reel: *779*. Ancestry.com

xl Historical Society of Pennsylvania; Philadelphia, Pennsylvania; Collection Name: *Historic Pennsylvania Church and Town Records*; Reel: *779*. Ancestry.com.

xli Year: *1860*; Census Place: *Philadelphia Ward 15, Philadelphia, Pennsylvania*; Roll: *M653_1165*; Page: *438*; Image: *444*; Family History Library Film: *805165*

xlii "Pennsylvania, Philadelphia City Death Certificates, 1803-1915," database with images, *FamilySearch* (https://familysearch.org/ark:/61903/1:1:J63G-WJN : 9 December 2014), William Letford, 09 Sep 1861; citing, Philadelphia City Archives and Historical Society of Pennsylvania, Philadelphia; FHL microfilm 1,977,567.

xliii Historical Society of Pennsylvania; Philadelphia, Pennsylvania; Collection Name: *Historic Pennsylvania Church and Town Records*; Reel: *779*. Ancestry.com.

xliv Will Books; Author: New Jersey. Surrogate's Court (Gloucester County); Probate Place: Gloucester, New Jersey. Ancestry.com

xlv Historical Society of Pennsylvania; Philadelphia, Pennsylvania; Collection Name: *Historic Pennsylvania Church and Town Records*; Reel: *779*. Ancestry.com.

xlvi Historical Society of Pennsylvania; Philadelphia, Pennsylvania; Collection Name: *Historic Pennsylvania Church and Town Records*; Reel: *779*. Ancestry.com.

xlvii England, Aquila B., Rev. Handwritten England family tree. England family file: Gloucester Historical Society, Woodbury, NJ.

xlviii Historical Society of Pennsylvania; Philadelphia, Pennsylvania; Collection Name: *Historic Pennsylvania Church and Town Records*; Reel: *779*. Ancestry.com.

xlix England, Aquila B., Rev. Handwritten England family tree. England family file: Gloucester Historical Society, Woodbury, NJ.

l England, Robert. Family group record. England family file. Gloucester Historical Society, Woodbury, NJ.

[li] "Pennsylvania, Philadelphia City Death Certificates, 1803-1915," database with images,*FamilySearch* (https://familysearch.org/ark:/61903/1:1:JDVB-BMS : 9 December 2014), L.D. England, 30 Mar 1879; citing , Philadelphia City Archives and Historical Society of Pennsylvania, Philadelphia; FHL microfilm 2,031,099.

[lii] Pennsylvania (State). Death certificates, 1906–1963. Series 11.90 (1,905 cartons). Records of the Pennsylvania Department of Health, Record Group 11. Pennsylvania Historical and Museum Commission, Harrisburg, Pennsylvania. Ancestry.com.

[liii] Historical Society of Pennsylvania; Philadelphia, Pennsylvania; Collection Name: *Historic Pennsylvania Church and Town Records*; Reel: *779*. Ancestry.com.

[liv] Ancestry.com. *New Jersey, Deaths and Burials Index, 1798-1971* [database on-line]. Provo, UT, USA: Ancestry.com Operations, Inc., 2011.

[lv] England, Robert. Family group record. England family file. Gloucester Historical Society, Woodbury, NJ.

[lvi] Ancestry.com. *New Jersey, Deaths and Burials Index, 1798-1971* [database on-line]. Provo, UT, USA: Ancestry.com Operations, Inc., 2011

[lvii] England, Robert. Family group record. England family file. Gloucester Historical Society, Woodbury, NJ.

[lviii] Historical Society of Pennsylvania; Philadelphia, Pennsylvania; Collection Name: *Historic Pennsylvania Church and Town Records*

[lix] England, Robert. Family group record. England family file. Gloucester Historical Society, Woodbury, NJ.

[lx] England, Robert. Family group record. England family file. Gloucester Historical Society, Woodbury, NJ

[lxi] Pennsylvania (State). Death certificates, 1906–1963. Series 11.90 (1,905 cartons). Records of the Pennsylvania Department of Health, Record Group 11. Pennsylvania Historical and Museum Commission, Harrisburg, Pennsylvania. Ancestry.com.

[lxii] "Pennsylvania, Philadelphia City Death Certificates, 1803-1915," atabasewithimages, *FamilySearch* (https://familysearch.org/ark:/61903/1:1:VK8P-G9P : 9 December 2014), Bodo England, 29 Jan 1891; citing v A p 60, Philadelphia City Archives and Historical Society of Pennsylvania, Philadelphia; FHL microfilm 1,011,821.

[lxiii] Historical Society of Pennsylvania; Philadelphia, Pennsylvania; Collection Name: Historic Pennsylvania Church and Town Records; Reel: 375. Ancestry.com.

[lxiv] "Pennsylvania, Philadelphia City Death Certificates, 1803-1915," databasewithimages,FamilySearch(https://familysearch.org/ark:/61903/1:1:J694-2HQ : 9 December 2014), Robert England, 29 Mar 1896; citing cn 20539, Philadelphia City Archives and Historical Society of Pennsylvania, Philadelphia; FHL microfilm 1,863,639.

[lxv] Historical Society of Pennsylvania; Philadelphia, Pennsylvania; Collection Name: *Historic Pennsylvania Church and Town Records*; Reel: *779*

[lxvi] Dodd, Jordan, Liahona Research, comp. *New Jersey Marriages, 1684-1895* [database on-line]. Provo, UT, USA: Ancestry.com Operations Inc, 2001.

[lxvii] England, Aquila B., Rev. Handwritten England family tree. England family file: Gloucester Historical Society, Woodbury, NJ.

[lxviii] Historical Society of Pennsylvania; Philadelphia, Pennsylvania; Collection Name: *Historic Pennsylvania Church and Town Records*; Reel: *779*

[lxix] "New Jersey, Deaths, 1670-1988," database, *FamilySearch* (https://familysearch.org/ark:/61903/1:1:FZKV-1M7 : 8 April 2016), Samuel Barber in entry for Daniel Barber, 15 Feb 1875; citing Woolwich, Gloucester, New Jersey, United States, Division of Archives and Record Management, New Jersey Department of State, Trenton.; FHL microfilm 584,598.

[lxx] "New Jersey, Deaths, 1670-1988," database, *FamilySearch*(https://familysearch.org/ark:/61903/1:1:FZHB-PWG : 8 April 2016), Wm. Barber, 12 Apr 1885; citing E. Greenwich, Gloucester, New Jersey, United States, Division of Archives and Record Management, New Jersey Department of State, Trenton.; FHL microfilm 589,837.

[lxxi] "New Jersey, Deaths, 1670-1988," database, *FamilySearch* (https://familysearch.org/ark:/61903/1:1:FZ23-BM9 : 8 April 2016), Hannah Barber, 10 Feb 1887; citing East Greenwich, Gloucester, New Jersey, United States, Division of Archives and Record Management, New Jersey Department of State, Trenton.; FHL microfilm 589,308.

[lxxii] Historical Society of Pennsylvania; Philadelphia, Pennsylvania; Collection Name: *Historic Pennsylvania Church and Town Records*; Reel: *779*

[lxxiii] Ancestry.com. *New Jersey, Deaths and Burials Index, 1798-1971* [database on-line]. Provo, UT, USA: Ancestry.com Operations, Inc., 2011.

[lxxiv] Historical Society of Pennsylvania; Philadelphia, Pennsylvania; Collection Name: *Historic Pennsylvania Church and Town Records*; Reel: *779*

[lxxv] Historical Society of Pennsylvania; Philadelphia, Pennsylvania; Collection Name: *Historic Pennsylvania Church and Town Records*; Reel: *779*

lxxvi Historical Society of Pennsylvania; Philadelphia, Pennsylvania; Collection Name: Historic Pennsylvania Church and Town Records; Reel: 779

lxxvii Historical Society of Pennsylvania; Philadelphia, Pennsylvania; Collection Name: *Historic Pennsylvania Church and Town Records*; Reel: *779*

lxxviii Ancestry.com. *New Jersey, Deaths and Burials Index, 1798-1971* [database on-line]. Provo, UT, USA: Ancestry.com Operations, Inc., 2011

lxxix Historical Society of Pennsylvania; Philadelphia, Pennsylvania; Collection Name: *Historic Pennsylvania Church and Town Records*; Reel: *779*

lxxx Year: *1850*; Census Place: *Brooklyn Ward 11, Kings, New York*; Roll: *M432_520*; Page: *337B*; Image: *615*

lxxxi Ancestry.com. *New York, New York, Death Index, 1862-1948* [database on-line]. Provo, UT, USA: Ancestry.com Operations, Inc., 2014.

lxxxii Year: *1850*; Census Place: *Brooklyn Ward 11, Kings, New York*; Roll: *M432_520*; Page: *337B*; Image: *615*

lxxxiii Ancestry.com. *New York, New York, Death Index, 1862-1948* [database on-line]. Provo, UT, USA: Ancestry.com Operations, Inc., 2014.

lxxxiv England, Aquila B., Rev. Handwritten England family tree. England family file: Gloucester Historical Society, Woodbury, NJ.

lxxxv England, Aquila B., Rev. Handwritten England family tree. England family file: Gloucester Historical Society, Woodbury, NJ.

lxxxvi Ancestry.com. *New Jersey, Deaths and Burials Index, 1798-1971* [database on-line]. Provo, UT, USA: Ancestry.com Operations, Inc., 2011.

lxxxvii Swarthmore College; Swarthmore, Pennsylvania; *Membership, 1897*; Collection: *Quaker Meeting Records*; Call Number: *MR-PH 237*

lxxxviii Swarthmore College; Swarthmore, Pennsylvania; *Membership, 1897*; Collection: *Quaker Meeting Records*; Call Number: *MR-PH 237*

lxxxix England, Aquila B., Rev. Handwritten England family tree. England family file: Gloucester Historical Society, Woodbury, NJ.

xc National Archives and Records Administration (NARA); Washington, D.C.; *Non-population Census Schedules for New Jersey, 1850-1880: Mortality*; Archive Collection: *M1810*; Archive Roll Number: *1*; Census Year: *1860*; Census Place: *Camden North Ward, Camden, New Jersey*

xci England, Aquila B., Rev. Handwritten England family tree. England family file: Gloucester Historical Society, Woodbury, NJ.

xcii Historical Society of Pennsylvania; Philadelphia, Pennsylvania; Collection Name: *Historic Pennsylvania Church and Town Records*; Reel: *1166*

xciii Greater New Jersey Annual Conference Commission on Archives and History; Madison, New Jersey; Description: *Methodist Church Records*

xciv England, Aquila B., Rev. Handwritten England family tree. England family file: Gloucester Historical Society, Woodbury, NJ.

xcv England, Aquila B., Rev. Handwritten England family tree. England family file: Gloucester Historical Society, Woodbury, NJ.

xcvi England, Aquila B., Rev. Handwritten England family tree. England family file: Gloucester Historical Society, Woodbury, NJ.

xcvii England, Aquila B., Rev. Handwritten England family tree. England family file: Gloucester Historical Society, Woodbury, NJ.

xcviii Ancestry.com. *New Jersey, Deaths and Burials Index, 1798-1971* [database on-line]. Provo, UT, USA: Ancestry.com Operations, Inc., 2011.

xcix Historical Society of Pennsylvania; Philadelphia, Pennsylvania; Collection Name: *Historic Pennsylvania Church and Town Records*; Reel: *779*

c Ancestry.com. *U.S., Find A Grave Index, 1600s-Current* [database on-line]. Provo, UT, USA: Ancestry.com Operations, Inc., 2012.

ci "New Jersey Deaths and Burials, 1720-1988," database, *FamilySearch* (https://familysearch.org/ark:/61903/1:1:FZHC-HTT : 12 December 2014), Eliza Campbell, 03 Oct 1858; citing Swedesboro, Woolwich Twp., Gloucester, N. J., reference 1 Jun 1858-1859; FHL microfilm 1,510,236.

cii *Will Books*; Author: *New Jersey. Surrogate's Court (Gloucester County)*; Probate Place: *Gloucester, New Jersey*

ciii Historical Society of Pennsylvania; Philadelphia, Pennsylvania; Collection Name: *Historic Pennsylvania Church and Town Records*; Reel: *779*

civ "New Jersey Deaths and Burials, 1720–1971." Index. FamilySearch, Salt Lake City, Utah, 2009, 2010. Index entries derived from digital copies of original and compiled records.

cv *Will Books*; Author: *New Jersey. Surrogate's Court (Gloucester County)*; Probate Place: *Gloucester, New Jersey*

cvi Historical Society of Pennsylvania; Philadelphia, Pennsylvania; Collection Name: *Historic Pennsylvania Church and Town Records*; Reel: *779*. Ancestry.com.

cvii Historical Society of Pennsylvania; Philadelphia, Pennsylvania; Collection Name: *Historic Pennsylvania Church and Town Records*; Reel: *779*. Ancestry.com.

cviii Historical Society of Pennsylvania; Philadelphia, Pennsylvania; Collection Name: *Historic Pennsylvania Church and Town Records*; Reel: *779*. Ancestry.com.

cix "Pennsylvania, Philadelphia City Death Certificates, 1803-1915," databasewithimages, *FamilySearch* (https://familysearch.org/ark:/61903/1:1:JDVB-BMS : 9 December 2014), L.D. England, 30 Mar 1879; citing , Philadelphia City Archives and Historical Society of Pennsylvania, Philadelphia; FHL microfilm 2,031,099.

cx Ancestry.com. *U.S., Find A Grave Index, 1600s-Current* [database on-line]. Provo, UT, USA: Ancestry.com Operations, Inc., 2012.

cxi Hosmer, Ralph S. *Genealogy of that branch of the Irwin family in New York founded in the Hudson River Valley by William Irwin, 1700-1787*. Ithaca, N.Y.: Privately printed for Dudley Marvin Irwin, 1938.

cxii Hosmer, Ralph S. *Genealogy of that branch of the Irwin family in New York founded in the Hudson River Valley by William Irwin, 1700-1787*. Ithaca, N.Y.: Privately printed for Dudley Marvin Irwin, 1938.

cxiii Ancestry.com. *Philadelphia, Pennsylvania, Death Certificates Index, 1803-1915* [database on-line]. Provo, UT, USA: Ancestry.com Operations, Inc., 2011.

cxiv *Genealogy of the Hannum family: descended from John and Margery Hannum, settlers in Chester County, Pennsylvania: with brief notices of other families allied with the name, and abstracts of early wills. Ancestry.com. North America, Family Histories, 1500-2000* [database on-line]. Provo, UT, USA: Ancestry.com Operations, Inc., 2016.

cxv Historical Society of Pennsylvania; Philadelphia, Pennsylvania; Collection Name: *Historic Pennsylvania Church and Town Records*; Reel: *779*. Ancestry.com.

cxvi Year: *1850*; Census Place: *Greenwich, Gloucester, New Jersey*; Roll: *M432_451*; Page: *134B*; Image: *275*. Ancestry.com.

cxvii "Pennsylvania, Philadelphia City Death Certificates, 1803-1915," database with images, *FamilySearch* (https://familysearch.org/ark:/61903/1:1:JDVB-BMS: 9 December 2014), L.D. England, 30 Mar 1879; citing, Philadelphia City Archives and Historical Society of Pennsylvania, Philadelphia; FHL microfilm 2,031,099.

cxviii Historical Society of Pennsylvania; Philadelphia, Pennsylvania; Collection Name: *Historic Pennsylvania Church and Town Records*; Reel: *166*

cxix Year: *1850*; Census Place: *Greenwich, Gloucester, New Jersey*; Roll: *M432_451*; Page: *134B*; Image: *275*

cxx "New Jersey Deaths and Burials, 1720–1971." Index. FamilySearch, Salt Lake City, Utah, 2009, 2010. Index entries derived from digital copies of original and compiled records.

cxxi Ancestry.com. *U.S., Sons of the American Revolution Membership Applications, 1889-1970* [database on-line]. Provo, UT, USA: Ancestry.com Operations, Inc., 2011.

cxxii Historical Society of Pennsylvania; Philadelphia, Pennsylvania; Collection Name: *Historic Pennsylvania Church and Town Records*; Reel: *1078*

cxxiii Ancestry.com. *New Jersey, Deaths and Burials Index, 1798-1971* [database on-line]. Provo, UT, USA: Ancestry.com Operations, Inc., 2011.

cxxiv England, Aquila B., Rev. Handwritten England family tree. England family file: Gloucester Historical Society, Woodbury, NJ.

cxxv NewJerseyBirthsandChristenings,1660-1980," database, *FamilySearch* (https://familysearch.org/ark:/61903/1:1:FZZG-VXX : 12 December 2014), Daniel England, 02 Nov 1862; citing NEWTON TWP,CAMDEN,NEW JERSEY, reference ; FHL microfilm 0493707 V. E.

cxxvi Ancestry.com. *Pennsylvania, Death Certificates, 1906-1963* [database on-line]. Provo, UT, USA: Ancestry.com Operations, Inc., 2014.

cxxvii Historical Society of Pennsylvania; Philadelphia, Pennsylvania; Collection Name: *Historic Pennsylvania Church and Town Records*; Reel: *1090*. Ancestry.com.

cxxviii Ancestry.com. *New Jersey, Births and Christenings Index, 1660-1931* [database on-line]. Provo, UT, USA: Ancestry.com Operations, Inc., 2011.

cxxix Ancestry.com. *New Jersey, Deaths and Burials Index, 1798-1971* [database on-line]. Provo, UT, USA: Ancestry.com Operations, Inc., 2011.

[cxxx] "New Jersey Births and Christenings, 1660-1980," database, *FamilySearch*(https://familysearch.org/ark:/61903/1:1:FZQM-W8Z : 12 December 2014), Hulings England, 06 Dec 1864; citing Haddenfield, Camden, New Jersey, reference Pg.-165 #3; FHL microfilm 493,707.

[cxxxi] "New Jersey, Births, 1670-1980," database, *FamilySearch*(https://familysearch.org/ark:/61903/1:1:FC18-9FP : 8 April 2016), Oscar England, 08 Feb 1868; citing Gloucester, Camden, New Jersey, United States, Division of Archives and Record Management, New Jersey Department of State, Trenton.; FHL microfilm 494,161.

[cxxxii] "Illinois Deaths and Stillbirths, 1916-1947," database, *FamilySearch*(https://familysearch.org/ark:/61903/1:1:N3Z4-WLL : 27 December 2014), Oscar B. England, 26 Apr 1937; Public Board of Health, Archives, Springfield; FHL microfilm 1,786,730.

[cxxxiii] "Illinois, Cook County Marriages, 1871-1920," database, *FamilySearch*(https://familysearch.org/ark:/61903/1:1:N7DK-LHZ : 26 December 2014), Oscar Bruce England and Frieda Ruedz, 27 Jun 1892; citing Cook, Illinois, , Cook County Courthouse, Chicago; FHL microfilm 1,030,215.

[cxxxiv] Year: *1900*; Census Place: *Chicago Ward 15, Cook, Illinois*; Roll: *264*; Page: *15B*; Enumeration District: *0479*; FHL microfilm: *1240264*

Year: *1900*; Census Place: *Chicago Ward 15, Cook, Illinois*; Roll: *264*; Page: *15B*; Enumeration District: *0479*; FHL microfilm: *1240264*[cxxxv]

[cxxxvi] 11 Mar 1948, Page 2 - Belvidere Daily Republican at Newspapers.com

[cxxxvii] Historical Society of Pennsylvania; Philadelphia, Pennsylvania; Collection Name: *Historic Pennsylvania Church and Town Records*; Reel: *779*

[cxxxviii] Ancestry.com. *New Jersey, Deaths and Burials Index, 1798-1971* [database on-line]. Provo, UT, USA: Ancestry.com Operations, Inc., 2011.

[cxxxix] Historical Society of Pennsylvania; Philadelphia, Pennsylvania; Collection Name: *Historic Pennsylvania Church and Town Records*; Reel: *779*

[cxl] Ancestry.com. *U.S., Find A Grave Index, 1600s-Current* [database on-line]. Provo, UT, USA: Ancestry.com Operations, Inc., 2012.

[cxli] Ancestry.com. *Philadelphia, Pennsylvania, Death Certificates Index, 1803-1915* [database on-line]. Provo, UT, USA: Ancestry.com Operations, Inc., 2011.

[cxlii] Ancestry.com. *Philadelphia, Pennsylvania, Death Certificates Index, 1803-1915* [database on-line]. Provo, UT, USA: Ancestry.com Operations, Inc., 2011.

[cxliii] Year: *1850*; Census Place: *Harrison, Gloucester, New Jersey*; Roll: *M432_451*; Page: *37A*; Image: *80*

[cxliv] Ancestry.com. *Philadelphia, Pennsylvania, Death Certificates Index, 1803-1915* [database on-line]. Provo, UT, USA: Ancestry.com Operations, Inc., 2011.

[cxlv] England, Aquila B., Rev. Handwritten England family tree. England family file: Gloucester Historical Society, Woodbury, NJ.

[cxlvi] Ancestry.com. *U.S., Find A Grave Index, 1600s-Current* [database on-line]. Provo, UT, USA: Ancestry.com Operations, Inc., 2012.

[cxlvii] Ancestry.com. *Pennsylvania, Death Certificates, 1906-1963* [database on-line]. Provo, UT, USA: Ancestry.com Operations, Inc., 2014.

[cxlviii] Book Title: *The descendants of Matthew Gill. Ancestry.com. North America, Family Histories, 1500-2000 [database on-line]. Provo, UT, USA: Ancestry.com Operations, Inc., 2016.*

[cxlix] Book Title: *The descendants of Matthew Gill. Ancestry.com. North America, Family Histories, 1500-2000 [database on-line]. Provo, UT, USA: Ancestry.com Operations, Inc., 2016.*

[cl] "Pennsylvania, Philadelphia City Death Certificates, 1803-1915," database with images, FamilySearch https://familysearch.org/ark:/61903/1:1:JDVB-BMS : 9 December 2014), L.D. England, 30 Mar 1879; citing , Philadelphia City Archives and Historical Society of Pennsylvania, Philadelphia; FHL microfilm 2,031,099.

[cli] Ancestry.com. Philadelphia, Pennsylvania, Death Certificates Index, 1803-1915 [database on-line]. Provo, UT, USA: Ancestry.com Operations, Inc., 2011.

[clii] Year: 1860; Census Place: Philadelphia Ward 24 Precinct 8, Philadelphia, Pennsylvania; Roll: M653_1175; Page: 1004; Image: 498; Family History Library Film: 805175

[cliii] Year: 1870; Census Place: Philadelphia Ward 27 District 89, Philadelphia, Pennsylvania; Roll: M593_1445; Page: 73B; Image: 35460; Family History Library Film: 552944

[cliv] Ancestry.com. U.S. City Directories, 1822-1995 [database on-line]. Provo, UT, USA: Ancestry.com Operations, Inc., 2011.

clv "Pennsylvania, Philadelphia City Death Certificates, 1803-1915," database with images, FamilySearch (https://familysearch.org/ark:/61903/1:1:JKQ1-FYM : 9 December 2014), Deborah England, 08 Mar 1844; citing 1833, Philadelphia City Archives and Historical Society of Pennsylvania, Philadelphia; FHL microfilm 1,906,031.

clvi Year: 1850; Census Place: West Philadelphia, Philadelphia, Pennsylvania; Roll: M432_823; Page: 505A; Image: 85

clvii "Pennsylvania Marriages, 1709-1940," database, FamilySearch(https://familysearch.org/ark:/61903/1:1:V26T-N4Q : 6 December 2014), William Strickland and Rebecca Nymos England, 08 Oct 1885; citing Philadelphia, Philadelphia, Pennsylvania; FHL microfilm 1,769,296.

clviii "Pennsylvania, Philadelphia City Death Certificates, 1803-1915," database with images, FamilySearch (https://familysearch.org/ark:/61903/1:1:JDGQ-WLH : 9 December 2014), Rebecca N. E. Strickland, 25 Jul 1896; citing cn 2305, Philadelphia City Archives and Historical Society of Pennsylvania, Philadelphia; FHL microfilm 1,863,645.

clix Year: 1860; Census Place: Philadelphia Ward 24 Precinct 8, Philadelphia, Pennsylvania; Roll: M653_1175; Page: 1004; Image: 498; Family History Library Film: 805175

clx Ancestry.com. Philadelphia, Pennsylvania, Death Certificates Index, 1803-1915 [database on-line]. Provo, UT, USA: Ancestry.com Operations, Inc., 2011.

clxi Year: 1900; Census Place: Newark Ward 9, Essex, New Jersey; Roll: 964; Page: 1A; Enumeration District:0083; FHL microfilm: 1240964

clxii Paint, Oil, and Drug Review, pg.287. https://play.google.com/books/reader?printsec=frontcover&output=reader&id=UP5YAAAAYAAJ

clxiii Ancestry.com. Philadelphia, Pennsylvania, Death Certificates Index, 1803-1915 [database on-line]. Provo, UT, USA: Ancestry.com Operations, Inc., 2011.

clxiv "Pennsylvania, Philadelphia City Death Certificates, 1803-1915," database with images, FamilySearch (https://familysearch.org/ark:/61903/1:1:JDP2-MH3 : 9 December 2014), Mary Baugh, 09 Dec 1907; citing cn 30037, Philadelphia City Archives and Historical Society of Pennsylvania, Philadelphia; FHL microfilm 1,402,918.

clxv Pennsylvania probate record; Probate Place: Philadelphia, Pennsylvania, Wills, No 071-096, 1908

clxvi Ancestry.com. Philadelphia, Pennsylvania, Death Certificates Index, 1803-1915 [database on-line]. Provo, UT, USA: Ancestry.com Operations, Inc., 2011.

clxvii Historical Data Systems, comp. U.S., Civil War Soldier Records and Profiles, 1861-1865 [database on-line]. Provo, UT, USA: Ancestry.com Operations Inc, 2009.

clxviii Year: 1850; Census Place: West Philadelphia, Philadelphia, Pennsylvania; Roll: M432_823; Page: 505A; Image: 85

clxix Historical Society of Pennsylvania; Philadelphia, Pennsylvania; Collection Name: Historic Pennsylvania Church and Town Records

clxx Ancestry.com. Pennsylvania, Death Certificates, 1906-1963 [database on-line]. Provo, UT, USA: Ancestry.com Operations, Inc., 2014.

clxxi "United States Census, 1900," database with images, FamilySearch (https://familysearch.org/ark:/61903/1:1:M3W4-2J5 : 22 January 2015), James M England in household of Joseph Baugh, Philadelphia city Ward 24, Philadelphia, Pennsylvania, United States; citing sheet 16B, family 314, NARA microfilm publication T623 (Washington, D.C.: National Archives and Records Administration, n.d.); FHL microfilm 1,241,465.

clxxii Year: 1920; Census Place: Philadelphia Ward 24, Philadelphia, Pennsylvania; Roll: T625_1627; Page: 9A; Enumeration District: 723; Image: 816

clxxiii Find A Grave. Find A Grave. http://www.findagrave.com/cgi-bin/fg.cgi.

clxxiv Find A Grave. Find A Grave. http://www.findagrave.com/cgi-bin/fg.cgi.

clxxv Find A Grave. Find A Grave. http://www.findagrave.com/cgi-bin/fg.cgi.

clxxvi Ancestry.com. U.S. City Directories, 1822-1995 [database on-line]. Provo, UT, USA: Ancestry.com Operations, Inc., 2011.

clxxvii Ancestry.com. U.S., Find A Grave Index, 1600s-Current [database on-line]. Provo, UT, USA: Ancestry.com Operations, Inc., 2012.

clxxviii "New Jersey, County Marriages, 1682-1956," database with images, FamilySearch (https://familysearch.org/ark:/61903/1:1:VKMD-GH3 : 12 December 2014), Oliver Crawford and Elisabeth Roberts, 18 Jan 1855; citing Somerset, New Jersey, United States, New Jersey

clxxix United States. Nonpopulation Census Schedules for New Jersey, 1850-1880: Mortality.M1810, 4 rolls. National Archives and Records Administration, Washington D.C.

clxxx Ancestry.com. New Jersey, Deaths and Burials Index, 1798-1971 [database on-line]. Provo, UT, USA: Ancestry.com Operations, Inc., 2011.

clxxxi "New Jersey Marriages, 1678-1985," database, FamilySearch(https://familysearch.org/ark:/61903/1:1:FZPZ-8D7 : 12 December 2014), Samuel B. Myers and Isabella E. Roberts, 01 Dec 1859; citing 584,565

clxxxii Year: 1850; Census Place: Woolwich, Gloucester, New Jersey; Roll: M432_451; Page: 140A; Image: 286

clxxxiii Year: *1860*; Census Place: *Woolwich, Gloucester, New Jersey*; Roll: *M653_691*; Page: *410*; Image: *414*; Family History Library Film: *803691*

clxxxivHistorical Society of Pennsylvania; Philadelphia, Pennsylvania; Collection Name: *Historic Pennsylvania Church and Town Records*; Reel: *779*

clxxxv "New Jersey Deaths and Burials, 1720-1988," database, FamilySearch (https://familysearch.org/ark:/61903/1:1:FZCC-GFF : 12 December 2014), Priscilla Roberts, 16 Feb 1889; citing Camden City, Camden, New Jersey, reference v 27 p 150; FHL microfilm 589,316.

clxxxvi Year: *1900*; Census Place: *Camden Ward 4, Camden, New Jersey*; Roll: *958*; Page: *8B*; Enumeration District:*0046*; FHL microfilm: *1240958*

clxxxvii Year: *1850*; Census Place: *Woolwich, Gloucester, New Jersey*; Roll: *M432_451*; Page: *155A*; Image: *318*

clxxxviii Year: *1910*; Census Place: *Camden Ward 10, Camden, New Jersey*; Roll: *T624_873*; Page: *8B*; Enumeration District: *0069*; FHL microfilm: *1374886*

clxxxix Greater New Jersey Annual Conference Commission on Archives and History; Madison, New Jersey; Description: *Methodist Church Records*

cxc Year: *1850*; Census Place: *Upper Penns Neck, Salem, New Jersey*; Roll: *M432_462*; Page: *188A*; Image: *376*

cxci Ancestry.com. *Pennsylvania, Death Certificates, 1906-1963* [database on-line]. Provo, UT, USA: Ancestry.com Operations, Inc., 2014.

cxcii Year: *1900*; Census Place: *Greenwich, Gloucester, New Jersey*; Roll: *971*; Page: *10A*; Enumeration District:*0157*; FHL microfilm: *1240971*

cxciii Year: *1870*; Census Place: *Upper Penns Neck, Salem, New Jersey*; Roll: *M593_887*; Page: *275A*; Image:*301705*; Family History Library Film: *552386*

cxciv Ancestry.com. *New Jersey, Births and Christenings Index, 1660-1931* [database on-line]. Provo, UT, USA: Ancestry.com Operations, Inc., 2011.

cxcvYear: *1900*; Census Place: *Camden Ward 9, Camden, New Jersey*; Roll: *959*; Page: *2A*; Enumeration District:*0076*; FHL microfilm: *124095*

cxcvi England, Robert. Family group record. England family file. Gloucester Historical Society, Woodbury, NJ.

cxcvii Historical Society of Pennsylvania; Philadelphia, Pennsylvania; Collection Name: *Historic Pennsylvania Church and Town Records*

cxcviii England, Robert. Family group record. England family file. Gloucester Historical Society, Woodbury, NJ.

cxcix England, Robert. Family group record. England family file. Gloucester Historical Society, Woodbury, NJ

cc Historical Society of Pennsylvania; Philadelphia, Pennsylvania; Collection Name: *Historic Pennsylvania Church and Town Records*; Reel: *1079*

cci Year: *1860*; Census Place: *Philadelphia Ward 8, Philadelphia, Pennsylvania*; Roll: *M653_1158*; Page: *588*; Image: *594*; Family History Library Film: *805158*

cciiHistorical Society of Pennsylvania; Philadelphia, Pennsylvania; Collection Name: *Historic Pennsylvania Church and Town Records*

cciii Ancestry.com. *Philadelphia, Pennsylvania, Death Certificates Index, 1803-1915* [database on-line]. Provo, UT, USA: Ancestry.com Operations, Inc., 2011.

cciv Historical Society of Pennsylvania; Philadelphia, Pennsylvania; Collection Name: *Historic Pennsylvania Church and Town Records*; Reel: *387*

ccv Ancestry.com. *Pennsylvania, Death Certificates, 1906-1963* [database on-line]. Provo, UT, USA: Ancestry.com Operations, Inc., 2014.

ccviAncestry.com. *Philadelphia, Pennsylvania, Marriage Index, 1885-1951* [database on-line]. Provo, UT, USA: Ancestry.com Operations, Inc., 2011.

ccvii England, Robert. Family group record. England family file. Gloucester Historical Society, Woodbury, NJ.

ccviii Pennsylvania (State). Death certificates, 1906–1963. Series 11.90 (1,905 cartons). Records of the Pennsylvania Department of Health, Record Group 11. Pennsylvania Historical and Museum Commission, Harrisburg, Pennsylvania. Ancestry.com.

ccixjttps://familysearch.org/ark:/61903/3:1:S3HT-63BQ-XN4?i=186&wc=9F5R-3TL%3A1073284501%3Fcc%3D1320976&cc=1320976

ccx Ancestry.com. *Pennsylvania, Civil War Muster Rolls, 1860-1869* [database on-line]. Provo, UT, USA: Ancestry.com Operations, Inc., 2015.

ccxi Year: *1870*; Census Place: *Philadelphia Ward 2 District 5, Philadelphia, Pennsylvania*; Roll: *M593_1388*; Page: *129A*; Image: *309314*; Family History Library Film: *552887* [ccxii]*Find A Grave*. Find A Grave. http://www.findagrave.com/cgi-bin/fg.cgi.

[ccxiii] Ancestry.com. *U.S., Find A Grave Index, 1600s-Current* [database on-line]. Provo, UT, USA: Ancestry.com Operations, Inc., 2012.

[ccxiv] Historical Society of Pennsylvania; Philadelphia, Pennsylvania; Collection Name: Historic Pennsylvania Church and Town Records; Reel: 375. Ancestry.com.

[ccxv] "Pennsylvania, Philadelphia City Death Certificates, 1803-1915," databasewithimages,FamilySearch(https://familysearch.org/ark:/61903/1:1:J694-2HQ : 9 December 2014), Robert England, 29 Mar 1896; citing cn 20539, Philadelphia City Archives and Historical Society of Pennsylvania, Philadelphia; FHL microfilm 1,863,639.

[ccxvi] Ancestry.com. *Pennsylvania, Death Certificates, 1906-1963* [database on-line]. Provo, UT, USA: Ancestry.com Operations, Inc., 2014.

[ccxvii] Ancestry.com. *Pennsylvania, Death Certificates, 1906-1963* [database on-line]. Provo, UT, USA: Ancestry.com Operations, Inc., 2014.

[ccxviii]Ancestry.com. *Philadelphia, Pennsylvania, Death Certificates Index, 1803-1915* [database on-line]. Provo, UT, USA: Ancestry.com Operations, Inc., 2011.

[ccxix] *Pennsylvania probate record*; Probate Place: *Philadelphia, Pennsylvania*

[ccxx] Ancestry.com. *Philadelphia, Pennsylvania, Death Certificates Index, 1803-1915* [database on-line]. Provo, UT, USA: Ancestry.com Operations, Inc., 2011.

[ccxxi] Historical Society of Pennsylvania; Philadelphia, Pennsylvania; Collection Name: *Historic Pennsylvania Church and Town Records*; Reel: *375*

[ccxxii] "Pennsylvania, Philadelphia City Death Certificates, 1803–1915." Index. FamilySearch, Salt Lake City, Utah, 2008, 2010. From originals housed at the Philadelphia City Archives. "Death Records.".

[ccxxiii] Historical Society of Pennsylvania; Philadelphia, Pennsylvania; Collection Name: *Historic Pennsylvania Church and Town Records*; Reel: *375*

[ccxxiv] Ancestry.com. *Pennsylvania and New Jersey, Church and Town Records, 1708-1985* [database on-line]. Provo, UT, USA: Ancestry.com Operations, Inc., 2011.

[ccxxv] Historical Society of Pennsylvania; Philadelphia, Pennsylvania; Collection Name: *Historic Pennsylvania Church and Town Records*; Reel: *335*

[ccxxvi] Ancestry.com. *Pennsylvania, Death Certificates, 1906-1963* [database on-line]. Provo, UT, USA: Ancestry.com Operations, Inc., 2014.

[ccxxvii] Ancestry.com. *Philadelphia, Pennsylvania, Death Certificates Index, 1803-1915* [database on-line]. Provo, UT, USA: Ancestry.com Operations, Inc., 2011.

[ccxxviii] Ancestry.com. *Pennsylvania, Death Certificates, 1906-1963* [database on-line]. Provo, UT, USA: Ancestry.com Operations, Inc., 2014.

[ccxxix] Ancestry.com. *Pennsylvania, Death Certificates, 1906-1963* [database on-line]. Provo, UT, USA: Ancestry.com Operations, Inc., 2014.

[ccxxx] Historical Society of Pennsylvania; Philadelphia, Pennsylvania; Collection Name: *Historic Pennsylvania Church and Town Records*; Reel: *779*

[ccxxxi] Ancestry.com. *New Jersey, Deaths and Burials Index, 1798-1971* [database on-line]. Provo, UT, USA: Ancestry.com Operations, Inc., 2011

[ccxxxii] Historical Society of Pennsylvania; Philadelphia, Pennsylvania; Collection Name: *Historic Pennsylvania Church and Town Records*; Reel: *779*

[ccxxxiii] Ancestry.com. *U.S., Find A Grave Index, 1600s-Current* [database on-line]. Provo, UT, USA: Ancestry.com Operations, Inc., 2012.

[ccxxxiv] Historical Society of Pennsylvania; Philadelphia, Pennsylvania; Collection Name: *Historic Pennsylvania Church and Town Records*; Reel: *779*

[ccxxxv] Historical Society of Pennsylvania; Philadelphia, Pennsylvania; Collection Name: *Historic Pennsylvania Church and Town Records*; Reel: *778*

[ccxxxvi] Year: *1900*; Census Place: *Elmwood, Peoria, Illinois*; Roll: *333*; Page: *16A*; Enumeration District: *0074*; FHL microfilm: *1240333*

[ccxxxvii] Ancestry.com. *U.S., Find A Grave Index, 1600s-Current* [database on-line]. Provo, UT, USA: Ancestry.com Operations, Inc., 2012.

[ccxxxviii] Year: *1850*; Census Place: *Brooklyn Ward 11, Kings, New York*; Roll: *M432_520*; Page: *337B*; Image: *615*

[ccxxxix] Ancestry.com. *New York, New York, Death Index, 1862-1948* [database on-line]. Provo, UT, USA: Ancestry.com Operations, Inc., 2014.

[ccxl] Year: *1850*; Census Place: *Brooklyn Ward 11, Kings, New York*; Roll: *M432_520*; Page: *337B*; Image: *615*

ccxli Ancestry.com. *New York, New York, Death Index, 1862-1948* [database on-line]. Provo, UT, USA: Ancestry.com Operations, Inc., 2014.

ccxlii Year: *1850*; Census Place: *Brooklyn Ward 11, Kings, New York*; Roll: *M432_520*; Page: *337B*; Image: *615*

ccxliii 16 Mar 1915, Page 20 - The Brooklyn Daily Eagle at Newspapers.com

ccxliv Ancestry.com. *New York, State Census, 1865* [database on-line]. Provo, UT, USA: Ancestry.com Operations, Inc., 2014.

ccxlv Ancestry.com. *New York, Death Newspaper Extracts, 1801-1890 (Barber Collection)* [database on-line]. Provo, UT, USA: Ancestry.com Operations Inc, 2005.

ccxlvi Ancestry.com. *New York, New York, Marriage Index 1866-1937* [database on-line]. Provo, UT, USA: Ancestry.com Operations, Inc., 2014.

ccxlvii 11 Jan 1897, Page 1 - The Brooklyn Daily Eagle at Newspapers.com

ccxlviii Year: *1900*; Census Place: *Brooklyn Ward 7, Kings, New York*; Roll: *1046*; Page: *5A*; Enumeration District:*0088*; FHL microfilm: *1241046*

ccxlix Year: *1900*; Census Place: *Brooklyn Ward 7, Kings, New York*; Roll: *1046*; Page: *5A*; Enumeration District:*0088*; FHL microfilm: *1241046*

ccl Year: *1900*; Census Place: *Brooklyn Ward 7, Kings, New York*; Roll: *1046*; Page: *5A*; Enumeration District:*0088*; FHL microfilm: *1241046*

ccli 18 Sep 1920, Page 16 - The Brooklyn Daily Eagle at Newspapers.com

cclii Year: *1850*; Census Place: *Brooklyn Ward 11, Kings, New York*; Roll: *M432_520*; Page: *337B*; Image: *615*

ccliii Year: *1870*; Census Place: *Brooklyn Ward 7, Kings, New York*; Roll: *M593_949*; Page: *448B*; Image: *372857*; Family History Library Film: *552448*

ccliv Ancestry.com. *New York, New York, Death Index, 1862-1948* [database on-line]. Provo, UT, USA: Ancestry.com Operations, Inc., 2014.

cclv *Wills and Indexes, 1787-1923*; Author: *New York. Surrogate's Court (Kings County)*; Probate Place: *Kings, New York*

cclvi Ancestry.com. *New York, New York, Death Index, 1862-1948* [database on-line]. Provo, UT, USA: Ancestry.com Operations, Inc., 2014.

cclvii Ancestry.com. *New York, New York, Death Index, 1862-1948* [database on-line]. Provo, UT, USA: Ancestry.com Operations, Inc., 2014.

cclviii Ancestry.com. *New York, New York, Death Index, 1862-1948* [database on-line]. Provo, UT, USA: Ancestry.com Operations, Inc., 2014.

cclix Ancestry.com. *New York, New York, Marriage Index 1866-1937* [database on-line]. Provo, UT, USA: Ancestry.com Operations, Inc., 2014.

cclx Ancestry.com. *New York, New York, Death Index, 1862-1948* [database on-line]. Provo, UT, USA: Ancestry.com Operations, Inc., 2014.

cclxi 14 Jun 1937, Page 13 - The Brooklyn Daily Eagle at Newspapers.com

cclxii England, Aquila B., Rev. Handwritten England family tree. England family file: Gloucester Historical Society, Woodbury, NJ.

cclxiii Ancestry.com. *New Jersey, Deaths and Burials Index, 1798-1971* [database on-line]. Provo, UT, USA: Ancestry.com Operations, Inc., 2011.

cclxiv Swarthmore College; Swarthmore, Pennsylvania; *Membership, 1897*; Collection: *Quaker Meeting Records*; Call Number: *MR-PH 237*

cclxv Swarthmore College; Swarthmore, Pennsylvania; *Membership, 1897*; Collection: *Quaker Meeting Records*; Call Number: *MR-PH 237*

cclxvi Year: *1860*; Census Place: *Upper Penns Neck, Salem, New Jersey*; Roll: *M653_707*; Page: *33*; Image: *419*; Family History Library Film: *803707*

cclxvii Ancestry.com. *U.S., Find A Grave Index, 1600s-Current* [database on-line]. Provo, UT, USA: Ancestry.com Operations, Inc., 2012.

cclxviii Year: *1900*; Census Place: *Oldmans, Salem, New Jersey*; Roll: *993*; Page: *3B*; Enumeration District: *0176*; FHL microfilm: *1240993*

cclxix United States, Selective Service System. *World War I Selective Service System Draft Registration Cards, 1917-1918*. Washington, D.C.: National Archives and Records Administration. M1509, 4,582 rolls. Imaged from Family History Library microfilm.

cclxx Year: *1900*; Census Place: *Woolwich, Gloucester, New Jersey*; Roll: *971*; Page: *5B*; Enumeration District: *0169*; FHL microfilm: *1240971*

cclxxi Ancestry.com. *New Jersey, Deaths and Burials Index, 1798-1971* [database on-line]. Provo, UT, USA: Ancestry.com Operations, Inc., 2011.

cclxxii Year: *1900*; Census Place: *Woolwich, Gloucester, New Jersey*; Roll: *971*; Page: *5B*; Enumeration District: *0169*; FHL microfilm: *1240971*

cclxxiii Year: *1900*; Census Place: *Woolwich, Gloucester, New Jersey*; Roll: *971*; Page: *5B*; Enumeration District: *0169*; FHL microfilm: *1240971*

cclxxiv Year: *1900*; Census Place: *Logan, Gloucester, New Jersey*; Roll: *971*; Page: *1B*; Enumeration District: *0159*; FHL microfilm: *1240971*

cclxxv Ancestry.com. *New Jersey, Deaths and Burials Index, 1798-1971* [database on-line]. Provo, UT, USA: Ancestry.com Operations, Inc., 2011.

cclxxvi "New Jersey, County Marriages, 1682-1956," database with images, *FamilySearch*(https://familysearch.org/ark:/61903/1:1:VW5L-BC1 : 12 December 2014), Stratton Mattson and Ella England, 04 Mar 1875; citing Gloucester, New Jersey, New Jersey State Archives, Trenton; FHL microfilm 846,905.

cclxxvii Ancestry.com. *Web: New Jersey, Find A Grave Index, 1664-2012* [database on-line]. Provo, UT, USA: Ancestry.com Operations, Inc., 2012.

cclxxviii Year: *1900*; Census Place: *Woolwich, Gloucester, New Jersey*; Roll: *971*; Page: *1B*; Enumeration District: *0168*; FHL microfilm: *1240971*

cclxxix Year: *1880*; Census Place: *Upper Penns Neck, Salem, New Jersey*; Roll: *797*; Family History Film: *1254797*; Page: *222B*; Enumeration District: *150*; Image: *0451*

cclxxx "New Jersey, Marriages, 1670-1980," database with images, *FamilySearch*(https://familysearch.org/ark:/61903/1:1:FZPW-1VC : 31 March 2016), William Harris and Sarah R. England, 31 Mar 1887; citing Cold Spring, Cape May, New Jersey, United States, Division of Archives and Record Management, New Jersey Department of State, Trenton.; FHL microfilm 495,705.

cclxxxi Ancestry.com. *U.S., Find A Grave Index, 1600s-Current* [database on-line]. Provo, UT, USA: Ancestry.com Operations, Inc., 2012.

cclxxxii New Jersey, Marriages, 1670-1980," database with images, *FamilySearch*(https://familysearch.org/ark:/61903/1:1:FZGF-W25 : 31 March 2016), Wm. W. England and Hannah R. Cheeseman, 27 Dec 1886; citing Woodstown, Salem, New Jersey, United States, Division of Archives and Record Management, New Jersey Department of State, Trenton.; FHL microfilm 495,704.

cclxxxiii Ancestry.com. *U.S., Find A Grave Index, 1600s-Current* [database on-line]. Provo, UT, USA: Ancestry.com Operations, Inc., 2012.

cclxxxiv Year: *1900*; Census Place: *Oldmans, Salem, New Jersey*; Roll: *993*; Page: *3A*; Enumeration District: *0176*; FHL microfilm: *1240993*

cclxxxv Ancestry.com. *U.S., Find A Grave Index, 1600s-Current* [database on-line]. Provo, UT, USA: Ancestry.com Operations, Inc., 2012.

cclxxxvi US Find a Grave, 1600's-current. Ancestry.com. 2012. Provo, UT.

cclxxxvii Ancestry.com. *1900 United States Federal Census* [database on-line]. Provo, UT, USA: Ancestry.com Operations Inc, 2004.

cclxxxviii US Find a Grave, 1600's-current. Ancestry.com. 2012. Provo, UT.

cclxxxix National Archives and Records Administration (NARA); Washington, D.C.; *Non-population Census Schedules for New Jersey, 1850-1880: Mortality*; Archive Collection: *M1810*; Archive Roll Number: *1*; Census Year: *1860*; Census Place: *Camden North Ward, Camden, New Jersey*

ccxc England, Aquila B., Rev. Handwritten England family tree. England family file: Gloucester Historical Society, Woodbury, NJ.

ccxci Historical Society of Pennsylvania; Philadelphia, Pennsylvania; Collection Name: *Historic Pennsylvania Church and Town Records*; Reel: *1166*

ccxcii Greater New Jersey Annual Conference Commission on Archives and History; Madison, New Jersey; Description: *Methodist Church Records*

ccxciii National Archives and Records Administration (NARA); Washington D.C.; NARA Series: *Passport Applications, 1795-1905*; Roll #: *265*; Volume #: *Roll 265 - 16 May 1884-16 Jun 1884*

ccxciv Historical Society of Pennsylvania; Philadelphia, Pennsylvania; Collection Name: *Historic Pennsylvania Church and Town Records*

ccxcv Historical Society of Pennsylvania; Philadelphia, Pennsylvania; Collection Name: *Historic Pennsylvania Church and Town Records*

ccxcvi Ancestry.com. *Pennsylvania, Death Certificates, 1906-1963* [database on-line]. Provo, UT, USA: Ancestry.com Operations, Inc., 2014.

ccxcvii Year: *1850*; Census Place: *Spring Garden Ward 3 Precinct 2, Philadelphia, Pennsylvania*; Roll: *M432_818*; Page: *15A*; Image: *523*

ccxcviii Year: *1900*; Census Place: *Camden Ward 3, Camden, New Jersey*; Roll: *958*; Page: *12A*; Enumeration District:*0043*; FHL microfilm: *1240958*

ccxcix Historical Society of Pennsylvania; Philadelphia, Pennsylvania; Collection Name: *Historic Pennsylvania Church and Town Records*; Reel: *1093*

ccc Year: *1900*; Census Place: *Camden Ward 3, Camden, New Jersey*; Roll: *958*; Page: *12A*; Enumeration District:*0043*; FHL microfilm: *1240958*

ccci Historical Society of Pennsylvania; Philadelphia, Pennsylvania; Collection Name: *Historic Pennsylvania Church and Town Records*; Reel: *1166*

cccii Ancestry.com. *U.S., Find A Grave Index, 1600s-Current* [database on-line]. Provo, UT, USA: Ancestry.com Operations, Inc., 2012.

ccciii Hosmer, Ralph S. *Genealogy of that branch of the Irwin family in New York founded in the Hudson River Valley by William Irwin, 1700-1787*. Ithaca, N.Y.: Privately printed for Dudley Marvin Irwin, 1938.

ccciv Hosmer, Ralph S. *Genealogy of that branch of the Irwin family in New York founded in the Hudson River Valley by William Irwin, 1700-1787*. Ithaca, N.Y.: Privately printed for Dudley Marvin Irwin, 1938.

cccv Ancestry.com. *Philadelphia, Pennsylvania, Death Certificates Index, 1803-1915* [database on-line]. Provo, UT, USA: Ancestry.com Operations, Inc., 2011.

cccvi *Genealogy of the Hannum family: descended from John and Margery Hannum, settlers in Chester County, Pennsylvania: with brief notices of other families allied with the name, and abstracts of early wills. Ancestry.com. North America, Family Histories, 1500-2000* [database on-line]. Provo, UT, USA: Ancestry.com Operations, Inc., 2016.

cccvii Historical Society of Pennsylvania; Philadelphia, Pennsylvania; Collection Name: *Historic Pennsylvania Church and Town Records*; Reel: *779*. Ancestry.com.

cccviii *Genealogy of the Hannum family: descended from John and Margery Hannum, settlers in Chester County, Pennsylvania: with brief notices of other families allied with the name, and abstracts of early wills. Ancestry.com. North America, Family Histories, 1500-2000* [database on-line]. Provo, UT, USA: Ancestry.com Operations, Inc., 2016.

cccix "Pennsylvania, Philadelphia City Death Certificates, 1803–1915." Index. FamilySearch, Salt Lake City, Utah, 2008, 2010. From originals housed at the Philadelphia City Archives. "Death Records.".

cccx Year: *1880*; Census Place: *Thornbury, Delaware, Pennsylvania*; Roll: *1126*; Family History Film: *1255126*; Page: *535A*; Enumeration District: *029*; Image: *0681*

cccxi Ancestry.com. *U.S., Find A Grave Index, 1600s-Current* [database on-line]. Provo, UT, USA: Ancestry.com Operations, Inc., 2012.

cccxii Year: *1940*; Census Place: *Greenburgh, Westchester, New York*; Roll: *T627_2803*; Page: *3A*; Enumeration District: *60-45*

cccxiii Ancestry.com. *U.S., Find A Grave Index, 1600s-Current* [database on-line]. Provo, UT, USA: Ancestry.com Operations, Inc., 2012.

cccxiv Ancestry.com. *U.S., Social Security Applications and Claims Index, 1936-2007* [database on-line]. Provo, UT, USA: Ancestry.com Operations, Inc., 2015.

cccxv 6 Jun 1895, Page 3 - The Times at Newspapers.com

cccxvi Historical Society of Pennsylvania; Philadelphia, Pennsylvania; Collection Name: *Historic Pennsylvania Church and Town Records*; Reel: *166*

cccxvii Year: *1850*; Census Place: *Greenwich, Gloucester, New Jersey*; Roll: *M432_451*; Page: *134B*; Image: *275*

cccxviii "New Jersey Deaths and Burials, 1720–1971." Index. FamilySearch, Salt Lake City, Utah, 2009, 2010. Index entries derived from digital copies of original and compiled records.

cccxix Ancestry.com. *U.S., Sons of the American Revolution Membership Applications, 1889-1970* [database on-line]. Provo, UT, USA: Ancestry.com Operations, Inc., 2011.

cccxx Historical Society of Pennsylvania; Philadelphia, Pennsylvania; Collection Name: *Historic Pennsylvania Church and Town Records*; Reel: *1078*

cccxxi Ancestry.com. *New Jersey, Deaths and Burials Index, 1798-1971* [database on-line]. Provo, UT, USA: Ancestry.com Operations, Inc., 2011.

cccxxii Year: *1880*; Census Place: *Woodbury, Gloucester, New Jersey*; Roll: *781*; Family History Film: *1254781*; Page:*518B*; Enumeration District: *102*; Image: *0679*

cccxxiii Ancestry.com. *U.S., Find A Grave Index, 1600s-Current* [database on-line]. Provo, UT, USA: Ancestry.com Operations, Inc., 2012.

[cccxxiv] *Sons of the American Revolution Membership Applications, 1889-1970*. Louisville, Kentucky: National Society of the Sons of the American Revolution. Microfilm, 508 rolls.

[cccxxv] Ancestry.com. *U.S., Find A Grave Index, 1600s-Current* [database on-line]. Provo, UT, USA: Ancestry.com Operations, Inc., 2012.

[cccxxvi] Ancestry.com. *New Jersey, Births and Christenings Index, 1660-1931* [database on-line]. Provo, UT, USA: Ancestry.com Operations, Inc., 2011.

[cccxxvii] Year: *1900*; Census Place: *Lansdowne, Delaware, Pennsylvania*; Roll: *1406*; Page: *21A*; Enumeration District:*0192*; FHL microfilm: *1241406*

[cccxxviii] NewJerseyBirthsandChristenings,1660-1980," database, *FamilySearch*(https://familysearch.org/ark:/61903/1:1:FZZG-VXX : 12 December 2014), Daniel England, 02 Nov 1862; citing NEWTON TWP,CAMDEN,NEW JERSEY, reference ; FHL microfilm 0493707 V. E.

[cccxxix] Ancestry.com. *Pennsylvania, Death Certificates, 1906-1963* [database on-line]. Provo, UT, USA: Ancestry.com Operations, Inc., 2014.

[cccxxx] Historical Society of Pennsylvania; Philadelphia, Pennsylvania; Collection Name: *Historic Pennsylvania Church and Town Records*; Reel: *1090*. Ancestry.com.

[cccxxxi] Ancestry.com. *New Jersey, Births and Christenings Index, 1660-1931* [database on-line]. Provo, UT, USA: Ancestry.com Operations, Inc., 2011.

[cccxxxii] Ancestry.com. *New Jersey, Deaths and Burials Index, 1798-1971* [database on-line]. Provo, UT, USA: Ancestry.com Operations, Inc., 2011.

[cccxxxiii] Social Security Administration. *Social Security Death Index, Master File*. Social Security Administration

[cccxxxiv] Historical Society of Pennsylvania; Philadelphia, Pennsylvania; Collection Name: *Historic Pennsylvania Church and Town Records*; Reel: *793*

[cccxxxv] "New Jersey Births and Christenings, 1660-1931." Index. FamilySearch, Salt Lake City, Utah, 2009, 2010. Index entries derived from digital copies of original and compiled records.

[cccxxxvi] Social Security Administration. *Social Security Death Index, Master File*. Social Security Administration.

[cccxxxvii] Year: *1930*; Census Place: *Woodbury, Gloucester, New Jersey*; Roll: *1346*; Page: *1A*; Enumeration District:*0045*; Image: *464.0*; FHL microfilm: *2341081*

[cccxxxviii] Year: *1930*; Census Place: *Woodbury, Gloucester, New Jersey*; Roll: *1346*; Page: *1A*; Enumeration District:*0045*; Image: *464.0*; FHL microfilm: *2341081*

[cccxxxix] "New Jersey Births and Christenings, 1660-1931." Index. FamilySearch, Salt Lake City, Utah, 2009, 2010. Index entries derived from digital copies of original and compiled records.

[cccxl] Social Security Administration. *Social Security Death Index, Master File*. Social Security Administration

[cccxli] Church Records. Greater New Jersey United Methodist Church Commission on Archives and History, Madison, New Jersey.

[cccxlii] Social Security Administration. *Social Security Death Index, Master File*. Social Security Administration.

[cccxliii] Social Security Administration. *Social Security Death Index, Master File*. Social Security Administration.

[cccxliv] Historical Society of Pennsylvania; Philadelphia, Pennsylvania; Collection Name: *Historic Pennsylvania Church and Town Records*

[cccxlv] Ancestry.com. *U.S., Social Security Applications and Claims Index, 1936-2007* [database on-line]. Provo, UT, USA: Ancestry.com Operations, Inc., 2015.

[cccxlvi] Year: *1910*; Census Place: *Manhattan Ward 12, New York, New York*; Roll: *T624_1021*; Page: *5B*; Enumeration District: *0516*; FHL microfilm: *1375034*

[cccxlvii] Ancestry.com. *Massachusetts, Birth Records, 1840-1915* [database on-line]. Provo, UT, USA: Ancestry.com Operations, Inc., 2013.

[cccxlviii] Virginia, Deaths, 1912–2014. Virginia Department of Health, Richmond, Virginia.

[cccxlix] "New Jersey Births and Christenings, 1660-1931." Index. FamilySearch, Salt Lake City, Utah, 2009, 2010. Index entries derived from digital copies of original and compiled records.

[cccl] England, Aquila B., Rev. Handwritten England family tree. England family file: Gloucester Historical Society, Woodbury, NJ.

[cccli] "New Jersey Deaths and Burials, 1720–1971." Index. FamilySearch, Salt Lake City, Utah, 2009, 2010. Index entries derived from digital copies of original and compiled records.

[ccclii] Kentucky. *Kentucky Birth, Marriage and Death Records – Microfilm (1852-1910)*. Microfilm rolls #994027-994058. Kentucky Department for Libraries and Archives, Frankfort, Kentucky.

[cccliii] England, Aquila B., Rev. Handwritten England family tree. England family file: Gloucester Historical Society, Woodbury, NJ.

cccliv Kentucky. *Kentucky Birth, Marriage and Death Records – Microfilm (1852-1910)*. Microfilm rolls #994027-994058. Kentucky Department for Libraries and Archives, Frankfort, Kentucky.

ccclv Pennsylvania (State). Death certificates, 1906–1963. Series 11.90 (1,905 cartons). Records of the Pennsylvania Department of Health, Record Group 11. Pennsylvania Historical and Museum Commission, Harrisburg, Pennsylvania.

ccclvi "Pennsylvania, Philadelphia Marriage Index, 1885–1951." Index. FamilySearch, Salt Lake City, Utah, 2009. Philadelphia County Pennsylvania Clerk of the Orphans' Court. "Pennsylvania, Philadelphia marriage license index, 1885-1951." Clerk of the Orphans' Court, Philadelphia, Pennsylvania.

ccclvii *Officer Down Memorial Page*. Officer Down Memorial Page, Inc. (http://www.odmp.org): accessed 3 November 2014.

ccclviii Supporting Heroes Foundation, Inc. *Officer Down Memorial Page*. Officer Down Memorial Page, Inc. (http://www.odmp.org): accessed 4 August 2016.

ccclix "New Jersey, Births, 1670-1980," database, *FamilySearch*(https://familysearch.org/ark:/61903/1:1:FC18-9FP : 8 April 2016), Oscar England, 08 Feb 1868; citing Gloucester, Camden, New Jersey, United States, Division of Archives and Record Management, New Jersey Department of State, Trenton.; FHL microfilm 494,161.

ccclx"Illinois Deaths and Stillbirths, 1916-1947," database, *FamilySearch*(https://familysearch.org/ark:/61903/1:1:N3Z4-WLL : 27 December 2014), Oscar B. England, 26 Apr 1937; Public Board of Health, Archives, Springfield; FHL microfilm 1,786,730.

ccclxi "Illinois, Cook County Marriages, 1871-1920," database, *FamilySearch*(https://familysearch.org/ark:/61903/1:1:N7DK-LHZ : 26 December 2014), Oscar Bruce England and Frieda Ruedz, 27 Jun 1892; citing Cook, Illinois, , Cook County Courthouse, Chicago; FHL microfilm 1,030,215.

ccclxii Year: *1900*; Census Place: *Chicago Ward 15, Cook, Illinois*; Roll: *264*; Page: *15B*; Enumeration District: *0479*; FHL microfilm: *1240264*

Year: *1900*; Census Place: *Chicago Ward 15, Cook, Illinois*; Roll: *264*; Page: *15B*; Enumeration District: *0479*; FHL microfilm: *1240264*ccclxiii

ccclxiv 11 Mar 1948, Page 2 - Belvidere Daily Republican at Newspapers.com

ccclxv Personal correspondence: Dorothy England Venables to Lorraine Venables Goodwillie, 14 Aug, unknown year.

ccclxvi Ancestry.com. *U.S., Find A Grave Index, 1600s-Current* [database on-line]. Provo, UT, USA: Ancestry.com Operations, Inc., 2012.

ccclxviiAncestry.com. *U.S., Find A Grave Index, 1600s-Current* [database on-line]. Provo, UT, USA: Ancestry.com Operations, Inc., 2012.

ccclxviii personal correspondence, email, jean bean west, 10 Mar 2010

ccclxix United States, Selective Service System. *World War I Selective Service System Draft Registration Cards, 1917-1918*. Washington, D.C.: National Archives and Records Administration. M1509, 4,582 rolls. Imaged from Family History Library microfilm.

ccclxx Social Security Administration. *Social Security Death Index, Master File*. Social Security Administration.

ccclxxi United States, Selective Service System. *World War I Selective Service System Draft Registration Cards, 1917-1918*. Washington, D.C.: National Archives and Records Administration. M1509, 4,582 rolls. Imaged from Family History Library microfilm.

ccclxxiiSocial Security Administration. *Social Security Death Index, Master File*. Social Security Administration.

ccclxxiii Social Security Applications and Claims, 1936-2007.

ccclxxiv Social Security Administration. *Social Security Death Index, Master File*. Social Security Administration.

ccclxxv Personal correspondence, collection of the author.

ccclxxvi United States, Selective Service System. *World War I Selective Service System Draft Registration Cards, 1917-1918*. Washington, D.C.: National Archives and Records Administration. M1509, 4,582 rolls. Imaged from Family History Library microfilm.

ccclxxvii Ancestry.com. *Cook County, Illinois Marriage Indexes, 1912-1942* [database on-line]. Provo, UT, USA: Ancestry.com Operations, Inc., 2011.

ccclxxviii State of Florida. *Florida Death Index, 1877-1998*. Florida: Florida Department of Health, Office of Vital Records, 1998.

ccclxxix Social Security Administration. *Social Security Death Index, Master File*. Social Security Administration.

ccclxxx 1 Apr 1953, Page 8 - Belvidere Daily Republican at Newspapers.com

ccclxxxi Winnebago County Clerk, comp. *Winnebago County Clerk Genealogy Records*. Winnebago, IL: Winnebago County Clerk, 2008.

ccclxxxii Winnebago County Clerk, comp. *Winnebago County Clerk Genealogy Records*. Winnebago, IL: Winnebago County Clerk, 2008.

ccclxxxiii The National Archives at St. Louis; St. Louis, Missouri; *Draft Registration Cards for Fourth Registration for Illinois, 04/27/1942 - 04/27/1942*; NAI Number: *623284*; Record Group Title: *Records of the Selective Service System*; Record Group Number: *147*

ccclxxxiv Social Security Administration. *Social Security Death Index, Master File*. Social Security Administration.

ccclxxxv Social Security Administration. *Social Security Death Index, Master File*. Social Security Administration.

ccclxxxvi Social Security Administration. *Social Security Death Index, Master File*. Social Security Administration.

ccclxxxvii Social Security Administration. *Social Security Death Index, Master File*. Social Security Administration

ccclxxxviii 20 Jun 1931, Page 8 - Belvidere Daily Republican at Newspapers.com

ccclxxxix National Archives and Records Administration (NARA); Washington, D.C.; *Soundex Index to Naturalization Petitions for the United States District and Circuit Courts, Northern District of Illinois and Immigration and Naturalization Service District 9, 1840-1950 (M1285)*; Microfilm Serial: *M1285*; Microfilm Roll: *172*

cccxc Ancestry.com. *U.S., Find A Grave Index, 1600s-Current* [database on-line]. Provo, UT, USA: Ancestry.com Operations, Inc., 2012.

cccxci Year: *1850*; Census Place: *Harrison, Gloucester, New Jersey*; Roll: *M432_451*; Page: *37A*; Image: *80*

cccxcii Ancestry.com. *Philadelphia, Pennsylvania, Death Certificates Index, 1803-1915* [database on-line]. Provo, UT, USA: Ancestry.com Operations, Inc., 2011.

cccxciii England, Aquila B., Rev. Handwritten England family tree. England family file: Gloucester Historical Society, Woodbury, NJ.

cccxciv Ancestry.com. *U.S., Find A Grave Index, 1600s-Current* [database on-line]. Provo, UT, USA: Ancestry.com Operations, Inc., 2012.

cccxcv Year: *1870*; Census Place: *Philadelphia Ward 20 District 67, Philadelphia, Pennsylvania*; Roll: *M593_1407*; Page: *568B*; Image: *11220*; Family History Library Film: *552906*

cccxcvi Year: *1870*; Census Place: *Philadelphia Ward 20 District 67, Philadelphia, Pennsylvania*; Roll: *M593_1407*; Page: *568B*; Image: *11222*; Family History Library Film: *552906*

cccxcvii "Pennsylvania, Philadelphia City Death Certificates, 1803–1915." Index. FamilySearch, Salt Lake City, Utah, 2008, 2010. From originals housed at the Philadelphia City Archives. "Death Records.".

cccxcviii "Pennsylvania, Philadelphia City Births, 1860-1906," database with images, *FamilySearch*(https://familysearch.org/ark:/61903/1:1:VBT4-7SL : 8 December 2014), Annie E. Cramer, 29 Jan 1871; citing bk 1871 p 153, Department of Records; FHL microfilm 1,289,313.

cccxcix Berks County Pennsylvania Register of Wills. *City of Reading PA Death Records 1873-1905*. Reading, PA, USA. Berksregofwills.com.

cd "Pennsylvania, Philadelphia Marriage Index, 1885–1951." Index. FamilySearch, Salt Lake City, Utah, 2009. Philadelphia County Pennsylvania Clerk of the Orphans' Court. "Pennsylvania, Philadelphia marriage license index, 1885-1951." Clerk of the Orphans' Court, Philadelphia, Pennsylvania.

cdi Year: *1900*; Census Place: *Reading Ward 5, Berks, Pennsylvania*; Roll: *1378*; Page: *8B*; Enumeration District:*0057*; FHL microfilm: *1241378*

cdii Ancestry.com. *Pennsylvania, Death Certificates, 1906-1963* [database on-line]. Provo, UT, USA: Ancestry.com Operations, Inc., 2014.

cdiii Book Title: *The descendants of Matthew Gill. Ancestry.com. North America, Family Histories, 1500-2000 [database on-line]. Provo, UT, USA: Ancestry.com Operations, Inc., 2016.*

cdiv Book Title: *The descendants of Matthew Gill. Ancestry.com. North America, Family Histories, 1500-2000 [database on-line]. Provo, UT, USA: Ancestry.com Operations, Inc., 2016.*

cdv Sheets, Oliver. "This was Paulsboro." *The Record*. May 13, 1965.

cdvi *The descendants of Matthew Gill.   Ancestry.com. North America, Family Histories, 1500-2000 [database on-line]. Provo, UT, USA: Ancestry.com Operations, Inc., 2016.*

cdvii "New Jersey Deaths and Burials, 1720–1971." Index. FamilySearch, Salt Lake City, Utah, 2009, 2010. Index entries derived from digital copies of original and compiled records.

cdviii *The descendants of Matthew Gill.   Ancestry.com. North America, Family Histories, 1500-2000 [database on-line]. Provo, UT, USA: Ancestry.com Operations, Inc., 2016.*

cdix Social Security Administration. *Social Security Death Index, Master File*. Social Security Administration

cdx *Find A Grave*. Find A Grave. http://www.findagrave.com/cgi-bin/fg.cgi.

cdxi *Find A Grave*. Find A Grave. http://www.findagrave.com/cgi-bin/fg.cgi.

cdxii *Find A Grave*. Find A Grave. http://www.findagrave.com/cgi-bin/fg.cgi.

cdxiii *Missouri Birth Records [Microfilm]*. Jefferson City, MO, USA: Missouri State Archives.

cdxiv State of Florida. *Florida Death Index, 1877-1998*. Florida: Florida Department of Health, Office of Vital Records, 1998.

cdxv Ancestry.com. *Florida Marriage Indexes, 1822-1875 and 1927-2001* [database on-line]. Provo, UT, USA: Ancestry.com Operations Inc, 2006.

cdxvi *Find A Grave*. Find A Grave. http://www.findagrave.com/cgi-bin/fg.cgi.

cdxvii *Missouri Birth Records [Microfilm]*. Jefferson City, MO, USA: Missouri State Archives.

[cdxviii] "Illinois, Cook County, Birth Certificates, 1871-1940,"
database, *FamilySearch*(https://familysearch.org/ark:/61903/1:1:NQY7-PGZ : 18 May 2016), Turner Kendall England, 05 Aug 1906; citing Chicago, Cook, Illinois, United States, reference/certificate 4155, Cook County Courthouse, Chicago; FHL microfilm 1,288,120.

[cdxix] "Illinois, Cook County Deaths, 1878-1994," database, *FamilySearch*(https://familysearch.org/ark:/61903/1:1:Q237-CLYM : 20 May 2016), Turner Kendall England, 14 Apr 1907; citing Chicago, Cook, Illinois, United States, source reference 3983, record number , Cook County Courthouse, Chicago; FHL microfilm 1,239,751.

[cdxx] Ancestry.com. *U.S., Find A Grave Index, 1600s-Current* [database on-line]. Provo, UT, USA: Ancestry.com Operations, Inc., 2012.

[cdxxi] United States. *Nonpopulation Census Schedules for New Jersey, 1850-1880: Mortality.*M1810, 4 rolls. National Archives and Records Administration, Washington D.C.

[cdxxii] Year: *1860*; Census Place: *Woolwich, Gloucester, New Jersey*; Roll: *M653_691*; Page: *409*; Image: *413*; Family History Library Film: *803691*

[cdxxiii] *Probate Records*; Author: *New Jersey. Surrogate's Court (Camden County)*; Probate Place: *Camden, New Jersey*

[cdxxiv] Year: *1860*; Census Place: *Woolwich, Gloucester, New Jersey*; Roll: *M653_691*; Page: *409*; Image: *413*; Family History Library Film: *803691*

[cdxxv] "New Jersey Births and Christenings, 1660-1980,"
database, *FamilySearch*(https://familysearch.org/ark:/61903/1:1:FCTW-GMK : 12 December 2014), Crawford, 17 Oct 1855; citing Gloucester, New Jersey, reference v O p 106; FHL microfilm 584,565.

[cdxxvi] "New Jersey Deaths and Burials, 1720-1988," database, *FamilySearch*(https://familysearch.org/ark:/61903/1:1:FZHC-W8Q : 12 December 2014), Oliver Crawford in entry for Crawford, 17 Oct 1855; citing Near Repaupo, Woolwich Twp., Gloucester, N. J., reference 1 Jun 1855-1856; FHL microfilm 1,510,236.

[cdxxvii] "New Jersey Deaths and Burials, 1720-1988," database, *FamilySearch*(https://familysearch.org/ark:/61903/1:1:FZHC-WTT : 12 December 2014), Oliver Crawford in entry for Crawford, 02 Feb 1856; citing Woolwich Twp., Gloucester, N. J., reference 1 Jun 1856-1857; FHL microfilm 1,510,236.

[cdxxviii] Year: *1860*; Census Place: *Woolwich, Gloucester, New Jersey*; Roll: *M653_691*; Page: *409*; Image: *413*; Family History Library Film: *803691*

[cdxxix] Year: *1870*; Census Place: *Upper Penns Neck, Salem, New Jersey*; Roll: *M593_887*; Page: *275B*; Image:*301747*; Family History Library Film: *552386*

[cdxxx] Historical Society of Pennsylvania; Philadelphia, Pennsylvania; Collection Name: *Historic Pennsylvania Church and Town Records*; Reel: *1096*

[cdxxxi] Year: *1880*; Census Place: *Camden, Camden, New Jersey*; Roll: *774*; Family History Film: *1254774*; Page:*215C*; Enumeration District: *047*; Image: *0072*

[cdxxxii] "New Jersey Births and Christenings, 1660-1980,"
database, *FamilySearch*(https://familysearch.org/ark:/61903/1:1:FCT4-ZH4 : 12 December 2014), Oliver Crawford in entry for Crawford, 11 Aug 1862; citing Centre Square, Gloucester, New Jersey, reference v O p 204; FHL microfilm 584,565.

[cdxxxiii] Year: *1870*; Census Place: *Upper Penns Neck, Salem, New Jersey*; Roll: *M593_887*; Page: *275B*; Image:*301748*; Family History Library Film: *552386*

[cdxxxiv] "New Jersey Births and Christenings, 1660-1931." Index. FamilySearch, Salt Lake City, Utah, 2009, 2010. Index entries derived from digital copies of original and compiled records.

[cdxxxv] Year: *1870*; Census Place: *Upper Penns Neck, Salem, New Jersey*; Roll: *M593_887*; Page: *275B*; Image:*301746*; Family History Library Film: *552386*

[cdxxxvi] Ancestry.com. *New Jersey, Deaths and Burials Index, 1798-1971* [database on-line]. Provo, UT, USA: Ancestry.com Operations, Inc., 2011.

[cdxxxvii] Year: *1850*; Census Place: *Woolwich, Gloucester, New Jersey*; Roll: *M432_451*; Page: *140A*; Image: *286*

[cdxxxviii] "New Jersey Births and Christenings, 1660-1931." Index. FamilySearch, Salt Lake City, Utah, 2009, 2010. Index entries derived from digital copies of original and compiled records.

[cdxxxix] Ancestry.com. *U.S., Find A Grave Index, 1600s-Current* [database on-line]. Provo, UT, USA: Ancestry.com Operations, Inc., 2012.

[cdxl] Year: *1900*; Census Place: *Oldmans, Salem, New Jersey*; Roll: *993*; Page: *6A*; Enumeration District: *0176*; FHL microfilm: *1240993*

[cdxli] "New Jersey Births and Christenings, 1660-1931." Index. FamilySearch, Salt Lake City, Utah, 2009, 2010. Index entries derived from digital copies of original and compiled records.

[cdxlii] Ancestry.com. *U.S., Find A Grave Index, 1600s-Current* [database on-line]. Provo, UT, USA: Ancestry.com Operations, Inc., 2012.

cdxliii Year: *1870*; Census Place: *Woolwich, Gloucester, New Jersey*; Roll: *M593_862*; Page: *247A*; Image: *415237*; Family History Library Film: *552361*

cdxliv Year: *1870*; Census Place: *Woolwich, Gloucester, New Jersey*; Roll: *M593_862*; Page: *247A*; Image: *415238*; Family History Library Film: *552361*

cdxlv *Find A Grave*. Find A Grave. http://www.findagrave.com/cgi-bin/fg.cgi.

cdxlvi Year: *1910*; Census Place: *Pleasantville Boro Ward 1, Atlantic, New Jersey*; Roll: *T624_867*; Page: *20B*; Enumeration District: *0037*; FHL microfilm: *1374880*

cdxlvii "New Jersey Births and Christenings, 1660-1931." Index. FamilySearch, Salt Lake City, Utah, 2009, 2010. Index entries derived from digital copies of original and compiled records.

"New Jersey Deaths and Burials, 1720–1971." Index. FamilySearch, Salt Lake City, Utah, 2009, 2010. Index entries derived from digital copies of original and compiled records.cdxlviii

cdxlix Year: *1910*; Census Place: *Pleasantville Boro Ward 1, Atlantic, New Jersey*; Roll: *T624_867*; Page: *20B*; Enumeration District: *0037*; FHL microfilm: *1374880*

cdl Historical Society of Pennsylvania; Philadelphia, Pennsylvania; Collection Name: *Historic Pennsylvania Church and Town Records*; Reel: *1101*

Year: *1880*; Census Place: *Harrisonville, Gloucester, New Jersey*; Roll: *781*; Family History Film: *1254781*; Page: *403D*; Enumeration District: *095*; Image: *0449*cdli

cdlii *Ancestry.com. Web: Burlington County, New Jersey, Death Index, 1814-2010 [database on-line]. Provo, UT, USA: Ancestry.com Operations, Inc., 2011.*

cdliii "New Jersey, Deaths, 1670-1988," database, *FamilySearch*(https://familysearch.org/ark:/61903/1:1:Q2S8-932H : 8 April 2016), Florence Myers, Dec 1874; citing Woolwich, Gloucester, New Jersey, United States, Division of Archives and Record Management, New Jersey Department of State, Trenton.; FHL microfilm 584,598.

cdliv "New Jersey, Deaths, 1670-1988," database, *FamilySearch*(https://familysearch.org/ark:/61903/1:1:FZDH-G62 : 8 April 2016), Harry Myers, 11 Nov 1876; citing , Auburn, New Jersey, United States, Division of Archives and Record Management, New Jersey Department of State, Trenton.; FHL microfilm 494,141.

cdlv "New Jersey, Births, 1670-1980," database, *FamilySearch*(https://familysearch.org/ark:/61903/1:1:FC58-P4K : 8 April 2016), Saml. B. Myers in entry for Clara Myers, 05 Nov 1875; citing Auburn, Gloucester, New Jersey, United States, Division of Archives and Record Management, New Jersey Department of State, Trenton.; FHL microfilm 494,179.

cdlvi "New Jersey, Births, 1670-1980," database, *FamilySearch*(https://familysearch.org/ark:/61903/1:1:FCJN-H9J : 8 April 2016), Saml. B. Myers in entry for Ella Myers, 05 Sep 1877; citing Woolich, Gloucester, New Jersey, United States, Division of Archives and Record Management, New Jersey Department of State, Trenton.; FHL microfilm 494,183.

cdlvii Year: *1860*; Census Place: *Woolwich, Gloucester, New Jersey*; Roll: *M653_691*; Page: *410*; Image: *414*; Family History Library Film: *803691*

cdlviii Historical Society of Pennsylvania; Philadelphia, Pennsylvania; Collection Name: *Historic Pennsylvania Church and Town Records*; Reel: *779*

cdlix "New Jersey Deaths and Burials, 1720-1988," database, FamilySearch (https://familysearch.org/ark:/61903/1:1:FZCC-GFF : 12 December 2014), Priscilla Roberts, 16 Feb 1889; citing Camden City, Camden, New Jersey, reference v 27 p 150; FHL microfilm 589,316.

cdlx http://www.dvrbs.com/people/camdenpeople-drjosepheroberts.htm

cdlxi "New Jersey Births and Christenings, 1660-1931." Index. FamilySearch, Salt Lake City, Utah, 2009, 2010. Index entries derived from digital copies of original and compiled records.

cdlxii Year: *1910*; Census Place: *Camden Ward 4, Camden, New Jersey*; Roll: *T624_872*; Page: *6A*; Enumeration District: *0023*; FHL microfilm: *1374885*

cdlxiii Year: *1900*; Census Place: *Camden Ward 4, Camden, New Jersey*; Roll: *958*; Page: *8B*; Enumeration District:*0046*; FHL microfilm: *1240958*

cdlxiv "New York, New York City Municipal Deaths, 1795-1949," database, FamilySearch (https://familysearch.org/ark:/61903/1:1:2WV1-W27 : 20 March 2015), Joseph English Roberts in entry for Joanna Roberts Brown, 25 Jan 1931; citing Death, Brooklyn, Kings, New York

cdlxv "New Jersey, Births, 1670-1980," database, *FamilySearch* (https://familysearch.org/ark:/61903/1:1:FC2Y-F58 : 8 April 2016), Wm. John Brown, 05 Mar 1871; citing Vineland, Cumberland, New Jersey, United States, Division of Archives and Record Management, New Jersey Department of State, Trenton.; FHL microfilm 494,168.

cdlxvi Year: *1900*; Census Place: *Camden Ward 4, Camden, New Jersey*; Roll: *958*; Page: *8B*; Enumeration District:*0046*; FHL microfilm: *1240958*

cdlxvii Year: *1930*; Census Place: *Haddonfield, Camden, New Jersey*; Roll: *1324*; Page: *8B*; Enumeration District:*0135*; Image: *252.0*; FHL microfilm: *2341059*

cdlxviii "New Jersey Births and Christenings, 1660-1931." Index. FamilySearch, Salt Lake City, Utah, 2009, 2010. Index entries derived from digital copies of original and compiled records.

cdlxix http://www.dvrbs.com/people/camdenpeople-drjosepheroberts.htm

cdlxx Social Security Administration. *Social Security Death Index, Master File*. Social Security Administration.

cdlxxi "New Jersey Births and Christenings, 1660-1931." Index. FamilySearch, Salt Lake City, Utah, 2009, 2010. Index entries derived from digital copies of original and compiled records.

cdlxxii "New Jersey Deaths and Burials, 1720–1971." Index. FamilySearch, Salt Lake City, Utah, 2009, 2010. Index entries derived from digital copies of original and compiled records.

cdlxxiii "New Jersey Births and Christenings, 1660-1931." Index. FamilySearch, Salt Lake City, Utah, 2009, 2010. Index entries derived from digital copies of original and compiled records.

cdlxxiv "New Jersey Births and Christenings, 1660-1931." Index. FamilySearch, Salt Lake City, Utah, 2009, 2010. Index entries derived from digital copies of original and compiled records.

cdlxxv Year: *1850*; Census Place: *Woolwich, Gloucester, New Jersey*; Roll: *M432_451*; Page: *155A*; Image: *318*

cdlxxvi Year: *1910*; Census Place: *Camden Ward 10, Camden, New Jersey*; Roll: *T624_873*; Page: *8B*; Enumeration District: *0069*; FHL microfilm: *1374886*

cdlxxvii Greater New Jersey Annual Conference Commission on Archives and History; Madison, New Jersey; Description: *Methodist Church Records*

cdlxxviii Year: *1850*; Census Place: *Upper Penns Neck, Salem, New Jersey*; Roll: *M432_462*; Page: *188A*; Image: *376*

cdlxxix Year: *1900*; Census Place: *Camden Ward 6, Camden, New Jersey*; Roll: *958*; Page: *6A*; Enumeration District:*0062*; FHL microfilm: *1240958*

cdlxxx Year: *1880*; Census Place: *Camden, Camden, New Jersey*; Roll: *774*; Family History Film: *1254774*; Page:*207C*; Enumeration District: *047*; Image: *0056*

cdlxxxi Public Archives Commission, Delaware Public Archives. *Marriage Records, 1744-1912*. Dover, Delaware: Delaware Public Archives. Record Group # RG 1325; Subgroup # 003; Series # 004.

cdlxxxii "Pennsylvania, Philadelphia City Death Certificates, 1803-1915," database with images, *FamilySearch* (https://familysearch.org/ark:/61903/1:1:JK95-62N : 9 December 2014), Hattie Harbeson, 20 Oct 1899; citing cn 7926, Philadelphia City Archives and Historical Society of Pennsylvania, Philadelphia; FHL microfilm 1,787,216.

cdlxxxiii *Find A Grave*. Find A Grave. http://www.findagrave.com/cgi-bin/fg.cgi.

cdlxxxiv Year: *1910*; Census Place: *Camden Ward 10, Camden, New Jersey*; Roll: *T624_873*; Page: *8B*; Enumeration District: *0069*; FHL microfilm: *1374886*

cdlxxxv "New Jersey Births and Christenings, 1660-1931." Index. FamilySearch, Salt Lake City, Utah, 2009, 2010. Index entries derived from digital copies of original and compiled records.

cdlxxxvi Newspapers.com - Courier-Post - 23 Jun 1953, Tue - Page 4

cdlxxxvii "New Jersey Births and Christenings, 1660-1931." Index. FamilySearch, Salt Lake City, Utah, 2009, 2010. Index entries derived from digital copies of original and compiled records.

cdlxxxviii Ancestry.com. *Pennsylvania, Death Certificates, 1906-1963* [database on-line]. Provo, UT, USA: Ancestry.com Operations, Inc., 2014.

cdlxxxix Year: *1900*; Census Place: *Greenwich, Gloucester, New Jersey*; Roll: *971*; Page: *10A*; Enumeration District:*0157*; FHL microfilm: *1240971*

cdxc Year: *1870*; Census Place: *Upper Penns Neck, Salem, New Jersey*; Roll: *M593_887*; Page: *275A*; Image:*301705*; Family History Library Film: *552386*

cdxci Year: *1880*; Census Place: *Camden, Camden, New Jersey*; Roll: *774*; Family History Film: *1254774*; Page:*190C*; Enumeration District: *046*; Image: *0021*

cdxcii "New Jersey State Census, 1885," database, *FamilySearch*(https://familysearch.org/ark:/61903/1:1:654K-H2M : 18 November 2014), Frank J Roberts, Camden, Ward 04, Camden, New Jersey; citing p. 262, Department of State, Trenton; FHL microfilm 888,604.

cdxciii Pennsylvania (State). Death certificates, 1906–1963. Series 11.90 (1,905 cartons). Records of the Pennsylvania Department of Health, Record Group 11. Pennsylvania Historical and Museum Commission, Harrisburg, Pennsylvania.

cdxciv Pennsylvania (State). Death certificates, 1906–1963. Series 11.90 (1,905 cartons). Records of the Pennsylvania Department of Health, Record Group 11. Pennsylvania Historical and Museum Commission, Harrisburg, Pennsylvania.

cdxcv "Pennsylvania, Philadelphia Marriage Index, 1885–1951." Index. FamilySearch, Salt Lake City, Utah, 2009. Philadelphia County Pennsylvania Clerk of the Orphans' Court. "Pennsylvania, Philadelphia marriage license index, 1885-1951." Clerk of the Orphans' Court, Philadelphia, Pennsylvania.

cdxcvi United States, Selective Service System. *World War I Selective Service System Draft Registration Cards, 1917-1918*. Washington, D.C.: National Archives and Records Administration. M1509, 4,582 rolls. Imaged from Family History Library microfilm.

cdxcvii "New Jersey, Births, 1670-1980," database, *FamilySearch*(https://familysearch.org/ark:/61903/1:1:FCGS-X86 : 8 April 2016), Rena F. Roberts, 01 Mar 1880; citing Camden City, Camden, New Jersey, United States, Division of Archives and Record Management, New Jersey Department of State, Trenton.; FHL microfilm 494,188.

cdxcviii Ancestry.com. *Philadelphia, Pennsylvania, Death Certificates Index, 1803-1915* [database on-line]. Provo, UT, USA: Ancestry.com Operations, Inc., 2011.

cdxcix Historical Society of Pennsylvania; Philadelphia, Pennsylvania; Collection Name: *Historic Pennsylvania Church and Town Records*; Reel: *387*

d Ancestry.com. *Pennsylvania, Death Certificates, 1906-1963* [database on-line]. Provo, UT, USA: Ancestry.com Operations, Inc., 2014.

di Ancestry.com. *Philadelphia, Pennsylvania, Marriage Index, 1885-1951* [database on-line]. Provo, UT, USA: Ancestry.com Operations, Inc., 2011.

dii Pennsylvania (State). Death certificates, 1906–1963. Series 11.90 (1,905 cartons). Records of the Pennsylvania Department of Health, Record Group 11. Pennsylvania Historical and Museum Commission, Harrisburg, Pennsylvania.

diii Historical Society of Pennsylvania; Philadelphia, Pennsylvania; Collection Name: *Historic Pennsylvania Church and Town Records*; Reel: *386*

div : Pennsylvania (State). Death certificates, 1906–1963. Series 11.90 (1,905 cartons). Records of the Pennsylvania Department of Health, Record Group 11. Pennsylvania Historical and Museum Commission, Harrisburg, Pennsylvania.

dv Year: *1900*; Census Place: *Pennsauken, Camden, New Jersey*; Roll: *959*; Page: *3A*; Enumeration District:*0104*; FHL microfilm: *1240959*

dvi Connecticut Department of Health. *Connecticut Death Index, 1949-2012* [database on-line]. Provo, UT, USA: Ancestry.com Operations, Inc., 2003.

dvii "Pennsylvania, Philadelphia Marriage Index, 1885–1951." Index. FamilySearch, Salt Lake City, Utah, 2009. Philadelphia County Pennsylvania Clerk of the Orphans' Court. "Pennsylvania, Philadelphia marriage license index, 1885-1951." Clerk of the Orphans' Court, Philadelphia, Pennsylvania.

dviii The National Archives at St. Louis; St. Louis, Missouri; *Draft Registration Cards for Fourth Registration for Pennsylvania, 04/27/1942 - 04/27/1942*; NAI Number: *563728*; Record Group Title: *Records of the Selective Service System*; Record Group Number: *147*

dix Connecticut Department of Health. *Connecticut Death Index, 1949-2012* [database on-line]. Provo, UT, USA: Ancestry.com Operations, Inc., 2003.

dx "Pennsylvania, Philadelphia City Death Certificates, 1803-1915," database with images,*FamilySearch* (https://familysearch.org/ark:/61903/1:1:JKSD-1MH : 9 December 2014), James Taws in entry for Willie Taws, 15 Mar 1888; citing , Philadelphia City Archives and Historical Society of Pennsylvania, Philadelphia; FHL microfilm 2,079,093.

dxi State of Florida. *Florida Death Index, 1877-1998*. Florida: Florida Department of Health, Office of Vital Records, 1998.

dxii Year: *1900*; Census Place: *Upper Darby, Delaware, Pennsylvania*; Roll: *1406*; Page: *8A*; Enumeration District:*0191*; FHL microfilm: *1241406*

dxiii Year: *1910*; Census Place: *Philadelphia Ward 44, Philadelphia, Pennsylvania*; Roll: *T624_1412*; Page: *1B*; Enumeration District: *1138*; FHL microfilm: *1375425*

dxiv "Pennsylvania, Philadelphia City Death Certificates, 1803–1915." Index. FamilySearch, Salt Lake City, Utah, 2008, 2010. From originals housed at the Philadelphia City Archives. "Death Records.".

dxv Ancestry.com. *U.S., Find A Grave Index, 1600s-Current* [database on-line]. Provo, UT, USA: Ancestry.com Operations, Inc., 2012.

dxvi Publication Number: M1279. Publication Title: <u>Case Files of Approved Pension Applications of Widows and Other Dependents of Civil War and Later Navy Veterans (Navy Widows' Certificates), 1861-1910</u> Publisher: NARA. National Archives Catalog ID: **561929**. National Archives Catalog Title: Case Files of Approved Pension Applications of Widows and Other Dependents of Navy Veterans, compiled ca. 1861 - ca. 1910. Record Group: 15. Date: 1861-1920

dxvii "Pennsylvania, Philadelphia City Births, 1860-1906," database with images, *FamilySearch*(https://familysearch.org/ark:/61903/1:1:V1MV-FLY : 8 December 2014), Anna Glessner England, 05 Dec 1866; citing bk 1866 p 405, Department of Records; FHL microfilm 1,289,310.

dxviii "Pennsylvania, Philadelphia City Death Certificates, 1803-1915," database with images, *FamilySearch* (https://familysearch.org/ark:/61903/1:1:VK87-8YH : 9 December 2014), Ann G. England, 13 Dec 1883; citing v 2 p 522, Philadelphia City Archives and Historical Society of Pennsylvania, Philadelphia; FHL microfilm 1,003,709.

dxix Year: *1870*; Census Place: *Philadelphia Ward 1 District 2, Philadelphia, Pennsylvania*; Roll: *M593_1387*; Page:*541A*; Image: *288426*; Family History Library Film: *552886*

dxx Pennsylvania (State). Death certificates, 1906–1963. Series 11.90 (1,905 cartons). Records of the Pennsylvania Department of Health, Record Group 11. Pennsylvania Historical and Museum Commission, Harrisburg, Pennsylvania.

dxxi Social Security Applications and Claims, 1936-2007.

dxxii Historical Society of Pennsylvania; Philadelphia, Pennsylvania; Collection Name: *Historic Pennsylvania Church and Town Records*

dxxiii Pennsylvania (State). Death certificates, 1906–1963. Series 11.90 (1,905 cartons). Records of the Pennsylvania Department of Health, Record Group 11. Pennsylvania Historical and Museum Commission, Harrisburg, Pennsylvania.

dxxiv Year: *1900*; Census Place: *Philadelphia Ward 2, Philadelphia, Pennsylvania*; Roll: *1452*; Page: *9B*; Enumeration District: *0035*; FHL microfilm: *1241452*

dxxv Newspapers.com - Evening Public Ledger - 3 Jun 1921, Fri - Page 3

dxxvi "Pennsylvania, Philadelphia City Births, 1860-1906," database with images, *FamilySearch*(https://familysearch.org/ark:/61903/1:1:VB13-SWJ : 8 December 2014), Gustavus England in entry for Mary O. England, 27 Mar 1873; citing bk 1873 p 73, Department of Records; FHL microfilm 1,289,314.

dxxvii "Pennsylvania, Philadelphia City Death Certificates, 1803-1915," database with images,*FamilySearch* (https://familysearch.org/ark:/61903/1:1:J6S8-NPD : 9 December 2014), May O. England, 15 Jan 1879; citing , Philadelphia City Archives and Historical Society of Pennsylvania, Philadelphia; FHL microfilm 2,030,839.

dxxviii Historical Society of Pennsylvania; Philadelphia, Pennsylvania; Collection Name: *Historic Pennsylvania Church and Town Records*; Reel: *375*

dxxix Ancestry.com. *Pennsylvania and New Jersey, Church and Town Records, 1708-1985* [database on-line]. Provo, UT, USA: Ancestry.com Operations, Inc., 2011.

dxxx Historical Society of Pennsylvania; Philadelphia, Pennsylvania; Collection Name: *Historic Pennsylvania Church and Town Records*; Reel: *335*

dxxxi Ancestry.com. *Pennsylvania, Death Certificates, 1906-1963* [database on-line]. Provo, UT, USA: Ancestry.com Operations, Inc., 2014.

dxxxii Newspapers.com - The Times - 21 Apr 1891, Tue - Page 4

dxxxiii "Pennsylvania, Philadelphia City Death Certificates, 1803-1915," database with images, *FamilySearch* (https://familysearch.org/ark:/61903/1:1:JD26-CJJ : 9 December 2014), Joseph W. England in entry for Ethel Virginia England, 28 Jun 1894; citing cn 27258, Philadelphia City Archives and Historical Society of Pennsylvania, Philadelphia; FHL microfilm 1,871,872.

dxxxiv Social Security Administration. *Social Security Death Index, Master File*. Social Security Administration

dxxxv Ancestry.com. *U.S., Find A Grave Index, 1600s-Current* [database on-line]. Provo, UT, USA: Ancestry.com Operations, Inc., 2012.

dxxxvi Year: *1870*; Census Place: *Woolwich, Gloucester, New Jersey*; Roll: *M593_862*; Page: *247A*; Image: *415250*; Family History Library Film: *552361*

dxxxvii *Find A Grave*. Find A Grave. http://www.findagrave.com/cgi-bin/fg.cgi.

dxxxviii *Will Books*; Author: *New Jersey. Surrogate's Court (Gloucester County)*; Probate Place: *Gloucester, New Jersey*

dxxxix "New Jersey Births and Christenings, 1660-1980," database, *FamilySearch*(https://familysearch.org/ark:/61903/1:1:FCTW-G95 : 12 December 2014), William Hurff in entry for Hurff, 09 Oct 1855; citing Gloucester, New Jersey, reference v O p 106; FHL microfilm 584,565.

dxl *Find A Grave*. Find A Grave. http://www.findagrave.com/cgi-bin/fg.cgi.

dxli *Find A Grave*. Find A Grave. http://www.findagrave.com/cgi-bin/fg.cgi.

dxlii *Find A Grave*. Find A Grave. http://www.findagrave.com/cgi-bin/fg.cgi.

dxliii Year: *1900*; Census Place: *Washington, Gloucester, New Jersey*; Roll: *971*; Page: *5B*; Enumeration District:*0164*; FHL microfilm: *1240971*

dxliv "New Jersey Deaths and Burials, 1720–1971." Index. FamilySearch, Salt Lake City, Utah, 2009, 2010. Index entries derived from digital copies of original and compiled records.

dxlv Historical Society of Pennsylvania; Philadelphia, Pennsylvania; Collection Name: *Historic Pennsylvania Church and Town Records*; Reel: *779*

dxlvi Historical Society of Pennsylvania; Philadelphia, Pennsylvania; Collection Name: *Historic Pennsylvania Church and Town Records*; Reel: *778*

dxlvii Year: *1900*; Census Place: *Elmwood, Peoria, Illinois*; Roll: *333*; Page: *16A*; Enumeration District: *0074*; FHL microfilm: *1240333*

dxlviii Ancestry.com. *U.S., Find A Grave Index, 1600s-Current* [database on-line]. Provo, UT, USA: Ancestry.com Operations, Inc., 2012.

dxlix The History of Peoria County, Illinois: Containing a History of the Northwest--history of Illinois--history of the County, Its Early Settlement, Growth, Development, Resources. Chicago: Johnson Publishing. 1880

dl *Find A Grave*. Find A Grave. http://www.findagrave.com/cgi-bin/fg.cgi

dli Year: *1910*; Census Place: *Marquette Ward 3, Marquette, Michigan*; Roll: *T624_662*; Page: *13A*; Enumeration District: *0190*; FHL microfilm: *1374675*

dlii *Find A Grave*. Find A Grave. http://www.findagrave.com/cgi-bin/fg.cgi.

dliii Year: *1910*; Census Place: *Marquette Ward 3, Marquette, Michigan*; Roll: *T624_662*; Page: *13A*; Enumeration District: *0190*; FHL microfilm: *1374675*

dliv 17 Dec 1955, Page 5 - The Daily Standard at Newspapers.com

dlv 22 Nov 1954, Page 1 - The Daily Standard at Newspapers.com

dlvi 22 Nov 1954, Page 1 - The Daily Standard at Newspapers.com

dlvii 29 Aug 1959, Page 10 - The Daily Standard at Newspapers.com

dlviii 29 Aug 1959, Page 10 - The Daily Standard at Newspapers.com

dlix Year: *1900*; Census Place: *Brooklyn Ward 7, Kings, New York*; Roll: *1046*; Page: *5A*; Enumeration District:*0088*; FHL microfilm: *1241046*

dlx Year: *1900*; Census Place: *Brooklyn Ward 7, Kings, New York*; Roll: *1046*; Page: *5A*; Enumeration District:*0088*; FHL microfilm: *1241046*

dlxi Year: *1900*; Census Place: *Brooklyn Ward 7, Kings, New York*; Roll: *1046*; Page: *5A*; Enumeration District:*0088*; FHL microfilm: *1241046*

dlxii 18 Sep 1920, Page 16 - The Brooklyn Daily Eagle at Newspapers.com

dlxiii 13 Jun 1922, Page 3 - The Brooklyn Daily Eagle at Newspapers.com

dlxiv "New York, New York City Births, 1846-1909," database, *FamilySearch*(https://familysearch.org/ark:/61903/1:1:2WZH-7RG : 20 March 2015), Ella A Ollis England in entry for Benjamin F England, 19 Mar 1869; citing Manhattan, New York, New York, United States, reference yr 1869 p 171 New York Municipal Archives, New York; FHL microfilm 447,543.

dlxv "Pennsylvania, Philadelphia City Death Certificates, 1803–1915." Index. FamilySearch, Salt Lake City, Utah, 2008, 2010. From originals housed at the Philadelphia City Archives. "Death Records.".

dlxvi Census of the state of New York, for 1875. Microfilm. New York State Archives, Albany, New York.

dlxvii Year: *1870*; Census Place: *Brooklyn Ward 7, Kings, New York*; Roll: *M593_949*; Page: *359B*; Image: *365816*; Family History Library Film: *552448*

dlxviii 12 Apr 1902, Page 18 - Brooklyn Life at Newspapers.com

dlxix Social Security Administration. *Social Security Death Index, Master File*. Social Security Administration

dlxx Year: *1880*; Census Place: *Brooklyn, Kings, New York*; Roll: *844*; Family History Film: *1254844*; Page: *242D*; Enumeration District: *056*; Image: *0054*

dlxxi Ancestry.com. *New York, New York, Death Index, 1862-1948* [database on-line]. Provo, UT, USA: Ancestry.com Operations, Inc., 2014.

dlxxii Ancestry.com. *New York, New York, Marriage Index 1866-1937* [database on-line]. Provo, UT, USA: Ancestry.com Operations, Inc., 2014.

dlxxiii Year: *1900*; Census Place: *Brooklyn Ward 23, Kings, New York*; Roll: *1061*; Page: *18A*; Enumeration District:*0399*; FHL microfilm: *1241061*

dlxxiv Census of the state of New York, for 1875. Microfilm. New York State Archives, Albany, New York.

dlxxv *New York State Abstracts of World War I Military Service, 1917–1919*. Adjutant General's Office. Series B0808. New York State Archives, Albany, New York.

Ancestry.com. *New York, New York, Death Index, 1862-1948* [database on-line]. Provo, UT, USA: Ancestry.com Operations, Inc., 2014.dlxxvi

dlxxvii Newspapers.com - The Brooklyn Daily Eagle - 24 Oct 1944, Tue - Page 10

dlxxviii *New York State Abstracts of World War I Military Service, 1917–1919*. Adjutant General's Office. Series B0808. New York State Archives, Albany, New York.

dlxxix"New York, New York City Municipal Deaths, 1795-1949,"

database, *FamilySearch*(https://familysearch.org/ark:/61903/1:1:2WTG-TMR : 20 March 2015), England, 07 Aug 1876; citing Death, Brooklyn, Kings, New York, United States, New York Municipal Archives, New York; FHL microfilm 1,323,727.

dlxxx Social Security Applications and Claims, 1936-2007

dlxxxi Ancestry.com. *New York, New York, Death Index, 1862-1948* [database on-line]. Provo, UT, USA: Ancestry.com Operations, Inc., 2014.

dlxxxii Ancestry.com. *New York, New York, Birth Index, 1878-1909* [database on-line]. Provo, UT, USA: Ancestry.com Operations, Inc., 2014.

dlxxxiii Ancestry.com. *New York, New York, Marriage Index 1866-1937* [database on-line]. Provo, UT, USA: Ancestry.com Operations, Inc., 2014.

dlxxxiv Year: *1910*; Census Place: *Brooklyn Ward 7, Kings, New York*; Roll: *T624_957*; Page: *2B*; Enumeration District:*0109*; FHL microfilm: *1374970*

dlxxxv Ancestry.com. *New York, New York, Death Index, 1862-1948* [database on-line]. Provo, UT, USA: Ancestry.com Operations, Inc., 2014.

dlxxxvi Ancestry.com. *New York, New York, Death Index, 1862-1948* [database on-line]. Provo, UT, USA: Ancestry.com Operations, Inc., 2014.

dlxxxvii "New York, New York City Municipal Deaths, 1795-1949," database, *FamilySearch*(https://familysearch.org/ark:/61903/1:1:2WTT-WQ8 : 20 March 2015), Thomas J Soden in entry for Elizabeth Burbank, 11 Aug 1943; citing Death, Brooklyn, Kings, New York, United States, New York Municipal Archives, New York; FHL microfilm 2,134,858.

dlxxxviii Ancestry.com. *New York, New York, Marriage Index 1866-1937* [database on-line]. Provo, UT, USA: Ancestry.com Operations, Inc., 2014.

dlxxxix Year: *1900*; Census Place: *Colorado Springs, El Paso, Colorado*; Roll: *124*; Page: *3B*; Enumeration District:*0029*; FHL microfilm: *1240124*

dxc Newspapers.com - The Brooklyn Daily Eagle - 25 Nov 1951, Sun - Page 21

dxci Year: *1900*; Census Place: *Brooklyn Ward 23, Kings, New York*; Roll: *1061*; Page: *12B*; Enumeration District:*0391*; FHL microfilm: *1241061*

dxcii Year: *1900*; Census Place: *Brooklyn Ward 23, Kings, New York*; Roll: *1061*; Page: *12B*; Enumeration District:*0391*; FHL microfilm: *1241061*

dxciii Office of the Judge Advocate General, Court Martial Records Nos. 36873 and 41304 Washington, DC: National Archives and Records Administration. Photo copy in author's possession.

dxciv Office of the Judge Advocate General, Court Martial Records No. 57454. Washington, DC: National Archives and Records Administration. Photo copy in author's possession.

dxcv Newspapers.com - The Brooklyn Daily Eagle - 11 Sep 1930, Thu - Page 15

dxcvi United States, Selective Service System. *World War I Selective Service System Draft Registration Cards, 1917-1918*. Washington, D.C.: National Archives and Records Administration. M1509, 4,582 rolls. Imaged from Family History Library microfilm.

dxcvii Ancestry.com. *Historical Newspapers, Birth, Marriage, & Death Announcements, 1851-2003* [database on-line]. Provo, UT, USA: Ancestry.com Operations Inc, 2006.

dxcviii Year: *1910*; Census Place: *Brooklyn Ward 24, Kings, New York*; Roll: *T624_974*; Page: *10A*; Enumeration District: *0621*; FHL microfilm: *1374987*

dxcix Ancestry.com. *New York, New York, Death Index, 1862-1948* [database on-line]. Provo, UT, USA: Ancestry.com Operations, Inc., 2014.

dc Year: *1860*; Census Place: *Upper Penns Neck, Salem, New Jersey*; Roll: *M653_707*; Page: *33*; Image: *419*; Family History Library Film: *803707*

dci Ancestry.com. *U.S., Find A Grave Index, 1600s-Current* [database on-line]. Provo, UT, USA: Ancestry.com Operations, Inc., 2012.

dcii Year: *1900*; Census Place: *Oldmans, Salem, New Jersey*; Roll: *993*; Page: *3B*; Enumeration District: *0176*; FHL microfilm: *1240993*

dciii United States, Selective Service System. *World War I Selective Service System Draft Registration Cards, 1917-1918*. Washington, D.C.: National Archives and Records Administration. M1509, 4,582 rolls. Imaged from Family History Library microfilm.

dciv "New Jersey Births and Christenings, 1660-1931." Index. FamilySearch, Salt Lake City, Utah, 2009, 2010. Index entries derived from digital copies of original and compiled records.

dcv "New Jersey Deaths and Burials, 1720–1971." Index. FamilySearch, Salt Lake City, Utah, 2009, 2010. Index entries derived from digital copies of original and compiled records.

dcvi *Find A Grave*. Find A Grave. http://www.findagrave.com/cgi-bin/fg.cgi.

dcvii "New Jersey Births and Christenings, 1660-1931." Index. FamilySearch, Salt Lake City, Utah, 2009, 2010. Index entries derived from digital copies of original and compiled records.

dcviii *Find A Grave.* Find A Grave. http://www.findagrave.com/cgi-bin/fg.cgi.

dcix Year: *1900*; Census Place: *Logan, Gloucester, New Jersey*; Roll: *971*; Page: *1B*; Enumeration District: *0159*; FHL microfilm: *1240971*

dcx Ancestry.com. *New Jersey, Deaths and Burials Index, 1798-1971* [database on-line]. Provo, UT, USA: Ancestry.com Operations, Inc., 2011.

dcxi "New Jersey, County Marriages, 1682-1956," database with images, *FamilySearch*(https://familysearch.org/ark:/61903/1:1:VW5L-BC1 : 12 December 2014), Stratton Mattson and Ella England, 04 Mar 1875; citing Gloucester, New Jersey, New Jersey State Archives, Trenton; FHL microfilm 846,905.

dcxii Ancestry.com. *Web: New Jersey, Find A Grave Index, 1664-2012* [database on-line]. Provo, UT, USA: Ancestry.com Operations, Inc., 2012.

dcxiii United States, Selective Service System. *World War I Selective Service System Draft Registration Cards, 1917-1918.* Washington, D.C.: National Archives and Records Administration. M1509, 4,582 rolls. Imaged from Family History Library microfilm.

dcxiv Rambo, Beverly Nelson and Beatty, Ronald Stephen. 2013. The Rambo Family Tree. http://sites.google.com/site/RamboFamilyTree

dcxv Rambo, Beverly Nelson and Beatty, Ronald Stephen. 2013. The Rambo Family Tree. http://sites.google.com/site/RamboFamilyTree

dcxvi Social Security Applications and Claims, 1936-2007.

dcxvii Rambo, Beverly Nelson and Beatty, Ronald Stephen. 2013. The Rambo Family Tree. http://sites.google.com/site/RamboFamilyTree

dcxviii United States, Selective Service System. *World War I Selective Service System Draft Registration Cards, 1917-1918.* Washington, D.C.: National Archives and Records Administration. M1509, 4,582 rolls. Imaged from Family History Library microfilm.

dcxix "New Jersey Deaths and Burials, 1720–1971." Index. FamilySearch, Salt Lake City, Utah, 2009, 2010. Index entries derived from digital copies of original and compiled records.

dcxx Rambo, Beverly Nelson and Beatty, Ronald Stephen. 2013. The Rambo Family Tree. http://sites.google.com/site/RamboFamilyTree

dcxxi Year: *1910*; Census Place: *Swedesboro, Gloucester, New Jersey*; Roll: *T624_885*; Page: *16A*; Enumeration District: *0135*; FHL microfilm: *1374898*

dcxxii Year: *1900*; Census Place: *Logan, Gloucester, New Jersey*; Roll: *971*; Page: *1B*; Enumeration District: *0159*; FHL microfilm: *1240971*

dcxxiii "New Jersey Deaths and Burials, 1720–1971." Index. FamilySearch, Salt Lake City, Utah, 2009, 2010. Index entries derived from digital copies of original and compiled records.

dcxxiv "New Jersey, Marriages, 1670-1980," database with images, *FamilySearch*(https://familysearch.org/ark:/61903/1:1:FZPP-S94 : 31 March 2016), Harry Hoffman and Mabel Mattson, 06 Sep 1897; citing Wenonah, Gloucester, New Jersey, United States, Division of Archives and Record Management, New Jersey Department of State, Trenton.; FHL microfilm 589,816.

dcxxv Rambo, Beverly Nelson and Beatty, Ronald Stephen. 2013. The Rambo Family Tree. http://sites.google.com/site/RamboFamilyTree

dcxxvi Year: *1910*; Census Place: *Logan, Gloucester, New Jersey*; Roll: *T624_885*; Page: *1A*; Enumeration District:*0127*; FHL microfilm: *1374898*

dcxxvii Records of the W. H. Hannold Funeral Home, Swedesboro, NJ.

dcxxviii "New Jersey Births and Christenings, 1660-1931." Index. FamilySearch, Salt Lake City, Utah, 2009, 2010. Index entries derived from digital copies of original and compiled records.

dcxxix "New Jersey Deaths and Burials, 1720–1971." Index. FamilySearch, Salt Lake City, Utah, 2009, 2010. Index entries derived from digital copies of original and compiled records.

dcxxx The National Archives at St. Louis; St. Louis, Missouri; *Draft Registration Cards for Fourth Registration for New Jersey, 04/27/1942 - 04/27/1942*; NAI Number: *2555983*; Record Group Title: *Records of the Selective Service System*; Record Group Number: *147*

dcxxxi Historical Society of Pennsylvania; Philadelphia, Pennsylvania; Collection Name: *Historic Pennsylvania Church and Town Records*; Reel: *779*

dcxxxii Social Security Applications and Claims, 1936-2007.

dcxxxiii Historical Society of Pennsylvania; Philadelphia, Pennsylvania; Collection Name: *Historic Pennsylvania Church and Town Records*; Reel: *779*

dcxxxiv Registration State: *New Jersey*; Registration County: *Gloucester*; Roll: *1712106*; Draft Board: *1*

dcxxxv"New Jersey Deaths and Burials, 1720–1971." Index. FamilySearch, Salt Lake City, Utah, 2009, 2010. Index entries derived from digital copies of original and compiled records.

dcxxxvi Year: *1920*; Census Place: *Woolwich, Gloucester, New Jersey*; Roll: *T625_1027*; Page: *2A*; Enumeration District: *163*; Image: *1145*

dcxxxvii Registration State: *New Jersey*; Registration County: *Gloucester*; Roll: *1712106*; Draft Board: *1*

dcxxxviii *Find A Grave.* Find A Grave. http://www.findagrave.com/cgi-bin/fg.cgi.

dcxxxix *Find A Grave.* Find A Grave. http://www.findagrave.com/cgi-bin/fg.cgi.

dcxl Social Security Administration. *Social Security Death Index, Master File*. Social Security Administration

dcxli Social Security Administration. *Social Security Death Index, Master File*. Social Security Administration

dcxlii Historical Society of Pennsylvania; Philadelphia, Pennsylvania; Collection Name: *Historic Pennsylvania Church and Town Records*; Reel: *1091*

dcxliii Registration State: *New Jersey*; Registration County: *Gloucester*; Roll: *1712106*; Draft Board: *1*

dcxliv "New Jersey Deaths and Burials, 1720–1971." Index. FamilySearch, Salt Lake City, Utah, 2009, 2010. Index entries derived from digital copies of original and compiled records.

dcxlv Rambo, Beverly Nelson and Beatty, Ronald Stephen. 2013. The Rambo Family Tree. http://sites.google.com/site/RamboFamilyTree.

dcxlvi Ancestry.com. *U.S., Find A Grave Index, 1600s-Current* [database on-line]. Provo, UT, USA: Ancestry.com Operations, Inc., 2012.

dcxlvii New Jersey, Marriages, 1670-1980," database with images, *FamilySearch*(https://familysearch.org/ark:/61903/1:1:FZGF-W25 : 31 March 2016), Wm. W. England and Hannah R. Cheeseman, 27 Dec 1886; citing Woodstown, Salem, New Jersey, United States, Division of Archives and Record Management, New Jersey Department of State, Trenton.; FHL microfilm 495,704.

dcxlviii Ancestry.com. *U.S., Find A Grave Index, 1600s-Current* [database on-line]. Provo, UT, USA: Ancestry.com Operations, Inc., 2012.

dcxlix "New Jersey Births and Christenings, 1660-1931." Index. FamilySearch, Salt Lake City, Utah, 2009, 2010. Index entries derived from digital copies of original and compiled records.

Social Security Administration. *Social Security Death Index, Master File*. Social Security Administration.dcl

dcli Year: *1900*; Census Place: *West Almond, Allegany, New York*; Roll: *1008*; Page: *10A*; Enumeration District:*0025*; FHL microfilm: *1241008*

dclii Social Security Administration. *Social Security Death Index, Master File*. Social Security Administration.

dcliii Registration State: *New Jersey*; Registration County: *Salem*; Roll: *1754437*; Draft Board: *1*

dcliv "BillionGraves Index," database, *FamilySearch*(https://familysearch.org/ark:/61903/1:1:QKKS-MW6M : 9 November 2015), Benjamin C. England, died 1960; citing *BillionGraves* (http://www.billiongraves.com : 2012), Burial at Lawnside Cemetery, Woodstown, Salem, New Jersey, United States.

dclv Social Security Applications and Claims, 1936-2007.

dclvi Pennsylvania (State). Death certificates, 1906–1963. Series 11.90 (1,905 cartons). Records of the Pennsylvania Department of Health, Record Group 11. Pennsylvania Historical and Museum Commission, Harrisburg, Pennsylvania.

dclvii Year: *1900*; Census Place: *Oldmans, Salem, New Jersey*; Roll: *993*; Page: *5A*; Enumeration District: *0176*; FHL microfilm: *1240993*

dclviii *Social Security Death Index, Master File*. Social Security Administration.

dclix "New Jersey Births and Christenings, 1660-1931." Index. FamilySearch, Salt Lake City, Utah, 2009, 2010. Index entries derived from digital copies of original and compiled records.

dclx Social Security Administration. *Social Security Death Index, Master File*. Social Security Administration.

dclxi Year: *1900*; Census Place: *Oldmans, Salem, New Jersey*; Roll: *993*; Page: *3A*; Enumeration District: *0176*; FHL microfilm: *1240993*

dclxii Ancestry.com. *U.S., Find A Grave Index, 1600s-Current* [database on-line]. Provo, UT, USA: Ancestry.com Operations, Inc., 2012.

dclxiii US Find a Grave, 1600's-current. Ancestry.com. 2012. Provo, UT.

dclxiv Ancestry.com. *1900 United States Federal Census* [database on-line]. Provo, UT, USA: Ancestry.com Operations Inc, 2004.

dclxvUS Find a Grave, 1600's-current. Ancestry.com. 2012. Provo, UT.

dclxvi Registration State: *New Jersey*; Registration County: *Salem*; Roll: *1754437*; Draft Board: *1*

dclxvii Social Security Administration. *Social Security Death Index, Master File*. Social Security Administration

dclxviii Social Security Administration. *Social Security Death Index, Master File*. Social Security Administration.

dclxix "New Jersey Deaths and Burials, 1720–1971." Index. FamilySearch, Salt Lake City, Utah, 2009, 2010. Index entries derived from digital copies of original and compiled records.

dclxx Registration State: *New Jersey*; Registration County: *Salem*; Roll: *1754437*; Draft Board: *1*

dclxxi "United States Social Security Death Index," database, *FamilySearch*(https://familysearch.org/ark:/61903/1:1:V3P6-223 : 20 May 2014), William England, Apr 1972; citing U.S. Social Security Administration, *Death Master File*, database (Alexandria, Virginia: National Technical Information Service, ongoing).

dclxxii Social Security Applications and Claims, 1936-2007.

dclxxiii "New Jersey Births and Christenings, 1660-1931." Index. FamilySearch, Salt Lake City, Utah, 2009, 2010. Index entries derived from digital copies of original and compiled records.

dclxxiv "BillionGraves Index," database, *FamilySearch* (https://familysearch.org/ark:/61903/1:1:QKKS-SH6K : 9 November 2015), J Davidson England, died 14 Sep 1983; citing *BillionGraves*(http://www.billiongraves.com : 2012), Burial at Lawnside Cemetery, Woodstown, Salem, New Jersey, United States.

dclxxvSocial Security Administration. *Social Security Death Index, Master File*. Social Security Administration.

dclxxvi Year: *1910*; Census Place: *Oldmans, Salem, New Jersey*; Roll: *T624_908*; Page: *11B*; Enumeration District:*0150*; FHL microfilm: *1374921*

dclxxviiVirginia, Deaths, 1912–2014. Virginia Department of Health, Richmond, Virginia.

dclxxviii *Find A Grave*. Find A Grave. http://www.findagrave.com/cgi-bin/fg.cgi: accessed 4 February 2013.

dclxxix District of Columbia Marriages, 1811-1950. Certificate 162037.

dclxxx Original data: Virginia, Deaths, 1912–2014. Virginia Department of Health, Richmond, Virginia.

dclxxxi *Find A Grave*. Find A Grave. http://www.findagrave.com/cgi-bin/fg.cgi: accessed 4 February 2013

dclxxxii National Archives and Records Administration (NARA); Washington D.C.; NARA Series: *Passport Applications, 1795-1905*; Roll #: *265*; Volume #: *Roll 265 - 16 May 1884-16 Jun 1884*

dclxxxiii Historical Society of Pennsylvania; Philadelphia, Pennsylvania; Collection Name: *Historic Pennsylvania Church and Town Records*

dclxxxiv Historical Society of Pennsylvania; Philadelphia, Pennsylvania; Collection Name: *Historic Pennsylvania Church and Town Records*

dclxxxv *Sons of the American Revolution Membership Applications, 1889-1970*. Louisville, Kentucky: National Society of the Sons of the American Revolution. Microfilm, 508 rolls.

dclxxxvi Ancestry.com. *Pennsylvania, Death Certificates, 1906-1963* [database on-line]. Provo, UT, USA: Ancestry.com Operations, Inc., 2014.

dclxxxvii *The Michigan Alumnus*, vol. 10. UM Alumni Association. UM Libraries, 1904.

dclxxxviii Pennsylvania (State). Death certificates, 1906–1963. Series 11.90 (1,905 cartons). Records of the Pennsylvania Department of Health, Record Group 11. Pennsylvania Historical and Museum Commission, Harrisburg, Pennsylvania.

dclxxxix"Illinois, Cook County Marriages, 1871–1920." Index. FamilySearch, Salt Lake City, Utah, 2010. Illinois Department of Public Health records. "Marriage Records, 1871–present." Division of Vital Records, Springfield, Illinois.

dcxc Pennsylvania (State). Death certificates, 1906–1963. Series 11.90 (1,905 cartons). Records of the Pennsylvania Department of Health, Record Group 11. Pennsylvania Historical and Museum Commission, Harrisburg, Pennsylvania.

dcxci Year: *1910*; Census Place: *Lyons, Cook, Illinois*; Roll: *T624_238*; Page: *7A*; Enumeration District: *0045*; FHL microfilm: *1374251*

dcxcii *Sons of the American Revolution Membership Applications, 1889-1970*. Louisville, Kentucky: National Society of the Sons of the American Revolution. Microfilm, 508 rolls.

dcxciii"Illinois, Cook County Marriages, 1871–1920." Index. FamilySearch, Salt Lake City, Utah, 2010. Illinois Department of Public Health records. "Marriage Records, 1871–present." Division of Vital Records, Springfield, Illinois.

dcxciv *Sons of the American Revolution Membership Applications, 1889-1970*. Louisville, Kentucky: National Society of the Sons of the American Revolution. Microfilm, 508 rolls.

dcxcv Year: *1900*; Census Place: *Camden Ward 3, Camden, New Jersey*; Roll: *958*; Page: *12A*; Enumeration District: *0043*; FHL microfilm: *1240958*

dcxcvi Historical Society of Pennsylvania; Philadelphia, Pennsylvania; Collection Name: *Historic Pennsylvania Church and Town Records*; Reel: *1093*

dcxcvii Year: *1900*; Census Place: *Camden Ward 3, Camden, New Jersey*; Roll: *958*; Page: *12A*; Enumeration District: *0043*; FHL microfilm: *1240958*

dcxcviii https://familysearch.org/ark:/61903/1:1:6544-GMM

dcxcix Newspapers.com - Courier-Post - 26 Mar 1965, Fri - Page 8

dcc Newspapers.com - Courier-Post - 26 Mar 1965, Fri - Page 8

dcci "New Jersey, Marriages, 1670-1980," database with images, *FamilySearch*(https://familysearch.org/ark:/61903/1:1:FZ2S-B2W : 31 March 2016), William M. Skaggs and Anna M. Allen, 19 Dec 1894; citing Camden, Camden, New Jersey, United States, Division of Archives and Record Management, New Jersey Department of State, Trenton.; FHL microfilm 495,719.

dccii Year: *1900*; Census Place: *Camden Ward 4, Camden, New Jersey*; Roll: *958*; Page: *1A*; Enumeration District: *0047*; FHL microfilm: *1240958*

dcciii Newspapers.com - Courier-Post - 4 Nov 1950, Sat - Page 5

dcciv United States, Selective Service System. *World War I Selective Service System Draft Registration Cards, 1917-1918*. Washington, D.C.: National Archives and Records Administration. M1509, 4,582 rolls. Imaged from Family History Library microfilm.

dccv Social Security Applications and Claims, 1936-2007.

dccvi Church Records. Greater New Jersey United Methodist Church Commission on Archives and History, Madison, New Jersey.

dccvii Year: *1900*; Census Place: *Camden Ward 8, Camden, New Jersey*; Roll: *959*; Page: *1A*; Enumeration District:*0072*; FHL microfilm: *1240959*

dccviii Social Security Administration. *Social Security Death Index, Master File*. Social Security Administration.

dccix Ancestry.com. *U.S., Social Security Applications and Claims Index, 1936-2007* [database on-line]. Provo, UT, USA: Ancestry.com Operations, Inc., 2015.

dccx 6 Jun 1895, Page 3 - The Times at Newspapers.com

dccxi Chamberlain, Joshua L. *University of Pennsylvania: Its History, Influence, Equipment and Characteristics with Biographical Sketches and Portraits of Founders, Benefactors, Officers and Alumni*. 1902. Boston: R. Herndon & Co.

dccxii United States, Selective Service System. *World War I Selective Service System Draft Registration Cards, 1917-1918*. Washington, D.C.: National Archives and Records Administration. M1509, 4,582 rolls. Imaged from Family History Library microfilm.

dccxiii Social Security Administration. *Social Security Death Index, Master File*. Social Security Administration.

dccxiv Ancestry.com. *Cook County, Illinois Marriage Indexes, 1912-1942* [database on-line]. Provo, UT, USA: Ancestry.com Operations, Inc., 2011.

dccxv Social Security Administration. *Social Security Death Index, Master File*. Social Security Administration.

dccxvi US Find a Grave, 1600's-current. Ancestry.com. 2012. Provo, UT

dccxvii National Archives and Records Administration (NARA); Washington D.C.; NARA Series: *Passport Applications, January 2, 1906 - March 31, 1925*; Roll #: *1326*; Volume #: *Roll 1326 - Certificates: 78500-78875, 05 Aug 1920-06 Aug 1920*

dccxviii Social Security Administration. *Social Security Death Index, Master File*. Social Security Administration.

dccxix Department of Public Health, Registry of Vital Records and Statistics. *Massachusetts Vital Records Index to Marriages [1916–1970]*. Volumes 76–166, 192– 207. Facsimile edition. Boston, MA: New England Historic Genealogical Society, Boston, Massachusetts.

dccxx "New York, New York City Municipal Deaths, 1795-1949," database, *FamilySearch*(https://familysearch.org/ark:/61903/1:1:2W13-PWB : 20 March 2015), William Irwin, 17 Oct 1922; citing Death, Manhattan, New York, New York, United States, New York Municipal Archives, New York; FHL microfilm 2,030,377.

dccxxi State of Massachusetts. *Massachusetts Death Index, 1970-2003*. Boston, MA, USA: Commonwealth of Massachusetts Department of Health Services, 2005.

dccxxii *Social Security Death Index, Master File*. Social Security Administration.

dccxxiii Year: *1880*; Census Place: *Woodbury, Gloucester, New Jersey*; Roll: *781*; Family History Film: *1254781*; Page:*518B*; Enumeration District: *102*; Image: *0679*

dccxxiv Ancestry.com. *U.S., Find A Grave Index, 1600s-Current* [database on-line]. Provo, UT, USA: Ancestry.com Operations, Inc., 2012.

dccxxv *Sons of the American Revolution Membership Applications, 1889-1970*. Louisville, Kentucky: National Society of the Sons of the American Revolution. Microfilm, 508 rolls.

dccxxvi Ancestry.com. *U.S., Find A Grave Index, 1600s-Current* [database on-line]. Provo, UT, USA: Ancestry.com Operations, Inc., 2012.

dccxxvii Social Security Administration. *Social Security Death Index, Master File*. Social Security Administration.

dccxxviii Social Security Administration. *Social Security Death Index, Master File*. Social Security Administration.

dccxxix "New Jersey Births and Christenings, 1660-1931." Index. FamilySearch, Salt Lake City, Utah, 2009, 2010. Index entries derived from digital copies of original and compiled records.

dccxxx New York State Archives; Albany, New York; *Abstracts of National Guard Service in World War I, 1917-1919*; Series: *13721*; Box: *2*; Volume: *5*

dccxxxi *Sons of the American Revolution Membership Applications, 1889-1970*. Louisville, Kentucky: National Society of the Sons of the American Revolution. Microfilm, 508 rolls.

dccxxxii Social Security Administration. *Social Security Death Index, Master File*. Social Security Administration.

dccxxxiii *Sons of the American Revolution Membership Applications, 1889-1970*. Louisville, Kentucky: National Society of the Sons of the American Revolution. Microfilm, 508 rolls.

dccxxxiv Social Security Administration. *Social Security Death Index, Master File*. Social Security Administration.

dccxxxv Year: *1930*; Census Place: *Schenectady, Schenectady, New York*; Roll: *1646*; Page: *9B*; Enumeration District:*0071*; Image: *543.0*; FHL microfilm: *2341380*

dccxxxvi Social Security Administration. *Social Security Death Index, Master File*. Social Security Administration.

dccxxxvii Social Security Administration. *Social Security Death Index, Master File*. Social Security Administration.

dccxxxviii Social Security Applications and Claims, 1936-2007.

dccxxxix *Find A Grave*. Find A Grave. http://www.findagrave.com/cgi-bin/fg.cgi.

dccxl *Find A Grave*. Find A Grave. http://www.findagrave.com/cgi-bin/fg.cgi.

dccxli Ancestry.com. *New Jersey, Births and Christenings Index, 1660-1931* [database on-line]. Provo, UT, USA: Ancestry.com Operations, Inc., 2011.

dccxlii Newspapers.com - Courier-Post - 9 Nov 1957, Sat - Page 4

dccxliii Year: *1900*; Census Place: *Lansdowne, Delaware, Pennsylvania*; Roll: *1406*; Page: *21A*; Enumeration District:*0192*; FHL microfilm: *1241406*

dccxliv Pennsylvania (State). World War II Veterans Compensation Applications, circa 1950s. Records of the Department of Military and Veterans Affairs, Record Group 19, Series 19.92 (877 cartons). Pennsylvania Historical and Museum Commission, Harrisburg, Pennsylvania.

dccxlv Social Security Administration. *Social Security Death Index, Master File*. Social Security Administration

dccxlvi "Pennsylvania, Philadelphia Marriage Index, 1885–1951." Index. FamilySearch, Salt Lake City, Utah, 2009. Philadelphia County Pennsylvania Clerk of the Orphans' Court. "Pennsylvania, Philadelphia marriage license index, 1885-1951." Clerk of the Orphans' Court, Philadelphia, Pennsylvania.

dccxlvii *Find A Grave*. Find A Grave. http://www.findagrave.com/cgi-bin/fg.cgi.

dccxlviii Pearl Harbor Muster Rolls, record group 31, roll 342. The National Archives, Bureau of Navy Personnel.

dccxlix Social Security Administration. *Social Security Death Index, Master File*. Social Security Administration.

dccl Social Security Administration. *Social Security Death Index, Master File*. Social Security Administration.

dccli *Find A Grave*. Find A Grave. http://www.findagrave.com/cgi-bin/fg.cgi

dcclii Year: *1920*; Census Place: *Philadelphia Ward 22, Philadelphia, Pennsylvania*; Roll: *T625_1623*; Page: *4B*; Enumeration District: *541*; Image: *58*

dccliii Social Security Administration. *Social Security Death Index, Master File*. Social Security Administration.

dccliv Historical Society of Pennsylvania; Philadelphia, Pennsylvania; Collection Name: *Historic Pennsylvania Church and Town Records*; Reel: *804*

dcclv http://www.legacy.com/obituaries/philly/obituary.aspx?page=lifestory&pid=160806777

dcclvi Ancestry.com. *U.S., Find A Grave Index, 1600s-Current* [database on-line]. Provo, UT, USA: Ancestry.com Operations, Inc., 2012.

dcclvii Ancestry.com. *U.S., Find A Grave Index, 1600s-Current* [database on-line]. Provo, UT, USA: Ancestry.com Operations, Inc., 2012.

dcclviii personal correspondence, email, jean bean west, 10 Mar 2010

dcclix United States, Selective Service System. *World War I Selective Service System Draft Registration Cards, 1917-1918*. Washington, D.C.: National Archives and Records Administration. M1509, 4,582 rolls. Imaged from Family History Library microfilm.

dcclx Social Security Administration. *Social Security Death Index, Master File*. Social Security Administration.

dcclxi 27 Mar 1945, Page 1 - Republican-Northwestern at Newspapers.com

dcclxii United States, Selective Service System. *World War I Selective Service System Draft Registration Cards, 1917-1918*. Washington, D.C.: National Archives and Records Administration. M1509, 4,582 rolls. Imaged from Family History Library microfilm.

dcclxiii Ancestry.com. *Cook County, Illinois Marriage Indexes, 1912-1942* [database on-line]. Provo, UT, USA: Ancestry.com Operations, Inc., 2011.

dcclxiv State of Florida. *Florida Death Index, 1877-1998*. Florida: Florida Department of Health, Office of Vital Records, 1998.

dcclxv National Tea Food Stores, Deep South News, employee newsletter, May 1966.

dcclxvi Cook County Clerk, comp. *Cook County Clerk Genealogy Records*. Cook County Clerk's Office, Chicago, IL: Cook County Clerk, 2008.

dcclxvii Social Security Applications and Claims, 1936-2007.

dcclxviii Cook County Clerk, comp. *Cook County Clerk Genealogy Records*. Cook County Clerk's Office, Chicago, IL: Cook County Clerk, 2008.

dcclxix Personal correspondence with the daughter of Constance R. England.

dcclxx Social Security Administration. *Social Security Death Index, Master File*. Social Security Administration.

dcclxxi Florida Department of Health. *Florida Marriage Index, 1927-2001*. Florida Department of Health, Jacksonville, Florida.

dcclxxii Social Security Administration. *Social Security Death Index, Master File*. Social Security Administration.

dcclxxiii 1 Apr 1953, Page 8 - Belvidere Daily Republican at Newspapers.com

dcclxxiv Winnebago County Clerk, comp. *Winnebago County Clerk Genealogy Records*. Winnebago, IL: Winnebago County Clerk, 2008.

dcclxxv Winnebago County Clerk, comp. *Winnebago County Clerk Genealogy Records*. Winnebago, IL: Winnebago County Clerk, 2008.

dcclxxvi The National Archives at St. Louis; St. Louis, Missouri; *Draft Registration Cards for Fourth Registration for Illinois, 04/27/1942 - 04/27/1942*; NAI Number: *623284*; Record Group Title: *Records of the Selective Service System*; Record Group Number: *147*

dcclxxvii Social Security Administration. *Social Security Death Index, Master File*. Social Security Administration.

dcclxxviii *Social Security Death Index, Master File*. Social Security Administration.

dcclxxix 12 Jan 1943, Page 3 - Republican-Northwestern at Newspapers.com

dcclxxx Year: *1930*; Census Place: *Rockford, Winnebago, Illinois*; Roll: *572*; Page: *3B*; Enumeration District: *0057*; Image: *814.0*; FHL microfilm: *2340307*

dcclxxxi Social Security Administration. *Social Security Death Index, Master File*. Social Security Administration

dcclxxxii "Pennsylvania, Philadelphia City Births, 1860-1906," database with images, *FamilySearch*(https://familysearch.org/ark:/61903/1:1:VBT4-7SL : 8 December 2014), Annie E. Cramer, 29 Jan 1871; citing bk 1871 p 153, Department of Records; FHL microfilm 1,289,313.

dcclxxxiii Berks County Pennsylvania Register of Wills. *City of Reading PA Death Records 1873-1905*. Reading, PA, USA. Berksregofwills.com.

dcclxxxiv "Pennsylvania, Philadelphia Marriage Index, 1885–1951." Index. FamilySearch, Salt Lake City, Utah, 2009. Philadelphia County Pennsylvania Clerk of the Orphans' Court. "Pennsylvania, Philadelphia marriage license index, 1885-1951." Clerk of the Orphans' Court, Philadelphia, Pennsylvania.

dcclxxxv Year: *1900*; Census Place: *Reading Ward 5, Berks, Pennsylvania*; Roll: *1378*; Page: *8B*; Enumeration District:*0057*; FHL microfilm: *1241378*

dcclxxxvi *Find A Grave*. Find A Grave. http://www.findagrave.com/cgi-bin/fg.cgi.

dcclxxxvii *Find A Grave*. Find A Grave. http://www.findagrave.com/cgi-bin/fg.cgi.

dcclxxxviii Town and City Clerks of Massachusetts. *Massachusetts Vital and Town Records*. Provo, UT: Holbrook Research Institute (Jay and Delene Holbrook).

dcclxxxix *Find A Grave*. Find A Grave. http://www.findagrave.com/cgi-bin/fg.cgi.

dccxc Year: *1900*; Census Place: *Reading Ward 5, Berks, Pennsylvania*; Roll: *1378*; Page: *8B*; Enumeration District:*0057*; FHL microfilm: *1241378*

dccxci Connecticut Department of Health. *Connecticut Death Index, 1949-2001*. Hartford, CT, USA: Connecticut Department of Health.

dccxcii The Archives of the Reformed Church in America; New Brunswick, New Jersey; *Park Hill First Church, Records, 1892-1964*

dccxciii United States, Selective Service System. *World War I Selective Service System Draft Registration Cards, 1917-1918*. Washington, D.C.: National Archives and Records Administration. M1509, 4,582 rolls. Imaged from Family History Library microfilm.

dccxciv Connecticut Department of Health. *Connecticut Death Index, 1949-2001*. Hartford, CT, USA: Connecticut Department of Health.

dccxcv National Archives and Records Administration (NARA); Washington, D.C.; *Indexes to Naturalization Petitons for United States District Courts, Connecticut, 1851-1992 (M2081)*; Microfilm Serial: *M2081*; Microfilm Roll: *13*

dccxcvi *Applications for Headstones for U.S. Military Veterans, 1925-1941*. Microfilm publication M1916, 134 rolls. ARC ID: 596118. Records of the Office of the Quartermaster General, Record Group 92. National Archives at Washington, D.C.

dccxcvii "Indiana Marriages, 1811-2007," database with images, *FamilySearch*(https://familysearch.org/ark:/61903/1:1:XXBY-PM7 : 21 January 2016), William Edwin Westney in entry for Harry England Westney and Grayce Kramer, 11 Jan 1934; citing Elkhart, Indiana, United States, various county clerk offices, Indiana; FHL microfilm 1,845,572.

dccxcviii "Indiana Marriages, 1811-2007," database with images, *FamilySearch*(https://familysearch.org/ark:/61903/1:1:XXBY-PM7 : 21 January 2016), William Edwin Westney in entry for Harry England Westney and Grayce Kramer, 11 Jan 1934; citing Elkhart, Indiana, United States, various county clerk offices, Indiana; FHL microfilm 1,845,572.

dccxcix Michigan, Marriage Records, 1867–1952. Michigan Department of Community Health, Division for Vital Records and Health Statistics.

dccc Year: *1870*; Census Place: *Upper Penns Neck, Salem, New Jersey*; Roll: *M593_887*; Page: *275B*; Image:*301747*; Family History Library Film: *552386*

dccci Historical Society of Pennsylvania; Philadelphia, Pennsylvania; Collection Name: *Historic Pennsylvania Church and Town Records*; Reel: *1096*

dcccii Year: *1880*; Census Place: *Camden, Camden, New Jersey*; Roll: *774*; Family History Film: *1254774*; Page:*215C*; Enumeration District: *047*; Image: *0072*

dccciii Year: 1880; Census Place: Camden, Camden, New Jersey; Roll: 774; Family History Film: 1254774; Page: 215C; Enumeration District: 047; Image: 0072

dccciv Year: 1880; Census Place: Camden, Camden, New Jersey; Roll: 774; Family History Film: 1254774; Page: 215C; Enumeration District: 047; Image: 0072

dcccv "Pennsylvania, Philadelphia City Death Certificates, 1803-1915," database with images, FamilySearch (https://familysearch.org/ark:/61903/1:1:JKSR-FLC : 9 December 2014), Jesse E. Smith, 11 Jul 1896; citing cn 935, Philadelphia City Archives and Historical Society of Pennsylvania, Philadelphia; FHL microfilm 1,863,644.

dcccvi "New Jersey Births and Christenings, 1660-1980," database, FamilySearch (https://familysearch.org/ark:/61903/1:1:FZHW-788 : 12 December 2014), Thomas W. Smith in entry for J. Mulford Smith, 19 Nov 1882; citing Camden, Camden, New Jersey, reference ; FHL microfilm 494,195.

dcccvii Newspapers.com - Courier-Post - 31 Jan 1975, Fri - Page 41

dcccviii "New Jersey Births and Christenings, 1660-1931." Index. FamilySearch, Salt Lake City, Utah, 2009, 2010. Index entries derived from digital copies of original and compiled records.

dcccix Ancestry.com. *U.S., Find A Grave Index, 1600s-Current* [database on-line]. Provo, UT, USA: Ancestry.com Operations, Inc., 2012.

dcccx Year: *1900*; Census Place: *Oldmans, Salem, New Jersey*; Roll: *993*; Page: *6A*; Enumeration District: *0176*; FHL microfilm: *1240993*

dcccxi "New Jersey Births and Christenings, 1660-1931." Index. FamilySearch, Salt Lake City, Utah, 2009, 2010. Index entries derived from digital copies of original and compiled records.

dcccxii Ancestry.com. *U.S., Find A Grave Index, 1600s-Current* [database on-line]. Provo, UT, USA: Ancestry.com Operations, Inc., 2012.

dcccxiii Year: *1880*; Census Place: *Upper Penns Neck, Salem, New Jersey*; Roll: *797*; Family History Film: *1254797*; Page: *215C*; Enumeration District: *150*; Image: *0436*

dcccxiv *Find A Grave*. Find A Grave. http://www.findagrave.com/cgi-bin/fg.cgi.

dcccxv Year: *1900*; Census Place: *Logan, Gloucester, New Jersey*; Roll: *971*; Page: *10A*; Enumeration District: *0159*; FHL microfilm: *1240971*

dcccxvi *Find A Grave*. Find A Grave. http://www.findagrave.com/cgi-bin/fg.cgi

dcccxvii United States, Selective Service System. *World War I Selective Service System Draft Registration Cards, 1917-1918*. Washington, D.C.: National Archives and Records Administration. M1509, 4,582 rolls. Imaged from Family History Library microfilm.

dcccxviii Newspapers.com - Courier-Post - 23 Oct 1957, Wed - Page 4

dcccxix "Pennsylvania, Philadelphia Marriage Index, 1885–1951." Index. FamilySearch, Salt Lake City, Utah, 2009. Philadelphia County Pennsylvania Clerk of the Orphans' Court. "Pennsylvania, Philadelphia marriage license index, 1885-1951." Clerk of the Orphans' Court, Philadelphia, Pennsylvania.

dcccxx Year: *1910*; Census Place: *Philadelphia Ward 44, Philadelphia, Pennsylvania*; Roll: *T624_1412*; Page: *1B*; Enumeration District: *1123*; FHL microfilm: *1375425*

dcccxxi Social Security Applications and Claims, 1936-2007.

dcccxxii Ancestry.com. *California, Death Index, 1940-1997* [database on-line]. Provo, UT, USA: Ancestry.com Operations Inc, 2000.

dcccxxiii Year: *1910*; Census Place: *Absecon Ward 1, Atlantic, New Jersey*; Roll: *T624_867*; Page: *1B*; Enumeration District: *0001*; FHL microfilm: *1374880*

dcccxxiv Ancestry.com. *California, Death Index, 1940-1997* [database on-line]. Provo, UT, USA: Ancestry.com Operations Inc, 2000.

dcccxxv "New Jersey, Births, 1670-1980," database, *FamilySearch* (https://familysearch.org/ark:/61903/1:1:FCRJ-4VC : 8 April 2016), Stacy C. Pancoast in entry for Pancoast, 04 Sep 1887; citing , Salem, New Jersey, United States, Division of Archives and Record Management, New Jersey Department of State, Trenton.; FHL microfilm 494,209.

dcccxxvi Social Security Administration. *Social Security Death Index, Master File*. Social Security Administration.

dcccxxvii Year: *1910*; Census Place: *Wilmington Ward 7, New Castle, Delaware*; Roll: *T624_147*; Page: *19A*; Enumeration District: *0041*; FHL microfilm: *1374160*

dcccxxviii Ancestry.com. *Delaware, Marriage Records, 1806-1933* [database on-line]. Provo, UT, USA: Ancestry.com Operations, Inc., 2010.

dcccxxix Ancestry.com. *Delaware, Birth Records, 1800-1932* [database on-line]. Provo, UT, USA: Ancestry.com Operations, Inc., 2010.

dcccxxx Newspapers.com - The Morning News - 7 May 1925, Thu - Page 7

dcccxxxi United States, Selective Service System. *World War I Selective Service System Draft Registration Cards, 1917-1918*. Washington, D.C.: National Archives and Records Administration. M1509, 4,582 rolls. Imaged from Family History Library microfilm.

dcccxxxii Ancestry.com. *Florida Death Index, 1877-1998* [database on-line]. Provo, UT, USA: Ancestry.com Operations Inc, 2004.

dcccxxxiii Year: *1930*; Census Place: *Upper Darby, Delaware, Pennsylvania*; Roll: *2033*; Page: *9A*; Enumeration District: *0151*; Image: *1042.0*; FHL microfilm: *2341767*

dcccxxxiv Delaware Public Archives; Dover, Delaware; Collection Number: *Birth Certificates - Delayed - 12*; Roll Number: *101*

dcccxxxv Newspapers.com - The News Journal - 2 Jan 2006, Mon - Page 10

dcccxxxvi Social Security Applications and Claims, 1936-2007.

dcccxxxvii *Find A Grave*. Find A Grave. http://www.findagrave.com/cgi-bin/fg.cgi

dcccxxxviii United States, Selective Service System. *World War I Selective Service System Draft Registration Cards, 1917-1918*. Washington, D.C.: National Archives and Records Administration. M1509, 4,582 rolls. Imaged from Family History Library microfilm.

dcccxxxix *Find A Grave*. Find A Grave. http://www.findagrave.com/cgi-bin/fg.cgi.

dcccxl *Find A Grave*. Find A Grave. http://www.findagrave.com/cgi-bin/fg.cgi

dcccxli "Pennsylvania, Philadelphia Marriage Index, 1885–1951." Index. FamilySearch, Salt Lake City, Utah, 2009. Philadelphia County Pennsylvania Clerk of the Orphans' Court. "Pennsylvania, Philadelphia marriage license index, 1885-1951." Clerk of the Orphans' Court, Philadelphia, Pennsylvania.

dcccxlii *Beneficiary Identification Records Locator Subsystem (BIRLS) Death File*. Washington, D.C.: U.S. Department of Veterans Affairs.

dcccxliii *Beneficiary Identification Records Locator Subsystem (BIRLS) Death File*. Washington, D.C.: U.S. Department of Veterans Affairs.

dcccxliv *Beneficiary Identification Records Locator Subsystem (BIRLS) Death File*. Washington, D.C.: U.S. Department of Veterans Affairs.

dcccxlv Year: *1910*; Census Place: *Pleasantville Boro Ward 1, Atlantic, New Jersey*; Roll: *T624_867*; Page: *20B*; Enumeration District: *0037*; FHL microfilm: *1374880*

dcccxlvi Historical Society of Pennsylvania; Philadelphia, Pennsylvania; Collection Name: *Historic Pennsylvania Church and Town Records*; Reel: *1101*

Year: *1880*; Census Place: *Harrisonville, Gloucester, New Jersey*; Roll: *781*; Family History Film: *1254781*; Page: *403D*; Enumeration District: *095*; Image: *0449*dcccxlvii

dcccxlviii *Ancestry.com. Web: Burlington County, New Jersey, Death Index, 1814-2010 [database on-line]. Provo, UT, USA: Ancestry.com Operations, Inc., 2011.*

dcccxlix United States, Selective Service System. *World War I Selective Service System Draft Registration Cards, 1917-1918*. Washington, D.C.: National Archives and Records Administration. M1509, 4,582 rolls. Imaged from Family History Library microfilm.

dcccl Find A Grave. http://www.findagrave.com/cgi-bin/fg.cgi

dcccli Historical Society of Pennsylvania; Philadelphia, Pennsylvania; Collection Name: *Historic Pennsylvania Church and Town Records*; Reel: *1101*

dccclii "New Jersey Births and Christenings, 1660-1931." Index. FamilySearch, Salt Lake City, Utah, 2009, 2010. Index entries derived from digital copies of original and compiled records.

dcccliii *Find A Grave*. Find A Grave. http://www.findagrave.com/cgi-bin/fg.cgi.

dccccliv "New Jersey Births and Christenings, 1660-1931." Index. FamilySearch, Salt Lake City, Utah, 2009, 2010. Index entries derived from digital copies of original and compiled records.

dccclv Year: *1910*; Census Place: *Pleasantville Boro Ward 1, Atlantic, New Jersey*; Roll: *T624_867*; Page: *20B*; Enumeration District: *0037*; FHL microfilm: *1374880*

dccclvi Year: *1910*; Census Place: *Pleasantville Boro Ward 1, Atlantic, New Jersey*; Roll: *T624_867*; Page: *20B*; Enumeration District: *0037*; FHL microfilm: *1374880*

dccclvii "New Jersey Births and Christenings, 1660-1931." Index. FamilySearch, Salt Lake City, Utah, 2009, 2010. Index entries derived from digital copies of original and compiled records.

dccclviii http://www.dvrbs.com/people/camdenpeople-drjosepheroberts.htm

dccclix Social Security Administration. *Social Security Death Index, Master File*. Social Security Administration.

dccclx http://www.dvrbs.com/people/camdenpeople-drjosepheroberts.htm

dccclxi Year: *1920*; Census Place: *Camden Ward 2, Camden, New Jersey*; Roll: *T625_1022*; Page: *9A*; Enumeration District: *11*; Image: *594*

dccclxii Newspapers.com - The Evening News - 25 Aug 1930, Mon - Page 2

dccclxiii Newspapers.com - The Evening News - 25 Aug 1930, Mon - Page 2

dccclxiv Year: *1930*; Census Place: *Haddonfield, Camden, New Jersey*; Roll: *1324*; Page: *8B*; Enumeration District:*0135*; Image: *252.0*; FHL microfilm: *2341059*

dccclxv Ancestry.com. *U.S., Department of Veterans Affairs BIRLS Death File, 1850-2010* [database on-line]. Provo, UT, USA: Ancestry.com Operations, Inc., 2011.

dccclxvi Ancestry.com. *U.S., Department of Veterans Affairs BIRLS Death File, 1850-2010* [database on-line]. Provo, UT, USA: Ancestry.com Operations, Inc., 2011.

dccclxvii http://obits.nj.com/obituaries/starledger/obituary.aspx?page=lifestory&pid=157645852

dccclxviii http://obits.nj.com/obituaries/starledger/obituary.aspx?page=lifestory&pid=157645852

dccclxix Newspapers.com - The Courier-News - 29 Aug 1949, Mon - Page 7

dccclxx Year: *1900*; Census Place: *Camden Ward 6, Camden, New Jersey*; Roll: *958*; Page: *6A*; Enumeration District:*0062*; FHL microfilm: *1240958*

dccclxxi United States, Selective Service System. *World War I Selective Service System Draft Registration Cards, 1917-1918*. Washington, D.C.: National Archives and Records Administration. M1509, 4,582 rolls. Imaged from Family History Library microfilm.

dccclxxii Ancestry.com. *New York, New York, Death Index, 1862-1948* [database on-line]. Provo, UT, USA: Ancestry.com Operations, Inc., 2014.

dccclxxiii *Alabama, Marriages, 1816-1957*. Salt Lake City, Utah: FamilySearch, 2013.

dccclxxiv Year: *1930*; Census Place: *Brooklyn, Kings, New York*; Roll: *1537*; Page: *12B*; Enumeration District: *0850*; Image: *536.0*; FHL microfilm: *2341272*

dccclxxv Social Security Administration. *Social Security Death Index, Master File*. Social Security Administration.

dccclxxvi Historical Society of Pennsylvania; Philadelphia, Pennsylvania; Collection Name: *Historic Pennsylvania Church and Town Records*; Reel: *1093*

dccclxxvii http://www.dvrbs.com/ccwd-kw/KW-WarrenPHarbison.htm

dccclxxviii Year: *1930*; Census Place: *Camden, Camden, New Jersey*; Roll: *1321*; Page: *6A*; Enumeration District: *0039*; Image: *340.0*; FHL microfilm: *2341056*

dccclxxix http://www.legacy.com/obituaries/courierpostonline/obituary.aspx?n=Ronald-G-Harbison&pid=163457072

dccclxxx Newspapers.com - The Times - 22 Oct 1899, Sun - Page 14

dccclxxxi *Find A Grave*. Find A Grave. http://www.findagrave.com/cgi-bin/fg.cgi.

dccclxxxii Year: *1910*; Census Place: *Camden Ward 10, Camden, New Jersey*; Roll: *T624_873*; Page: *8B*; Enumeration District: *0069*; FHL microfilm: *1374886*

dccclxxxiii Year: *1910*; Census Place: *Camden Ward 10, Camden, New Jersey*; Roll: *T624_873*; Page: *8B*; Enumeration District: *0069*; FHL microfilm: *1374886*

dccclxxxiv Year: *1920*; Census Place: *Camden Ward 1, Camden, New Jersey*; Roll: *T625_1022*; Page: *7B*; Enumeration District: *10*; Image: *148*

dccclxxxv *The Courier Post*, Camden, NJ. 5 March 1960, pg. 6. Newspapers.com

dccclxxxvi "New Jersey Births and Christenings, 1660-1931." Index. FamilySearch, Salt Lake City, Utah, 2009, 2010. Index entries derived from digital copies of original and compiled records.

dccclxxxvii "New Jersey Births and Christenings, 1660-1931." Index. FamilySearch, Salt Lake City, Utah, 2009, 2010. Index entries derived from digital copies of original and compiled records.

dccclxxxviii Year: *1910*; Census Place: *Camden Ward 9, Camden, New Jersey*; Roll: *T624_874*; Page: *5B*; Enumeration District: *0063*; FHL microfilm: *1374887*

dccclxxxix *The Courier-Post*, Camden, NJ. 2 January 1968, p.22. Newspapers.com

dcccxc Newspapers.com - Courier-Post - 6 Sep 1991, Fri - Page 34

dcccxci Social Security Applications and Claims, 1936-2007.

dcccxcii http://www.legacy.com/obituaries/courierpostonline/obituary.aspx?n=neil-b-harbison&pid=131055812

dcccxciii Social Security Administration. *Social Security Death Index, Master File.* Social Security Administration

dcccxciv Pennsylvania (State). Death certificates, 1906–1963. Series 11.90 (1,905 cartons). Records of the Pennsylvania Department of Health, Record Group 11. Pennsylvania Historical and Museum Commission, Harrisburg, Pennsylvania.

dcccxcv Historical Society of Pennsylvania; Philadelphia, Pennsylvania; Collection Name: *Historic Pennsylvania Church and Town Records*; Reel: *386*

dcccxcvi : Pennsylvania (State). Death certificates, 1906–1963. Series 11.90 (1,905 cartons). Records of the Pennsylvania Department of Health, Record Group 11. Pennsylvania Historical and Museum Commission, Harrisburg, Pennsylvania.

dcccxcvii Historical Society of Pennsylvania; Philadelphia, Pennsylvania; Collection Name: *Historic Pennsylvania Church and Town Records*; Reel: *386*

dcccxcviii Newspapers.com - The Morning News - 11 Oct 1945, Thu - Page 4

dcccxcix "Pennsylvania, Philadelphia Marriage Index, 1885–1951." Index. FamilySearch, Salt Lake City, Utah, 2009. Philadelphia County Pennsylvania Clerk of the Orphans' Court. "Pennsylvania, Philadelphia marriage license index, 1885-1951." Clerk of the Orphans' Court, Philadelphia, Pennsylvania.

cm Year: *1930*; Census Place: *Philadelphia, Philadelphia, Pennsylvania*; Roll: *2119*; Page: *19B*; Enumeration District: *0436*; Image: *867.0*; FHL microfilm: *2341853*

cmi Pennsylvania (State). Birth certificates, 1906–1908. Series 11.89 (50 cartons). Records of the Pennsylvania Department of Health, Record Group 11. Pennsylvania Historical and Museum Commission, Harrisburg, Pennsylvania.

cmii "Pennsylvania, Philadelphia City Death Certificates, 1803–1915." Index. FamilySearch, Salt Lake City, Utah, 2008, 2010. From originals housed at the Philadelphia City Archives. "Death Records.".

cmiii Pennsylvania (State). World War II Veterans Compensation Applications, circa 1950s. Records of the Department of Military and Veterans Affairs, Record Group 19, Series 19.92 (877 cartons). Pennsylvania Historical and Museum Commission, Harrisburg, Pennsylvania.

cmiv *Find A Grave*. Find A Grave. http://www.findagrave.com/cgi-bin/fg.cgi.

cmv *Find A Grave*. Find A Grave. http://www.findagrave.com/cgi-bin/fg.cgi.

cmvi Year: *1900*; Census Place: *Pennsauken, Camden, New Jersey*; Roll: *959*; Page: *3A*; Enumeration District:*0104*; FHL microfilm: *1240959*

cmvii Connecticut Department of Health. *Connecticut Death Index, 1949-2012* [database on-line]. Provo, UT, USA: Ancestry.com Operations, Inc., 2003.

cmviii "Pennsylvania, Philadelphia Marriage Index, 1885–1951." Index. FamilySearch, Salt Lake City, Utah, 2009. Philadelphia County Pennsylvania Clerk of the Orphans' Court. "Pennsylvania, Philadelphia marriage license index, 1885-1951." Clerk of the Orphans' Court, Philadelphia, Pennsylvania.

cmix The National Archives at St. Louis; St. Louis, Missouri; *Draft Registration Cards for Fourth Registration for Pennsylvania, 04/27/1942 - 04/27/1942*; NAI Number: *563728*; Record Group Title: *Records of the Selective Service System*; Record Group Number: *147*

cmx Connecticut Department of Health. *Connecticut Death Index, 1949-2012* [database on-line]. Provo, UT, USA: Ancestry.com Operations, Inc., 2003.

cmxi United States, Selective Service System. *World War I Selective Service System Draft Registration Cards, 1917-1918.* Washington, D.C.: National Archives and Records Administration. M1509, 4,582 rolls. Imaged from Family History Library microfilm.

cmxii Pennsylvania (State). Birth certificates, 1906–1908. Series 11.89 (50 cartons). Records of the Pennsylvania Department of Health, Record Group 11. Pennsylvania Historical and Museum Commission, Harrisburg, Pennsylvania.

cmxiii Social Security Administration. *Social Security Death Index, Master File.* Social Security Administration.

cmxiv Year: *1930*; Census Place: *Philadelphia, Philadelphia, Pennsylvania*; Roll: *2108*; Page: *24A*; Enumeration District: *0378*; Image: *135.0*; FHL microfilm: *2341842*

cmxvSocial Security Applications and Claims, 1936-2007.

cmxvi Social Security Administration. *Social Security Death Index, Master File.* Social Security Administration.

cmxvii "Pennsylvania, Philadelphia Marriage Index, 1885–1951." Index. FamilySearch, Salt Lake City, Utah, 2009. Philadelphia County Pennsylvania Clerk of the Orphans' Court. "Pennsylvania, Philadelphia marriage license index, 1885-1951." Clerk of the Orphans' Court, Philadelphia, Pennsylvania.

cmxviii Social Security Administration. *Social Security Death Index, Master File.* Social Security Administration

cmxix *Find A Grave*. Find A Grave. http://www.findagrave.com/cgi-bin/fg.cgi.

cmxx Social Security Applications and Claims, 1936-2007.

cmxxi Social Security Administration. *Social Security Death Index, Master File*. Social Security Administration

cmxxii "Pennsylvania, Philadelphia Marriage Index, 1885–1951." Index. FamilySearch, Salt Lake City, Utah, 2009. Philadelphia County Pennsylvania Clerk of the Orphans' Court. "Pennsylvania, Philadelphia marriage license index, 1885-1951." Clerk of the Orphans' Court, Philadelphia, Pennsylvania.

cmxxiii Pennsylvania (State). World War II Veterans Compensation Applications, circa 1950s. Records of the Department of Military and Veterans Affairs, Record Group 19, Series 19.92 (877 cartons). Pennsylvania Historical and Museum Commission, Harrisburg, Pennsylvania.

cmxxiv Social Security Administration. *Social Security Death Index, Master File*. Social Security Administration

cmxxv Historical Society of Pennsylvania; Philadelphia, Pennsylvania; Collection Name: *Historic Pennsylvania Church and Town Records*; Reel: *930*

cmxxvi Connecticut Department of Health. *Connecticut Death Index, 1949-2012* [database on-line]. Provo, UT, USA: Ancestry.com Operations, Inc., 2003.

cmxxvii Pennsylvania (State). Death certificates, 1906–1963. Series 11.90 (1,905 cartons). Records of the Pennsylvania Department of Health, Record Group 11. Pennsylvania Historical and Museum Commission, Harrisburg, Pennsylvania.

cmxxviii Year: *1900*; Census Place: *Philadelphia Ward 2, Philadelphia, Pennsylvania*; Roll: *1452*; Page: *9B*; Enumeration District: *0035*; FHL microfilm: *1241452*

cmxxix Newspapers.com - Evening Public Ledger - 3 Jun 1921, Fri - Page 3

cmxxx United States, Selective Service System. *World War I Selective Service System Draft Registration Cards, 1917-1918*. Washington, D.C.: National Archives and Records Administration. M1509, 4,582 rolls. Imaged from Family History Library microfilm.

cmxxxi Pennsylvania (State). Death certificates, 1906–1963. Series 11.90 (1,905 cartons). Records of the Pennsylvania Department of Health, Record Group 11. Pennsylvania Historical and Museum Commission, Harrisburg, Pennsylvania.

cmxxxii "Pennsylvania, Philadelphia Marriage Index, 1885–1951." Index. FamilySearch, Salt Lake City, Utah, 2009. Philadelphia County Pennsylvania Clerk of the Orphans' Court. "Pennsylvania, Philadelphia marriage license index, 1885-1951." Clerk of the Orphans' Court, Philadelphia, Pennsylvania.

cmxxxiii Year: *1900*; Census Place: *Philadelphia Ward 24, Philadelphia, Pennsylvania*; Roll: *1466*; Page: *1B*; Enumeration District: *0567*; FHL microfilm: *1241466*

cmxxxiv World War I Veterans Service and Compensation File, 1934–1948. RG 19, Series 19.91. Pennsylvania Historical and Museum Commission, Harrisburg Pennsylvania.

cmxxxv Loomis, Ernest L. *History of the 304th Ammunition Train*. 1920. Boston: The Gorham Press. Available at Google books.

cmxxxvi DeLong, Thomas F. *A History and Roster of the 103rd Ammunition Train*. Allentown PA: the 103rd Publishing Co. Available at hathitrust.org.

cmxxxvii The National Archives at St. Louis; St. Louis, Missouri; *Draft Registration Cards for Fourth Registration for Pennsylvania, 04/27/1942 - 04/27/1942*; NAI Number: *563728*; Record Group Title: *Records of the Selective Service System*; Record Group Number: *147*

cmxxxviii State of Florida. *Florida Death Index, 1877-1998*. Florida: Florida Department of Health, Office of Vital Records, 1998.

cmxxxix "Pennsylvania, Philadelphia Marriage Index, 1885–1951." Index. FamilySearch, Salt Lake City, Utah, 2009. Philadelphia County Pennsylvania Clerk of the Orphans' Court. "Pennsylvania, Philadelphia marriage license index, 1885-1951." Clerk of the Orphans' Court, Philadelphia, Pennsylvania.

cmxl *Find A Grave*. Find A Grave. http://www.findagrave.com/cgi-bin/fg.cgi.

cmxli *Find A Grave*. Find A Grave. http://www.findagrave.com/cgi-bin/fg.cgi.

cmxlii *Find A Grave*. Find A Grave. http://www.findagrave.com/cgi-bin/fg.cgi.

cmxliii Social Security Administration. *Social Security Death Index, Master File*. Social Security Administration

cmxliv "Pennsylvania, Philadelphia City Death Certificates, 1803-1915," database with images,*FamilySearch* (https://familysearch.org/ark:/61903/1:1:JDTH-42N : 9 December 2014), Elizabeth Hoffman, 02 Aug 1899; citing cn 2767, Philadelphia City Archives and Historical Society of Pennsylvania, Philadelphia; FHL microfilm 1,769,851.

cmxlv Historical Society of Pennsylvania; Philadelphia, Pennsylvania; Collection Name: *Historic Pennsylvania Church and Town Records*; Reel: *366*

cmxlvi Social Security Administration. *Social Security Death Index, Master File*. Social Security Administration

cmxlvii Social Security Administration. *Social Security Death Index, Master File*. Social Security Administration

cmxlviii Social Security Administration. *Social Security Death Index, Master File*. Social Security Administration

cmxlix Newspapers.com - Courier-Post - 4 Dec 1993, Sat - Page 15 cml Pennsylvania (State). Death certificates, 1906–1963. Series 11.90 (1,905 cartons). Records of the Pennsylvania Department of Health, Record Group 11. Pennsylvania Historical and Museum Commission, Harrisburg, Pennsylvania.

cmli "New Jersey Births and Christenings, 1660-1980," database, *FamilySearch*(https://familysearch.org/ark:/61903/1:1:FCTW-G95 : 12 December 2014), William Hurff in entry for Hurff, 09 Oct 1855; citing Gloucester, New Jersey, reference v O p 106; FHL microfilm 584,565.

cmlii *Find A Grave*. Find A Grave. http://www.findagrave.com/cgi-bin/fg.cgi.

cmliii *Find A Grave*. Find A Grave. http://www.findagrave.com/cgi-bin/fg.cgi.

cmliv Social Security Administration. *Social Security Death Index, Master File*. Social Security Administration.

cmlv Social Security Administration. *Social Security Death Index, Master File*. Social Security Administration.

cmlvi Year: *1910*; Census Place: *Oaklyn, Camden, New Jersey*; Roll: *T624_874*; Page: *6B*; Enumeration District:*0107*; FHL microfilm: *1374887*

cmlvii Ancestry.com. *U.S., World War I Draft Registration Cards, 1917-1918* [database on-line]. Provo, UT, USA: Ancestry.com Operations Inc, 2005.

cmlviii Ancestry.com. *Pennsylvania, Death Certificates, 1906-1963* [database on-line]. Provo, UT, USA: Ancestry.com Operations, Inc., 2014.

cmlix United States, Selective Service System. *World War I Selective Service System Draft Registration Cards, 1917-1918*. Washington, D.C.: National Archives and Records Administration. M1509, 4,582 rolls. Imaged from Family History Library microfilm.

cmlx Social Security Administration. *Social Security Death Index, Master File*. Social Security Administration.

cmlxi Social Security Administration. *Social Security Death Index, Master File*. Social Security Administration.

cmlxii Social Security Administration. *Social Security Death Index, Master File*. Social Security Administration.

cmlxiii Year: *1920*; Census Place: *Haddonfield, Camden, New Jersey*; Roll: *T625_1025*; Page: *15B*; Enumeration District: *120*; Image: *94*

cmlxiv *Find A Grave*. Find A Grave. http://www.findagrave.com/cgi-bin/fg.cgi.

cmlxv Year: *1900*; Census Place: *Washington, Gloucester, New Jersey*; Roll: *971*; Page: *5B*; Enumeration District:*0164*; FHL microfilm: *1240971*

cmlxvi "New Jersey Deaths and Burials, 1720–1971." Index. FamilySearch, Salt Lake City, Utah, 2009, 2010. Index entries derived from digital copies of original and compiled records.

cmlxvii "New Jersey Births and Christenings, 1660-1931." Index. FamilySearch, Salt Lake City, Utah, 2009, 2010.

cmlxviii Year: *1900*; Census Place: *Washington, Gloucester, New Jersey*; Roll: *971*; Page: *5B*; Enumeration District:*0164*; FHL microfilm: *1240971*

cmlxix Ancestry.com. *Washington, Deaths, 1883-1960* [database on-line]. Provo, UT, USA: Ancestry.com Operations Inc, 2008.

cmlxx Historical Society of Pennsylvania; Philadelphia, Pennsylvania; Collection Name: *Historic Pennsylvania Church and Town Records*; Reel: *774*

cmlxxi The National Archives at St. Louis; St. Louis, Missouri; *Draft Registration Cards for Fourth Registration for Colorado, 04/27/1942 - 04/27/1942*; NAI Number: *923647*; Record Group Title: *Records of the Selective Service System*; Record Group Number: *147*

cmlxxii "Washington Death Certificates, 1907-1960," database, *FamilySearch*(https://familysearch.org/ark:/61903/1:1:NQM1-147 : 5 December 2014), William Campbell, 21 Oct 1950; citing Seattle, King, Washington, United States, reference 17254, Bureau of Vital Statistics, Olympia; FHL microfilm 2,032,914.

cmlxxiii The National Archives at St. Louis; St. Louis, Missouri; *Draft Registration Cards for Fourth Registration for New Jersey, 04/27/1942 - 04/27/1942*; NAI Number: *2555983*; Record Group Title: *Records of the Selective Service System*; Record Group Number: *147*

cmlxxiv "New Jersey Deaths and Burials, 1720-1988," database, *FamilySearch*(https://familysearch.org/ark:/61903/1:1:FZ32-3M8 : 12 December 2014), Walter H. Hurff, 09 Feb 1948; citing , reference ; FHL microfilm 1,001,900.

cmlxxv *Find A Grave*. Find A Grave. http://www.findagrave.com/cgi-bin/fg.cgi.

cmlxxvi Social Security Administration. *Social Security Death Index, Master File*. Social Security Administration

cmlxxvii "New Jersey Births and Christenings, 1660-1980," database, *FamilySearch*(https://familysearch.org/ark:/61903/1:1:FZDK-T4V : 12 December 2014), Grover C. Huff, 14 Jan 1884; citing Gloucester, New Jersey, reference ; FHL microfilm 494,200.

cmlxxviii "New Jersey Deaths and Burials, 1720-1988," database, *FamilySearch*(https://familysearch.org/ark:/61903/1:1:FZ32-S26 : 12 December 2014), Grover C. Hurff, 16 Oct 1964; citing , reference ; FHL microfilm 1,001,900.

cmlxxix *Find A Grave*. Find A Grave. http://www.findagrave.com/cgi-bin/fg.cgi.

cmlxxx "New Jersey Births and Christenings, 1660-1980,"
database, *FamilySearch*(https://familysearch.org/ark:/61903/1:1:FZ81-JZH : 12 December 2014), Henry L. Hurff in entry for Ella Hurff, 21 Sep 1886; citing Wn , Gloucester, New Jersey, reference ; FHL microfilm 494,205.

cmlxxxi "New Jersey, Deaths, 1670-1988," database, *FamilySearch*(https://familysearch.org/ark:/61903/1:1:FZ2Q-MMQ : 8 April 2016), Ella Hurff, 11 Oct 1886; citing Washington, Gloucester, New Jersey, United States, Division of Archives and Record Management, New Jersey Department of State, Trenton.; FHL microfilm 589,308.

cmlxxxii Year: *1880*; Census Place: *Brooklyn, Kings, New York*; Roll: *844*; Family History Film: *1254844*; Page: *242D*; Enumeration District: *056*; Image: *0054*

cmlxxxiii Ancestry.com. *New York, New York, Death Index, 1862-1948* [database on-line]. Provo, UT, USA: Ancestry.com Operations, Inc., 2014.

cmlxxxiv Ancestry.com. *New York, New York, Marriage Index 1866-1937* [database on-line]. Provo, UT, USA: Ancestry.com Operations, Inc., 2014.

cmlxxxv Year: *1900*; Census Place: *Brooklyn Ward 23, Kings, New York*; Roll: *1061*; Page: *18A*; Enumeration District:*0399*; FHL microfilm: *1241061*

cmlxxxvi Newspapers.com - The Brooklyn Daily Eagle - 5 Oct 1919, Sun - Page 68

cmlxxxvii https://familysearch.org/ark:/61903/1:1:2CHD-3F2

cmlxxxviii Year: *1900*; Census Place: *Brooklyn Ward 23, Kings, New York*; Roll: *1061*; Page: *18A*; Enumeration District:*0399*; FHL microfilm: *1241061*

cmlxxxix "New York, New York City Municipal Deaths, 1795-1949,"
database, *FamilySearch*(https://familysearch.org/ark:/61903/1:1:2WQ3-WLV : 20 March 2015), Florence Violet England, 18 Aug 1912; citing Death, New York City, Queens, New York, United States, New York Municipal Archives, New York; FHL microfilm 1,323,430.

cmxc "United States World War I Draft Registration Cards, 1917-1918," database with images,
FamilySearch (https://familysearch.org/ark:/61903/1:1:KXYV-PB4 : 12 December 2014), Harold F England, 1917-1918; citing New York City no 64, New York, United States, NARA microfilm publication M1509 (Washington D.C.: National Archives and Records Administration, n.d.); FHL microfilm 1,754,591.

cmxci Ancestry.com. *California, Death Index, 1940-1997* [database on-line]. Provo, UT, USA: Ancestry.com Operations Inc, 2000

cmxcii Social Security Administration. *Social Security Death Index, Master File*. Social Security Administration.

cmxciii *Find A Grave*. Find A Grave. http://www.findagrave.com/cgi-bin/fg.cgi.

cmxciv Ancestry.com. *New York, New York, Marriage Index 1866-1937* [database on-line]. Provo, UT, USA: Ancestry.com Operations, Inc., 2014.

cmxcv Social Security Administration. *Social Security Death Index, Master File*. Social Security Administration

cmxcvi *Find A Grave*. Find A Grave. http://www.findagrave.com/cgi-bin/fg.cgi.

cmxcvii *Beneficiary Identification Records Locator Subsystem (BIRLS) Death File*. Washington, D.C.: U.S. Department of Veterans Affairs.

cmxcviii "New York, New York City Births, 1846-1909," database, *FamilySearch*(https://familysearch.org/ark:/61903/1:1:27YD-ZTV : 20 March 2015), Ethel B. O. Johnson England in entry for Ethel Lillian England, 15 Aug 1909; citing Manhattan, New York, New York, United States, reference Item 5 cn 3792 New York Municipal Archives, New York; FHL microfilm 2,022,367.

cmxcix Social Security Applications and Claims, 1936-2007.

m http://www.npwelch.com/obituary/ethel-l-bonnington/

mi Ancestry.com. *New York, New York, Birth Index, 1878-1909* [database on-line]. Provo, UT, USA: Ancestry.com Operations, Inc., 2014.

mii Ancestry.com. *New York, New York, Marriage Index 1866-1937* [database on-line]. Provo, UT, USA: Ancestry.com Operations, Inc., 2014.

miii Year: *1910*; Census Place: *Brooklyn Ward 7, Kings, New York*; Roll: *T624_957*; Page: *2B*; Enumeration District:*0109*; FHL microfilm: *1374970*

miv Ancestry.com. *New York, New York, Birth Index, 1878-1909* [database on-line]. Provo, UT, USA: Ancestry.com Operations, Inc., 2014.

mv Social Security Administration. *Social Security Death Index, Master File*. Social Security Administration.

mvi Newspapers.com - The Brooklyn Daily Eagle - 15 Sep 1929, Sun - Page 29

mvii Ancestry.com. *U.S. Public Records Index, 1950-1993, Volume 1* [database on-line]. Provo, UT, USA: Ancestry.com Operations, Inc., 2010.

mviii Ancestry.com. *Florida Death Index, 1877-1998* [database on-line]. Provo, UT, USA: Ancestry.com Operations Inc, 2004.

mix United States, Selective Service System. *World War I Selective Service System Draft Registration Cards, 1917-1918*. Washington, D.C.: National Archives and Records Administration. M1509, 4,582 rolls. Imaged from Family History Library microfilm.

mx Social Security Applications and Claims, 1936-2007.

mxi "New Jersey, Deaths, 1670-1988," database, *FamilySearch*(https://familysearch.org/ark:/61903/1:1:Q2S8-QQL4 : 8 April 2016), Joseph S Mattson, Nov 1929; citing , , New Jersey, United States, Division of Archives and Record Management, New Jersey Department of State, Trenton.; FHL microfilm 1,543,562.

mxii "New Jersey, Marriages, 1670-1980," database with images, *FamilySearch*(https://familysearch.org/ark:/61903/1:1:Q29L-QHDK : 31 March 2016), Joseph S. Mattson and Helen Homan, Sep 1923; citing , , New Jersey, United States, Division of Archives and Record Management, New Jersey Department of State, Trenton.; FHL microfilm 1,543,473.

mxiii Historical Society of Pennsylvania; Philadelphia, Pennsylvania; Collection Name: *Historic Pennsylvania Church and Town Records*; Reel: *779*

mxiv *Find A Grave*. Find A Grave. http://www.findagrave.com/cgi-bin/fg.cgi.

mxv United States, Selective Service System. *World War I Selective Service System Draft Registration Cards, 1917-1918*. Washington, D.C.: National Archives and Records Administration. M1509, 4,582 rolls. Imaged from Family History Library microfilm.

mxvi "New Jersey Deaths and Burials, 1720–1971." Index. FamilySearch, Salt Lake City, Utah, 2009, 2010. Index entries derived from digital copies of original and compiled records.

mxvii Rambo, Beverly Nelson and Beatty, Ronald Stephen. 2013. The Rambo Family Tree. http://sites.google.com/site/RamboFamilyTree

mxviii Year: *1910*; Census Place: *Swedesboro, Gloucester, New Jersey*; Roll: *T624_885*; Page: *16A*; Enumeration District: *0135*; FHL microfilm: *1374898*

mxix Social Security Administration. *Social Security Death Index, Master File*. Social Security Administration.

mxx Social Security Administration. *Social Security Death Index, Master File*. Social Security Administration.

mxxi Year: *1920*; Census Place: *Swedesboro, Gloucester, New Jersey*; Roll: *T625_1027*; Page: *7A*; Enumeration District: *189*; Image: *867*

mxxii Rambo, Beverly Nelson and Beatty, Ronald Stephen. 2013. *The Rambo Family Tree.* http://sites.google.com/site/RamboFamilyTree.

mxxiii Greater New Jersey Annual Conference Commission on Archives and History; Madison, New Jersey; Description: *Methodist Church Records*

mxxiv New Jersey, Deaths, 1670-1988," database, *FamilySearch*(https://familysearch.org/ark:/61903/1:1:FZ3V-2YX : 8 April 2016), Blanche E. Mattson Gibbons, 19 Dec 1965; citing , Gloucester, New Jersey, United States, Division of Archives and Record Management, New Jersey Department of State, Trenton.; FHL microfilm 1,001,899.

mxxv Rambo, Beverly Nelson and Beatty, Ronald Stephen. 2013. *The Rambo Family Tree.* http://sites.google.com/site/RamboFamilyTree.

mxxvi World War I Veterans Service and Compensation File, 1934–1948. RG 19, Series 19.91. Pennsylvania Historical and Museum Commission, Harrisburg Pennsylvania.

mxxvii Newspapers.com - Courier-Post - 21 Jun 1956, Thu - Page 8

mxxviii "New Jersey, Marriages, 1670-1980," database with images, *FamilySearch*(https://familysearch.org/ark:/61903/1:1:Q29L-7FRW : 31 March 2016), Eugene T. Gibbons and Blanche E. Anderson, 29 Sep 1956; citing , , New Jersey, United States, Division of Archives and Record Management, New Jersey Department of State, Trenton.; FHL microfilm 1,543,529.

mxxix Year: *1900*; Census Place: *Logan, Gloucester, New Jersey*; Roll: *971*; Page: *1B*; Enumeration District: *0159*; FHL microfilm: *1240971*

mxxx "New Jersey Deaths and Burials, 1720–1971." Index. FamilySearch, Salt Lake City, Utah, 2009, 2010. Index entries derived from digital copies of original and compiled records.

mxxxi Year: *1910*; Census Place: *Logan, Gloucester, New Jersey*; Roll: *T624_885*; Page: *1A*; Enumeration District:*0127*; FHL microfilm: *1374898*

mxxxii Rambo, Beverly Nelson and Beatty, Ronald Stephen. 2013. *The Rambo Family Tree.* http://sites.google.com/site/RamboFamilyTree.

mxxxiii "United States Social Security Death Index," database, *FamilySearch*(https://familysearch.org/ark:/61903/1:1:JPZ7-JWG : 20 May 2014), Myrtle Carson, Nov 1980; citing U.S. Social Security Administration, *Death Master File*, database (Alexandria, Virginia: National Technical Information Service, ongoing).

mxxxiv "New Jersey, Marriages, 1670-1980," database with images, *FamilySearch*(https://familysearch.org/ark:/61903/1:1:Q29L-QHS3 : 31 March 2016), Leon Wilson and Myrtle M. Hoffman, 24 Jun 1915; citing Gibbstown, Gloucester, New Jersey, United States, Division of Archives and Record Management, New Jersey Department of State, Trenton.; FHL microfilm 1,543,473.

mxxxv Year: *1900*; Census Place: *Greenwich, Gloucester, New Jersey*; Roll: *971*; Page: *2B*; Enumeration District:*0157*; FHL microfilm: *1240971*

mxxxvi "New Jersey, Deaths, 1670-1988," database, *FamilySearch*(https://familysearch.org/ark:/61903/1:1:FZWT-SQF : 8 April 2016), Leon Wilson, 17 May 1916; citing , Gloucester, New Jersey, United States, Division of Archives and Record Management, New Jersey Department of State, Trenton.; FHL microfilm 1,543,567.

mxxxvii United States, Selective Service System. *World War I Selective Service System Draft Registration Cards, 1917-1918*. Washington, D.C.: National Archives and Records Administration. M1509, 4,582 rolls. Imaged from Family History Library microfilm.

mxxxviii Pennsylvania (State). Death certificates, 1906–1963. Series 11.90 (1,905 cartons). Records of the Pennsylvania Department of Health, Record Group 11. Pennsylvania Historical and Museum Commission, Harrisburg, Pennsylvania.

mxxxix The National Archives at St. Louis; St. Louis, Missouri; *Draft Registration Cards for Fourth Registration for New Jersey, 04/27/1942 - 04/27/1942*; NAI Number: *2555983*; Record Group Title: *Records of the Selective Service System*; Record Group Number: *147*

mxl Historical Society of Pennsylvania; Philadelphia, Pennsylvania; Collection Name: *Historic Pennsylvania Church and Town Records*; Reel: *779*

mxli Social Security Applications and Claims, 1936-2007.

mxlii Historical Society of Pennsylvania; Philadelphia, Pennsylvania; Collection Name: *Historic Pennsylvania Church and Town Records*; Reel: *779*

mxliii Historical Society of Pennsylvania; Philadelphia, Pennsylvania; Collection Name: *Historic Pennsylvania Church and Town Records*; Reel: *779*

mxliv Social Security Administration. *Social Security Death Index, Master File*. Social Security Administration.

mxlv Social Security Applications and Claims, 1936-2007.

mxlvi Social Security Administration. *Social Security Death Index, Master File*. Social Security Administration.

mxlvii Social Security Administration. *Social Security Death Index, Master File*. Social Security Administration.

mxlviii Social Security Applications and Claims, 1936-2007

mxlix Social Security Administration. *Social Security Death Index, Master File*. Social Security Administration

ml Ancestry.com. *U.S. City Directories, 1822-1995* [database on-line]. Provo, UT, USA: Ancestry.com Operations, Inc., 2011.

mli Year: *1930*; Census Place: *Woolwich, Gloucester, New Jersey*; Roll: *1346*; Page: *6A*; Enumeration District: *0047*; Image: *508.0*; FHL microfilm: *2341081*

mlii Social Security Applications and Claims, 1936-2007.

mliii Social Security Administration. *Social Security Death Index, Master File*. Social Security Administration

mliv "Illinois, Cook County, Birth Certificates, 1871-1940," database, *FamilySearch*(https://familysearch.org/ark:/61903/1:1:N738-J2G : 18 May 2016), Theresa Asta, 24 Jan 1920; citing Oak Park, Cook, Illinois, United States, reference/certificate , Cook County Courthouse, Chicago; FHL microfilm 1,308,627.

mlv Year: *1940*; Census Place: *Woolwich, Gloucester, New Jersey*; Roll: *T627_2343*; Page: *7B*; Enumeration District: *8-68*

mlvi Social Security Applications and Claims, 1936-2007.

mlvii Social Security Administration. *Social Security Death Index, Master File*. Social Security Administration.

mlviii *Beneficiary Identification Records Locator Subsystem (BIRLS) Death File*. Washington, D.C.: U.S. Department of Veterans Affairs.

mlix "New Jersey Births and Christenings, 1660-1931." Index. FamilySearch, Salt Lake City, Utah, 2009, 2010. Index entries derived from digital copies of original and compiled records.

mlx Social Security Administration. *Social Security Death Index, Master File*. Social Security Administration.

mlxi Year: *1900*; Census Place: *West Almond, Allegany, New York*; Roll: *1008*; Page: *10A*; Enumeration District:*0025*; FHL microfilm: *1241008*

mlxii Social Security Administration. *Social Security Death Index, Master File*. Social Security Administration.

mlxiii Social Security Applications and Claims, 1936-2007.

mlxiv Social Security Applications and Claims, 1936-2007.

mlxv Social Security Applications and Claims, 1936-2007.

mlxvi Social Security Administration. *Social Security Death Index, Master File*. Social Security Administration.

mlxvii National Cemetery Administration. *Nationwide Gravesite Locator*.

mlxviii *Find A Grave*. Find A Grave. http://www.findagrave.com/cgi-bin/fg.cgi.

mlxix *Find A Grave*. Find A Grave. http://www.findagrave.com/cgi-bin/fg.cgi.

mlxx Virginia, Marriages, 1936-2014. Virginia Department of Health, Richmond, Virginia.

mlxxi *Beneficiary Identification Records Locator Subsystem (BIRLS) Death File*. Washington, D.C.: U.S. Department of Veterans Affairs.

mlxxii *Beneficiary Identification Records Locator Subsystem (BIRLS) Death File*. Washington, D.C.: U.S. Department of Veterans Affairs.

mlxxiii *Beneficiary Identification Records Locator Subsystem (BIRLS) Death File*. Washington, D.C.: U.S. Department of Veterans Affairs.

mlxxiv North Carolina County Registers of Deeds. Microfilm. Record Group 048. North Carolina State Archives, Raleigh, NC.

mlxxv Virginia, Births, 1864–2014. Virginia Department of Health, Richmond, Virginia.

mlxxvi Social Security Administration. *Social Security Death Index, Master File*. Social Security Administration

mlxxviii *Find A Grave*. Find A Grave. http://www.findagrave.com/cgi-bin/fg.cgi.

mlxxix Registration State: *New Jersey*; Registration County: *Salem*; Roll: *1754437*; Draft Board: *1*

mlxxx Social Security Applications and Claims, 1936-2007.

mlxxxi Pennsylvania (State). Death certificates, 1906–1963. Series 11.90 (1,905 cartons). Records of the Pennsylvania Department of Health, Record Group 11. Pennsylvania Historical and Museum Commission, Harrisburg, Pennsylvania.

mlxxxii Social Security Administration. *Social Security Death Index, Master File*. Social Security Administration

mlxxxiii Social Security Administration. *Social Security Death Index, Master File*. Social Security Administration

mlxxxiv Social Security Administration. *Social Security Death Index, Master File*. Social Security Administration

mlxxxv Social Security Applications and Claims, 1936-2007.

mlxxxvi Social Security Applications and Claims, 1936-2007.

mlxxxvii Social Security Administration. *Social Security Death Index, Master File*. Social Security Administration.

mlxxxviii Social Security Administration. *Social Security Death Index, Master File*. Social Security Administration.

mlxxxix "New Jersey Births and Christenings, 1660-1931." Index. FamilySearch, Salt Lake City, Utah, 2009, 2010. Index entries derived from digital copies of original and compiled records.

mxc "BillionGraves Index," database, *FamilySearch* (https://familysearch.org/ark:/61903/1:1:QKKS-SH6K : 9 November 2015), J Davidson England, died 14 Sep 1983; citing *BillionGraves*(http://www.billiongraves.com : 2012), Burial at Lawnside Cemetery, Woodstown, Salem, New Jersey, United States.

mxci Social Security Administration. *Social Security Death Index, Master File*. Social Security Administration.

mxcii Historical Society of Pennsylvania; Philadelphia, Pennsylvania; Collection Name: *Historic Pennsylvania Church and Town Records*; Reel: *779*

mxciii Year: *1910*; Census Place: *Oldmans, Salem, New Jersey*; Roll: *T624_908*; Page: *11B*; Enumeration District:*0150*; FHL microfilm: *1374921*

mxciv Virginia, Deaths, 1912–2014. Virginia Department of Health, Richmond, Virginia.

mxcv *Find A Grave*. Find A Grave. http://www.findagrave.com/cgi-bin/fg.cgi: accessed 4 February 2013.

mxcvi District of Columbia Marriages, 1811-1950. Certificate 162037.

mxcvii Original data: Virginia, Deaths, 1912–2014. Virginia Department of Health, Richmond, Virginia.

mxcviii *Find A Grave*. Find A Grave. http://www.findagrave.com/cgi-bin/fg.cgi: accessed 4 February 2013

mxcix *Find A Grave*. Find A Grave. http://www.findagrave.com/cgi-bin/fg.cgi.

mc *Find A Grave*. Find A Grave. http://www.findagrave.com/cgi-bin/fg.cgi

mci *Sons of the American Revolution Membership Applications, 1889-1970*. Louisville, Kentucky: National Society of the Sons of the American Revolution. Microfilm, 508 rolls.

mcii "Illinois, Cook County Marriages, 1871–1920." Index. FamilySearch, Salt Lake City, Utah, 2010. Illinois Department of Public Health records. "Marriage Records, 1871–present." Division of Vital Records, Springfield, Illinois.

mciii *Sons of the American Revolution Membership Applications, 1889-1970*. Louisville, Kentucky: National Society of the Sons of the American Revolution. Microfilm, 508 rolls.

mciv *Sons of the American Revolution Membership Applications, 1889-1970*. Louisville, Kentucky: National Society of the Sons of the American Revolution. Microfilm, 508 rolls.

mcv *Sons of the American Revolution Membership Applications, 1889-1970*. Louisville, Kentucky: National Society of the Sons of the American Revolution. Microfilm, 508 rolls.

mcvi *Sons of the American Revolution Membership Applications, 1889-1970*. Louisville, Kentucky: National Society of the Sons of the American Revolution. Microfilm, 508 rolls.

mcvii *Find A Grave*. Find A Grave. http://www.findagrave.com/cgi-bin/fg.cgi.

mcviii https://familysearch.org/ark:/61903/1:1:6544-GMM

mcix Newspapers.com - Courier-Post - 26 Mar 1965, Fri - Page 8

mcx Newspapers.com - Courier-Post - 26 Mar 1965, Fri - Page 8

mcxi "New Jersey, Marriages, 1670-1980," database with images, *FamilySearch*(https://familysearch.org/ark:/61903/1:1:FZ2S-B2W : 31 March 2016), William M. Skaggs and Anna M. Allen, 19 Dec 1894; citing Camden, Camden, New Jersey, United States, Division of Archives and Record Management, New Jersey Department of State, Trenton.; FHL microfilm 495,719.

mcxii Year: *1900*; Census Place: *Camden Ward 4, Camden, New Jersey*; Roll: *958*; Page: *1A*; Enumeration District: *0047*; FHL microfilm: *1240958*

mcxiii Newspapers.com - Courier-Post - 4 Nov 1950, Sat - Page 5

mcxiv Social Security Administration. *Social Security Death Index, Master File*. Social Security Administration.

mcxv Newspapers.com - Courier-Post - 2 May 1975, Fri - Page 8

mcxvi Newspapers.com - Courier-Post - 25 Jan 1960, Mon - Page 1

mcxvii Year: *1930*; Census Place: *Schenectady, Schenectady, New York*; Roll: *1646*; Page: *9B*; Enumeration District:*0071*; Image: *543.0*; FHL microfilm: *2341380*

mcxviii Social Security Administration. *Social Security Death Index, Master File*. Social Security Administration.

mcxix Social Security Administration. *Social Security Death Index, Master File*. Social Security Administration.

mcxx Social Security Applications and Claims, 1936-2007.

mcxxi Year: *1880*; Census Place: *Upper Penns Neck, Salem, New Jersey*; Roll: *797*; Family History Film: *1254797*; Page: *215C*; Enumeration District: *150*; Image: *0436*

mcxxii *Find A Grave*. Find A Grave. http://www.findagrave.com/cgi-bin/fg.cgi.

mcxxiii Year: *1900*; Census Place: *Logan, Gloucester, New Jersey*; Roll: *971*; Page: *10A*; Enumeration District: *0159*; FHL microfilm: *1240971*

mcxxiv *Find A Grave*. Find A Grave. http://www.findagrave.com/cgi-bin/fg.cgi

mcxxv Social Security Administration. *Social Security Death Index, Master File*. Social Security Administration.

mcxxvi *Find A Grave*. Find A Grave. http://www.findagrave.com/cgi-bin/fg.cgi.

mcxxvii Year: *1930*; Census Place: *Logan, Gloucester, New Jersey*; Roll: *1345*; Page: *17A*; Enumeration District: *0016*; Image: *526.0*; FHL microfilm: *2341080*

mcxxviii *Find A Grave*. Find A Grave. http://www.findagrave.com/cgi-bin/fg.cgi.

mcxxix Social Security Administration. *Social Security Death Index, Master File*. Social Security Administration.

mcxxx Social Security Administration. *Social Security Death Index, Master File*. Social Security Administration.

mcxxxi Year: *1930*; Census Place: *Swedesboro, Gloucester, New Jersey*; Roll: *1346*; Page: *21B*; Enumeration District: *0031*; Image: *57.0*; FHL microfilm: *2341081*

mcxxxii "New Jersey Deaths and Burials, 1720-1988," database, *FamilySearch* (https://familysearch.org/ark:/61903/1:1:FZ3J-45L : 12 December 2014), Clementine S. Mrs. Dawson, 25 Apr 1969; citing , reference ; FHL microfilm 1,001,898.

mcxxxiii *Find A Grave*. Find A Grave. http://www.findagrave.com/cgi-bin/fg.cgi.

mcxxxiv*Find A Grave*. Find A Grave. http://www.findagrave.com/cgi-bin/fg.cgi.

mcxxxv *Find A Grave*. Find A Grave. http://www.findagrave.com/cgi-bin/fg.cgi.

mcxxxvi Social Security Applications and Claims, 1936-2007.

mcxxxvii Social Security Administration. *Social Security Death Index, Master File*. Social Security Administration.

mcxxxviii *Find A Grave*. Find A Grave. http://www.findagrave.com/cgi-bin/fg.cgi.

mcxxxix Year: *1920*; Census Place: *Logan, Gloucester, New Jersey*; Roll: *T625_1027*; Page: *14B*; Enumeration District: *145*; Image: *518*

mcxl "New Jersey, Marriages, 1670-1980," database with images, *FamilySearch* (https://familysearch.org/ark:/61903/1:1:Q29L-Q3C9 : 31 March 2016), William Krouse and Elva Viola Dawson, 03 Aug 1931; citing , Bel Air, Maryland, United States, Division of Archives and Record Management, New Jersey Department of State, Trenton.; FHL microfilm 1,543,469.

mcxli United States, Selective Service System. *World War I Selective Service System Draft Registration Cards, 1917-1918*. Washington, D.C.: National Archives and Records Administration. M1509, 4,582 rolls. Imaged from Family History Library microfilm.

mcxlii Newspapers.com - Courier-Post - 23 Oct 1957, Wed - Page 4

mcxliii "Pennsylvania, Philadelphia Marriage Index, 1885–1951." Index. FamilySearch, Salt Lake City, Utah, 2009. Philadelphia County Pennsylvania Clerk of the Orphans' Court. "Pennsylvania, Philadelphia marriage license index, 1885-1951." Clerk of the Orphans' Court, Philadelphia, Pennsylvania.

mcxliv Year: *1910*; Census Place: *Philadelphia Ward 44, Philadelphia, Pennsylvania*; Roll: *T624_1412*; Page: *1B*; Enumeration District: *1123*; FHL microfilm: *1375425*

mcxlv Pennsylvania (State). World War II Veterans Compensation Applications, circa 1950s. Records of the Department of Military and Veterans Affairs, Record Group 19, Series 19.92 (877 cartons). Pennsylvania Historical and Museum Commission, Harrisburg, Pennsylvania.

mcxlvi Social Security Administration. *Social Security Death Index, Master File*. Social Security Administration.

mcxlvii Newspapers.com - The Philadelphia Inquirer - 11 Oct 1972, Wed - Page 36

mcxlviii Pennsylvania (State). World War II Veterans Compensation Applications, circa 1950s. Records of the Department of Military and Veterans Affairs, Record Group 19, Series 19.92 (877 cartons). Pennsylvania Historical and Museum Commission, Harrisburg, Pennsylvania.

mcxlix Social Security Applications and Claims, 1936-2007.

mcl Social Security Administration. *Social Security Death Index, Master File*. Social Security Administration.

mcli http://www.legacy.com/obituaries/wickedlocal-ipswich/obituary.aspx?pid=160598168

mclii *Find A Grave*. Find A Grave. http://www.findagrave.com/cgi-bin/fg.cgi.

mcliii "Oklahoma, County Marriages, 1890-1995", database with images, *FamilySearch* (https://familysearch.org/ark:/61903/1:1:Q29M-319G : 2 February 2016), Raymond W Pancoast and Jane Calvert, 1956.

mcliv Social Security Applications and Claims, 1936-2007.

mclv *Find A Grave*. Find A Grave. http://www.findagrave.com/cgi-bin/fg.cgi.

mclvi Newspapers.com - The Philadelphia Inquirer - 6 Sep 1990, Thu - Page 9

mclvii Social Security Applications and Claims, 1936-2007.

mclviii Ancestry.com. *California, Death Index, 1940-1997* [database on-line]. Provo, UT, USA: Ancestry.com Operations Inc, 2000.

mclix Year: *1910*; Census Place: *Absecon Ward 1, Atlantic, New Jersey*; Roll: *T624_867*; Page: *1B*; Enumeration District: *0001*; FHL microfilm: *1374880*

mclx Ancestry.com. *California, Death Index, 1940-1997* [database on-line]. Provo, UT, USA: Ancestry.com Operations Inc, 2000.

mclxi Ancestry.com. *California, Death Index, 1940-1997* [database on-line]. Provo, UT, USA: Ancestry.com Operations Inc, 2000.

mclxii Ancestry.com. *California, Death Index, 1940-1997* [database on-line]. Provo, UT, USA: Ancestry.com Operations Inc, 2000.

mclxiii Ancestry.com. *California, Death Index, 1940-1997* [database on-line]. Provo, UT, USA: Ancestry.com Operations Inc, 2000.

mclxiv Ancestry.com. *California, Death Index, 1940-1997* [database on-line]. Provo, UT, USA: Ancestry.com Operations Inc, 2000.

mclxv Year: *1920*; Census Place: *Los Angeles Assembly District 66, Los Angeles, California*; Roll: *T625_110*; Page: *5A*; Enumeration District: *263*; Image: *524*

mclxvi *Find A Grave*. Find A Grave. http://www.findagrave.com/cgi-bin/fg.cgi

mclxvii Ancestry.com. *Historical Newspapers, Birth, Marriage, & Death Announcements, 1851-2003* [database on-line]. Provo, UT, USA: Ancestry.com Operations Inc, 2006.

mclxviii Newspapers.com - The Los Angeles Times - 30 Jan 1935, Wed - Page 15

mclxix *Find A Grave*. Find A Grave. http://www.findagrave.com/cgi-bin/fg.cgi.

mclxx *Find A Grave*. Find A Grave. http://www.findagrave.com/cgi-bin/fg.cgi.

mclxxi Ancestry.com. *California Birth Index, 1905-1995* [database on-line]. Provo, UT, USA: Ancestry.com Operations Inc, 2005.

mclxxii Ancestry.com. *California, Death Index, 1905-1939* [database on-line]. Provo, UT, USA: Ancestry.com Operations, Inc., 2013.

mclxxiii Ancestry.com. *California Birth Index, 1905-1995* [database on-line]. Provo, UT, USA: Ancestry.com Operations Inc, 2005.

mclxxiv Find A Grave. http://www.findagrave.com/cgi-bin/fg.cgi.

mclxxv Ancestry.com. *California Birth Index, 1905-1995* [database on-line]. Provo, UT, USA: Ancestry.com Operations Inc, 2005.

mclxxvi Ancestry.com. *California, Death Index, 1940-1997* [database on-line]. Provo, UT, USA: Ancestry.com Operations Inc, 2000.

mclxxvii Ancestry.com. *California, Marriage Index, 1949-1959* [database on-line]. Provo, UT, USA: Ancestry.com Operations, Inc., 2013.

mclxxviii Social Security Applications and Claims, 1936-2007

mclxxix Ancestry.com. *California, Divorce Index, 1966-1984* [database on-line]. Provo, UT, USA: Ancestry.com Operations Inc, 2007.

mclxxx *Beneficiary Identification Records Locator Subsystem (BIRLS) Death File*. Washington, D.C.: U.S. Department of Veterans Affairs.

mclxxxi "New Jersey, Births, 1670-1980," database, *FamilySearch* (https://familysearch.org/ark:/61903/1:1:FCRJ-4VC : 8 April 2016), Stacy C. Pancoast in entry for Pancoast, 04 Sep 1887; citing , Salem, New Jersey, United States, Division of Archives and Record Management, New Jersey Department of State, Trenton.; FHL microfilm 494,209.

mclxxxii Social Security Administration. *Social Security Death Index, Master File*. Social Security Administration.

mclxxxiii Year: *1910*; Census Place: *Wilmington Ward 7, New Castle, Delaware*; Roll: *T624_147*; Page: *19A*; Enumeration District: *0041*; FHL microfilm: *1374160*

mclxxxiv Ancestry.com. *Delaware, Marriage Records, 1806-1933* [database on-line]. Provo, UT, USA: Ancestry.com Operations, Inc., 2010.

mclxxxv Ancestry.com. *Delaware, Birth Records, 1800-1932* [database on-line]. Provo, UT, USA: Ancestry.com Operations, Inc., 2010.

mclxxxvi Newspapers.com - The Morning News - 7 May 1925, Thu - Page 7

mclxxxvii Delaware Public Archives; Dover, Delaware; Collection Number: *Birth Records - 88*; Roll Number: *88*

mclxxxviii Ancestry.com. *North Carolina, Death Indexes, 1908-2004* [database on-line]. Provo, UT, USA: Ancestry.com Operations, Inc., 2007.

mclxxxix Ancestry.com. *Delaware, Marriage Records, 1806-1933* [database on-line]. Provo, UT, USA: Ancestry.com Operations, Inc., 2010.

mcxc Delaware Public Archives; Dover, Delaware; Collection Number: *Birth Records - 84*; Roll Number: *84*

mcxci Ancestry.com. *North Carolina, Death Indexes, 1908-2004* [database on-line]. Provo, UT, USA: Ancestry.com Operations, Inc., 2007.

mcxcii Newspapers.com - The High Point Enterprise - 20 Mar 1960, Sun - Page 15

mcxciii http://www.greensboro.com/obituaries/article_da0fc38e-a129-5c40-882b-17fde552c8a8.html

mcxciv Delaware Public Archives; Dover, Delaware; Collection Number: *Register of Births - 4*; Roll Number: *107*

mcxcv Social Security Administration. *Social Security Death Index, Master File*. Social Security Administration.

mcxcvi Delaware Public Archives; Dover, Delaware; Collection Number: *Register of Births - 3*; Roll Number: *106*

mcxcvii Find A Grave. http://www.findagrave.com/cgi-bin/fg.cgi.

mcxcviii Newspapers.com - The News Journal - 18 Sep 1944, Mon - Page 11

mcxcix *Find A Grave*. Find A Grave. http://www.findagrave.com/cgi-bin/fg.cgi.

mcc *Find A Grave*. Find A Grave. http://www.findagrave.com/cgi-bin/fg.cgi.

mcci http://www.legacy.com/obituaries/delawareonline/obituary.aspx?pid=163382857

mccii Delaware Public Archives; Dover, Delaware; Collection Number: *Register of Births - 4*; Roll Number: *107*

mcciii *Find A Grave*. Find A Grave. http://www.findagrave.com/cgi-bin/fg.cgi.

mcciv Newspapers.com - The Morning News - 7 Sep 1936, Mon - Page 9

mccv *Find A Grave*. Find A Grave. http://www.findagrave.com/cgi-bin/fg.cgi.

mccvi *Find A Grave*. Find A Grave. http://www.findagrave.com/cgi-bin/fg.cgi.

mccvii Social Security Applications and Claims, 1936-2007.

mccviii Social Security Administration. *Social Security Death Index, Master File*. Social Security Administration.

mccix National Archives and Records Administration. Electronic Army Serial Number Merged File, 1938-1946 [Archival Database]; ARC: 1263923. World War II Army Enlistment Records; Records of the National Archives and Records Administration, Record Group 64; National Archives at College Park. College Park, Maryland, U.S.A.

mccx "Oklahoma, County Marriages, 1890-1995", database with images, *FamilySearch* (https://familysearch.org/ark:/61903/1:1:VXL2-WVW : 12 December 2014), Roger S Pancoast and Lilian Ann Curtin, 1942.

mccxi Social Security Applications and Claims, 1936-2007

mccxii *Find A Grave*. Find A Grave. http://www.findagrave.com/cgi-bin/fg.cgi.

mccxiii *Find A Grave*. Find A Grave. http://www.findagrave.com/cgi-bin/fg.cgi.

mccxiv *Find A Grave*. Find A Grave. http://www.findagrave.com/cgi-bin/fg.cgi.

mccxv Social Security Applications and Claims, 1936-2007.

mccxvi Social Security Administration. *Social Security Death Index, Master File*. Social Security Administration.

mccxvii http://www.newarkpostonline.com/obituaries/article_3285073e-ce53-5410-a7f0-72d9b1b5117a.html

mccxviii Social Security Applications and Claims, 1936-2007

mccxix Newspapers.com - The News Journal - 31 Aug 1983, Wed - Page 1

mccxx United States, Selective Service System. *World War I Selective Service System Draft Registration Cards, 1917-1918*. Washington, D.C.: National Archives and Records Administration. M1509, 4,582 rolls. Imaged from Family History Library microfilm.

mccxxi Ancestry.com. *Florida Death Index, 1877-1998* [database on-line]. Provo, UT, USA: Ancestry.com Operations Inc, 2004.

mccxxii Year: *1930*; Census Place: *Upper Darby, Delaware, Pennsylvania*; Roll: *2033*; Page: *9A*; Enumeration District: *0151*; Image: *1042.0*; FHL microfilm: *2341767*

mccxxiii Newspapers.com - The News Journal - 4 May 1931, Mon - Page 1

mccxxiv Delaware Public Archives; Dover, Delaware; Collection Number: *Birth Certificates - Delayed - 12*; Roll Number: *101*

mccxxv Newspapers.com - The News Journal - 2 Jan 2006, Mon - Page 10

mccxxvi Social Security Applications and Claims, 1936-2007

mccxxvii Newspapers.com - The News Journal - 7 Apr 1992, Tue - Page 7

mccxxviii Newspapers.com - The News Journal - 15 Jan 1938, Sat - Page 5

mccxxix Social Security Applications and Claims, 1936-2007

mccxxx Social Security Administration. *Social Security Death Index, Master File*. Social Security Administration.

mccxxxi Newspapers.com - The News Journal - 23 Dec 1998, Wed - Page 18

mccxxxii Newspapers.com - The News Journal - 11 May 1970, Mon - Page 25

mccxxxiii United States, Selective Service System. *World War I Selective Service System Draft Registration Cards, 1917-1918*. Washington, D.C.: National Archives and Records Administration. M1509, 4,582 rolls. Imaged from Family History Library microfilm.

mccxxxiv Ancestry.com. *New York, New York, Death Index, 1862-1948* [database on-line]. Provo, UT, USA: Ancestry.com Operations, Inc., 2014.

mccxxxv *Alabama, Marriages, 1816-1957*. Salt Lake City, Utah: FamilySearch, 2013.

mccxxxvi Year: *1930*; Census Place: *Brooklyn, Kings, New York*; Roll: *1537*; Page: *12B*; Enumeration District: *0850*; Image: *536.0*; FHL microfilm: *2341272*

mccxxxvii Social Security Administration. *Social Security Death Index, Master File*. Social Security Administration.

mccxxxviii *Find A Grave*. Find A Grave. http://www.findagrave.com/cgi-bin/fg.cgi.

mccxxxix *Social Security Death Index, Master File*. Social Security Administration.

mccxl Pennsylvania (State). World War II Veterans Compensation Applications, circa 1950s. Records of the Department of Military and Veterans Affairs, Record Group 19, Series 19.92 (877 cartons). Pennsylvania Historical and Museum Commission, Harrisburg, Pennsylvania.

mccxli *Find A Grave*. Find A Grave. http://www.findagrave.com/cgi-bin/fg.cgi.

mccxlii *Find A Grave*. Find A Grave. http://www.findagrave.com/cgi-bin/fg.cgi.

mccxliii Social Security Applications and Claims, 1936-2007.

mccxliv Social Security Applications and Claims, 1936-2007.

mccxlv *Missouri Marriage Records*. Jefferson City, MO, USA: Missouri State Archives. Microfilm.

mccxlvi Florida Department of Health. *Florida Divorce Index, 1927-2001*. Jacksonville, FL, USA: Florida Department of Health.

mccxlvii E-mail communication with Robyn Sheets, 9 Sep 2016

mccxlviii National Cemetery Administration. *Nationwide Gravesite Locator*.

mccxlix E-mail communication with Robyn Sheets, 9 Sep 2016

mccl E-mail communication with Robyn Sheets, 9 Sep 2016

mccli Social Security Applications and Claims, 1936-2007.

mcclii Social Security Administration. *Social Security Death Index, Master File*. Social Security Administration.

mccliii Pennsylvania (State). Birth certificates, 1906–1908. Series 11.89 (50 cartons). Records of the Pennsylvania Department of Health, Record Group 11. Pennsylvania Historical and Museum Commission, Harrisburg, Pennsylvania.

mccliv Social Security Administration. *Social Security Death Index, Master File*. Social Security Administration.

mcclv Year: *1930*; Census Place: *Philadelphia, Philadelphia, Pennsylvania*; Roll: *2108*; Page: *24A*; Enumeration District: *0378*; Image: *135.0*; FHL microfilm: *2341842*

mcclvi Social Security Applications and Claims, 1936-2007.

mcclvii *Social Security Death Index, Master File*. Social Security Administration.

mcclviii http://www.legacy.com/obituaries/gjsentinel/obituary.aspx?n=barbara-edith-martin-baker&pid=16049190

mcclix Social Security Applications and Claims, 1936-2007.

mcclx Social Security Administration. *Social Security Death Index, Master File*. Social Security Administration.

mcclxi Social Security Administration. *Social Security Death Index, Master File*. Social Security Administration.

mcclxii Social Security Administration. *Social Security Death Index, Master File*. Social Security Administration.

mcclxiii Year: *1910*; Census Place: *Oaklyn, Camden, New Jersey*; Roll: *T624_874*; Page: *6B*; Enumeration District: *0107*; FHL microfilm: *1374887*

mcclxiv Ancestry.com. *U.S., World War I Draft Registration Cards, 1917-1918* [database on-line]. Provo, UT, USA: Ancestry.com Operations Inc, 2005.

mcclxv Ancestry.com. *Pennsylvania, Death Certificates, 1906-1963* [database on-line]. Provo, UT, USA: Ancestry.com Operations, Inc., 2014.

mcclxvi Swarthmore College; Swarthmore, Pennsylvania; *Births and Deaths, 1755-1935*; Collection: *Quaker Meeting Records*; Call Number: *MR-PH 237*

mcclxvii Year: *1910*; Census Place: *Oaklyn, Camden, New Jersey*; Roll: *T624_874*; Page: *6B*; Enumeration District: *0107*; FHL microfilm: *1374887*

mcclxviii United States, Selective Service System. *World War I Selective Service System Draft Registration Cards, 1917-1918*. Washington, D.C.: National Archives and Records Administration. M1509, 4,582 rolls. Imaged from Family History Library microfilm.

mcclxix Swarthmore College; Swarthmore, Pennsylvania; *Births and Deaths, 1755-1935*; Collection: *Quaker Meeting Records*; Call Number: *MR-PH 237*

mcclxx Year: *1920*; Census Place: *Haddonfield, Camden, New Jersey*; Roll: *T625_1025*; Page: *11B*; Enumeration District: *121*; Image: *158*

mcclxxiSocial Security Administration. *Social Security Death Index, Master File*. Social Security Administration.

mcclxxii Social Security Administration. *Social Security Death Index, Master File*. Social Security Administration.

mcclxxiii Social Security Administration. *Social Security Death Index, Master File*. Social Security Administration.

mcclxxiv Year: *1920*; Census Place: *Haddonfield, Camden, New Jersey*; Roll: *T625_1025*; Page: *15B*; Enumeration District: *120*; Image: *94*

mcclxxv Social Security Applications and Claims, 1936-2007.

mcclxxvi Newspapers.com - Courier-Post - 27 Mar 1990, Tue - Page 12

mcclxxvii Historical Society of Pennsylvania; Philadelphia, Pennsylvania; Collection Name: *Historic Pennsylvania Church and Town Records*; Reel: *804*

mcclxxviii Social Security Applications and Claims, 1936-2007.

mcclxxix Social Security Administration. *Social Security Death Index, Master File*. Social Security Administration.

mcclxxx Newspapers.com - Courier-Post - 5 Sep 2006, Tue - Page 20

mcclxxxi Newspapers.com - Courier-Post - 21 Oct 2001, Sun - Page 24

mcclxxxii Year: *1900*; Census Place: *Washington, Gloucester, New Jersey*; Roll: *971*; Page: *5B*; Enumeration District:*0164*; FHL microfilm: *1240971*

mcclxxxiii Ancestry.com. *Washington, Deaths, 1883-1960* [database on-line]. Provo, UT, USA: Ancestry.com Operations Inc, 2008.

mcclxxxiv Historical Society of Pennsylvania; Philadelphia, Pennsylvania; Collection Name: *Historic Pennsylvania Church and Town Records*; Reel: *774*

mcclxxxv The National Archives at St. Louis; St. Louis, Missouri; *Draft Registration Cards for Fourth Registration for Colorado, 04/27/1942 - 04/27/1942*; NAI Number: *923647*; Record Group Title: *Records of the Selective Service System*; Record Group Number: *147*

mcclxxxvi "Washington Death Certificates, 1907-1960," database, *FamilySearch*(https://familysearch.org/ark:/61903/1:1:NQM1-147 : 5 December 2014), William Campbell, 21 Oct 1950; citing Seattle, King, Washington, United States, reference 17254, Bureau of Vital Statistics, Olympia; FHL microfilm 2,032,914.

mcclxxxvii Ohio Deaths, 1908-1953," database with images, *FamilySearch* (https://familysearch.org/ark:/61903/1:1:X64G-85Z : 8 December 2014), Raymond H Campbell, 25 Dec 1929; citing Lakewood, Cuyahoga, Ohio, reference fn 76365; FHL microfilm 1,992,028.

mcclxxxviii Ohio Deaths, 1908-1953," database with images, *FamilySearch* (https://familysearch.org/ark:/61903/1:1:X64G-85Z : 8 December 2014), Raymond H Campbell, 25 Dec 1929; citing Lakewood, Cuyahoga, Ohio, reference fn 76365; FHL microfilm 1,992,028.

mcclxxxix Historical Society of Pennsylvania; Philadelphia, Pennsylvania; Collection Name: *Historic Pennsylvania Church and Town Records*; Reel: *774*

mccxc *Washington, Death Certificates, 1907-1960*. Salt Lake City, Utah: FamilySearch, 2013

mccxci State of California. *California Death Index, 1940-1997*. Sacramento, CA, USA: State of California Department of Health Services, Center for Health Statistics.

mccxciiThe National Archives at St. Louis; St. Louis, Missouri; *Draft Registration Cards for Fourth Registration for New Jersey, 04/27/1942 - 04/27/1942*; NAI Number: *2555983*; Record Group Title: *Records of the Selective Service System*; Record Group Number: *147*

mccxciii "New Jersey Deaths and Burials, 1720-1988," database, *FamilySearch*(https://familysearch.org/ark:/61903/1:1:FZ32-3M8 : 12 December 2014), Walter H. Hurff, 09 Feb 1948; citing , reference ; FHL microfilm 1,001,900.

mccxciv *Find A Grave*. Find A Grave. http://www.findagrave.com/cgi-bin/fg.cgi.

[mccxcv] Social Security Administration. *Social Security Death Index, Master File*. Social Security Administration

[mccxcvi] Social Security Applications and Claims, 1936-2007.

[mccxcvii] *Social Security Death Index, Master File*. Social Security Administration.

[mccxcviii] Social Security Applications and Claims, 1936-2007.

[mccxcix] Social Security Applications and Claims, 1936-2007.

[mccc] Social Security Applications and Claims, 1936-2007

[mccci] Social Security Administration. *Social Security Death Index, Master File*. Social Security Administration.

[mcccii] *Beneficiary Identification Records Locator Subsystem (BIRLS) Death File*. Washington, D.C.: U.S. Department of Veterans Affairs.

[mccciii] *Beneficiary Identification Records Locator Subsystem (BIRLS) Death File*. Washington, D.C.: U.S. Department of Veterans Affairs.

[mccciv] Newspapers.com - Courier-Post - Thu, Nov 20, 1975 - Page 68

[mcccv] "New Jersey Births and Christenings, 1660-1980," database, *FamilySearch*(https://familysearch.org/ark:/61903/1:1:FZDK-T4V : 12 December 2014), Grover C. Huff, 14 Jan 1884; citing Gloucester, New Jersey, reference ; FHL microfilm 494,200.

[mcccvi] "New Jersey Deaths and Burials, 1720-1988," database, *FamilySearch*(https://familysearch.org/ark:/61903/1:1:FZ32-S26 : 12 December 2014), Grover C. Hurff, 16 Oct 1964; citing , reference ; FHL microfilm 1,001,900.

[mcccvii] *Find A Grave*. Find A Grave. http://www.findagrave.com/cgi-bin/fg.cgi.

[mcccviii] Social Security Applications and Claims, 1936-2007

[mcccix] Social Security Administration. *Social Security Death Index, Master File*. Social Security Administration.

[mcccx] Social Security Administration. *Social Security Death Index, Master File*. Social Security Administration.

[mcccxi] Newspapers.com - Courier-Post - 5 Dec 1986, Fri - Page 44

[mcccxii] *Find A Grave*. Find A Grave. http://www.findagrave.com/cgi-bin/fg.cgi: accessed 4 February 2013.

[mcccxiii] *Find A Grave*. Find A Grave. http://www.findagrave.com/cgi-bin/fg.cgi: accessed 4 February 2013.

[mcccxiv] Greater New Jersey Annual Conference Commission on Archives and History; Madison, New Jersey; Description: *Methodist Church Records*

[mcccxv] Newspapers.com - Courier-Post - 16 Nov 2000, Thu - Page 25

[mcccxvi] Greater New Jersey Annual Conference Commission on Archives and History; Madison, New Jersey; Description: *Methodist Church Records*

[mcccxvii] http://www.legacy.com/obituaries/thedailyjournal/obituary.aspx?page=lifestory&pid=183258187

[mcccxviii] Social Security Administration. *Social Security Death Index, Master File*. Social Security Administration.

[mcccxix] Social Security Administration. *Social Security Death Index, Master File*. Social Security Administration.

[mcccxx] Social Security Administration. *Social Security Death Index, Master File*. Social Security Administration.

[mcccxxi] Social Security Administration. *Social Security Death Index, Master File*. Social Security Administration.

[mcccxxii] Year: *1920*; Census Place: *Swedesboro, Gloucester, New Jersey*; Roll: *T625_1027*; Page: *7A*; Enumeration District: *189*; Image: *867*

[mcccxxiii] Rambo, Beverly Nelson and Beatty, Ronald Stephen. 2013. *The Rambo Family Tree*. http://sites.google.com/site/RamboFamilyTree.

[mcccxxiv] Greater New Jersey Annual Conference Commission on Archives and History; Madison, New Jersey; Description: *Methodist Church Records*

[mcccxxv] Social Security Applications and Claims, 1936-2007

[mcccxxvi] Social Security Administration. *Social Security Death Index, Master File*. Social Security Administration.

[mcccxxvii] Social Security Administration. *Social Security Death Index, Master File*. Social Security Administration

[mcccxxviii] Social Security Administration. *Social Security Death Index, Master File*. Social Security Administration

[mcccxxix] *Find A Grave*. Find A Grave. http://www.findagrave.com/cgi-bin/fg.cgi.

[mcccxxx] Social Security Applications and Claims, 1936-2007

[mcccxxxi] Social Security Applications and Claims, 1936-2007

[mcccxxxii] *Beneficiary Identification Records Locator Subsystem (BIRLS) Death File*. Washington, D.C.: U.S. Department of Veterans Affairs.

[mcccxxxiii] Rambo, Beverly Nelson and Beatty, Ronald Stephen. 2013. *The Rambo Family Tree*. http://sites.google.com/site/RamboFamilyTree.

[mcccxxxiv] "United States Social Security Death Index," database, *FamilySearch*(https://familysearch.org/ark:/61903/1:1:JPZ7-JWG : 20 May 2014), Myrtle Carson, Nov 1980; citing U.S. Social Security Administration, *Death Master File*, database (Alexandria, Virginia: National Technical Information Service, ongoing).

mcccxxxv "New Jersey, Marriages, 1670-1980," database with images, *FamilySearch*(https://familysearch.org/ark:/61903/1:1:Q29L-QHS3 : 31 March 2016), Leon Wilson and Myrtle M. Hoffman, 24 Jun 1915; citing Gibbstown, Gloucester, New Jersey, United States, Division of Archives and Record Management, New Jersey Department of State, Trenton.; FHL microfilm 1,543,473.

mcccxxxvi Year: *1900*; Census Place: *Greenwich, Gloucester, New Jersey*; Roll: *971*; Page: *2B*; Enumeration District:*0157*; FHL microfilm: *1240971*

mcccxxxvii "New Jersey, Deaths, 1670-1988," database, *FamilySearch*(https://familysearch.org/ark:/61903/1:1:FZWT-SQF : 8 April 2016), Leon Wilson, 17 May 1916; citing , Gloucester, New Jersey, United States, Division of Archives and Record Management, New Jersey Department of State, Trenton.; FHL microfilm 1,543,567.

mcccxxxviii United States, Selective Service System. *World War I Selective Service System Draft Registration Cards, 1917-1918*. Washington, D.C.: National Archives and Records Administration. M1509, 4,582 rolls. Imaged from Family History Library microfilm.

mcccxxxix Pennsylvania (State). Death certificates, 1906–1963. Series 11.90 (1,905 cartons). Records of the Pennsylvania Department of Health, Record Group 11. Pennsylvania Historical and Museum Commission, Harrisburg, Pennsylvania.

mcccxl Social Security Applications and Claims, 1936-2007.

mcccxli *Social Security Death Index, Master File*. Social Security Administration.

mcccxlii Newspapers.com - Courier-Post - 28 Dec 1995, Thu - Page 14

mcccxliii Social Security Applications and Claims, 1936-2007.

mcccxliv Social Security Applications and Claims, 1936-2007.

mcccxlv Social Security Applications and Claims, 1936-2007.

mcccxlvi Social Security Applications and Claims, 1936-2007.

mcccxlvii Social Security Applications and Claims, 1936-2007.

mcccxlviii Social Security Administration. *Social Security Death Index, Master File*. Social Security Administration.